Global Food a
Institutions

This pioneering text brings together for the first time the global institutions on the front line of the campaign against hunger and poverty.

The institutions examined in this book—the Food and Agriculture Organization (FAO), the International Fund for Agricultural Development (IFAD), the World Bank, the World Food Programme (WFP) and the Consultative Group on International Agricultural Research (CGIAR)—play important roles in achieving and maintaining world food security, which is essential for human existence, economic and social development, and world peace.

By analyzing the origins, functions, successes, and difficulties of these global institutions, D. John Shaw highlights the continuing relevance of these bodies in their quest to meet the challenges of the twenty-first century. In the light of the current world food crisis, this book provides a particularly pertinent commentary on a highly topical issue that is never far from the media spotlight.

This book is essential reading for all students, academics, and readers with an interest in international organizations, agricultural development, and economic and humanitarian affairs.

D. John Shaw is currently on the International Editorial Board of the journal *Food Policy*. He served for over 30 years with the United Nations World Food Programme at its headquarters in Rome, Italy, latterly as its Economic Adviser and Chief of WFP's Policy Affairs Service. He was also a consultant for both FAO and the World Bank.

Routledge Global Institutions
Edited by Thomas G. Weiss
The CUNY Graduate Center, New York, USA
and Rorden Wilkinson
University of Manchester, UK

About the Series

The Global Institutions Series is designed to provide readers with comprehensive, accessible, and informative guides to the history, structure, and activities of key international organizations. Every volume stands on its own as a thorough and insightful treatment of a particular topic, but the series as a whole contributes to a coherent and complementary portrait of the phenomenon of global institutions at the dawn of the millennium.

Books are written by recognized experts, conform to a similar structure, and cover a range of themes and debates common to the series. These areas of shared concern include the general purpose and rationale for organizations, developments over time, membership, structure, decision-making procedures, and key functions. Moreover, current debates are placed in historical perspective alongside informed analysis and critique. Each book also contains an annotated bibliography and guide to electronic information as well as any annexes appropriate to the subject matter at hand.

The volumes currently published or under contract include:

The United Nations and Human Rights (2005)
A guide for a new era
by Julie Mertus (American University)

The UN Secretary General and Secretariat (2005)
by Leon Gordenker (Princeton University)

United Nations Global Conferences (2005)
by Michael G. Schechter (Michigan State University)

The UN General Assembly (2005)
by M.J. Peterson (University of Massachusetts, Amherst)

Internal Displacement (2006)
Conceptualization and its consequences
by Thomas G. Weiss (The CUNY Graduate Center) and David A. Korn

Global Environmental Institutions (2006)
by Elizabeth R. DeSombre (Wellesley College)

The UN Security Council (2006)
Practice and promise
by Edward C. Luck *(Columbia University)*

The World Intellectual Property Organization (2006)
Resurgence and the development agenda
by Chris May *(University of Lancaster)*

The North Atlantic Treaty Organization (2007)
The enduring alliance
by Julian Lindley-French *(European Union Centre for Security Studies)*

The International Monetary Fund (2007)
Politics of conditional lending
by James Raymond Vreeland *(Yale University)*

The Group of 7/8 (2007)
by Hugo Dobson *(University of Sheffield)*

The World Economic Forum (2007)
A multi-stakeholder approach to global governance
by Geoffrey Allen Pigman *(Bennington College)*

The International Committee of the Red Cross (2007)
A neutral humanitarian actor
by David P. Forsythe *(University of Nebraska)* and
Barbara Ann Rieffer-Flanagan *(Central Washington University)*

The Organization for Security and Co-operation in Europe (2007)
by David J. Galbreath *(University of Aberdeen)*

United Nations Conference on Trade and Development (UNCTAD) (2007)
by Ian Taylor *(University of St. Andrews)* and Karen Smith *(University of Stellenbosch)*

A Crisis of Global Institutions? (2007)
Multilateralism and international security
by Edward Newman *(University of Birmingham)*

The World Trade Organization (2007)
Law, economics, and politics
by Bernard M. Hoekman *(World Bank)* and Petros C. Mavroidis *(Columbia University)*

The African Union (2008)
Challenges of globalization, security, and governance
by Samuel M. Makinda *(Murdoch University)* and
F. Wafula Okumu *(Institute for Security Studies)*

Commonwealth (2008)
Inter- and non-state contributions to global governance
by Timothy M. Shaw *(Royal Roads University and University of the West Indies)*

The European Union (2008)
by Clive Archer *(Manchester Metropolitan University)*

The World Bank (2008)
From reconstruction to development to equity
by Katherine Marshall *(Georgetown University)*

Contemporary Human Rights Ideas (2008)
by Bertrand G. Ramcharan *(Geneva Graduate Institute of International and Development Studies)*

The United Nations High Commissioner for Refugees (UNHCR) (2008)
The politics and practice of refugee protection into the twenty-first century
by Gil Loescher *(University of Oxford)*, Alexander Betts *(University of Oxford)*, and James Milner *(University of Toronto)*

The International Olympic Committee and the Olympic System (2008)
The governance of world sport
by Jean-Loup Chappelet *(IDHEAP Swiss Graduate School of Public Administration)* and Brenda Kübler-Mabbott

Institutions of the Asia-Pacific (2009)
ASEAN, APEC, and beyond
by Mark Beeson *(University of Birmingham)*

Internet Governance (2009)
The new frontier of global institutions
by John Mathiason *(Syracuse University)*

The World Health Organization (2009)
by Kelley Lee *(London School of Hygiene and Tropical Medicine)*

International Judicial Institutions (2009)
The architecture of international justice at home and abroad
by Richard J. Goldstone *(Retired Justice of the Constitutional Court of South Africa)* and Adam M. Smith

Institutions of the Global South (2009)
by Jacqueline Anne Braveboy-Wagner *(City College of New York)*

Global Food and Agricultural Institutions (2009)
by John Shaw

Shaping the Humanitarian World (2009)
by Peter Walker *(Tufts University)* and Daniel G. Maxwell *(Tufts University)*

The International Organization for Standardization and the Global Economy (2009)
Setting standards
by Craig N. Murphy *(Wellesley College)* and JoAnne Yates *(Massachusetts Institute of Technology)*

Organisation for Economic Co-operation and Development
by Richard Woodward *(University of Hull)*

Non-Governmental Organizations in Global Politics
by Peter Willetts *(City University, London)*

The International Labour Organization
by Steve Hughes *(University of Newcastle)* and Nigel Haworth *(The University of Auckland Business School)*

Global Institutions and the HIV/AIDS Epidemic
Responding to an international crisis
by Franklyn Lisk *(University of Warwick)*

African Economic Institutions
by Kwame Akonor (Seton Hall University)

The United Nations Development Programme (UNDP)
by Elizabeth A. Mandeville (Tufts University) and
Craig N. Murphy (Wellesley College)

The Regional Development Banks
Lending with a regional flavor
by Jonathan R. Strand (University of Nevada, Las Vegas)

Multilateral Cooperation Against Terrorism
by Peter Romaniuk (John Jay College of Criminal Justice, CUNY)

Transnational Organized Crime
by Frank Madsen (University of Cambridge)

Peacebuilding
From concept to commission
by Robert Jenkins (University of London)

Governing Climate Change
by Peter Newell (University of East Anglia) and
Harriet A. Bulkeley (Durham University)

Millennium Development Goals (MDGs)
For a people-centered development agenda?
by Sakiko Fukada-Parr (The New School)

Regional Security
The capacity of international organizations
by Rodrigo Tavares (United Nations University)

Human Development
by Maggie Black

Human Security
by Dan Hubert (University of Ottawa)

For further information regarding the series, please contact:

Craig Fowlie, Publisher, Politics & International Studies
Taylor & Francis
2 Park Square, Milton Park, Abingdon
Oxford OX14 4RN, UK

+44 (0)207 842 2057 Tel
+44 (0)207 842 2302 Fax

Craig.Fowlie@tandf.co.uk
www.routledge.com

Global Food and Agricultural Institutions

D. John Shaw

LONDON AND NEW YORK

First published 2009
by Routledge
2 Park Square, Milton Park, Abingdon, Oxon OX14 4RN

Simultaneously published in the U.S.A. and Canada
by Routledge
270 Madison Avenue, New York, NY 10016

Routledge is an imprint of the Taylor & Francis Group, an informa business

Transferred to Digital Printing 2010

© 2009 D. John Shaw

Typeset in Times New Roman by
Taylor & Francis Books

All rights reserved. No part of this book may be reprinted or reproduced or utilised in any form or by any electronic, mechanical, or other means, now known or hereafter invented, including photocopying and recording, or in any information storage or retrieval system, without permission in writing from the publishers.

British Library Cataloguing in Publication Data
A catalogue record for this book is available from the British Library

Library of Congress Cataloging in Publication Data
Shaw, D. John.
　Global food and agricultural institutions / D. John Shaw.
　　p. cm.—(Global institutions)
　Includes bibliographical references and index.
　　1. Food-supply—International cooperation. 2. Food relief—International cooperation. 3. Agricultural assistance—Developing countries. 4. Economic assistance—Developing countries. I. Title.
　HD9000.6.S48 2008
　　338.1'9091724—dc22
　　　　　　　　　　　2008021727

ISBN 978-0-415-44503-0 (hbk)
ISBN 978-0-415-44504-7 (pbk)
ISBN 978-0-203-88727-1 (ebk)

Dedicated to past and present staff members of the Global Food and Agricultural Institutions included in this book for their professionalism and devotion to the cause of world food security.

And he gave it his opinion, that whoever could make two ears of corn or two blades of grass to grow upon a spot of ground where only one grew before, would deserve better of mankind, and do more essential service to his country than the whole race of politicians put together.
Jonathan Swift, *Gulliver's Travels*

One man's hunger is every man's hunger—one man's freedom from hunger is neither a free nor secure freedom until all men are free from hunger.
John Donne

Democracy is a word that rumbles meaninglessly in empty bellies.
Lord Richie Calder

Contents

List of illustrations xiv
Foreword xvi
Acknowledgments xix
List of abbreviations xxii

   Introduction 1

1 Background 4

2 Origins 53

3 Mandates, governance, and finance 67

4 Policies, programs, and projects 95

5 Future directions 172

   Postscript 217

Notes 218
Web sites and select bibliography 231
Index 235

Illustrations

Tables

I.1	The five global food and agricultural institutions covered in this book	2
1.1	World grain production, consumption and stocks	7
1.2	Cereal import bill in low-income, food-deficit countries	7
1.3	Undernutrition in the developing world, 1979–81 to 2001–6	9
1.4	Number of people living below U.S.$1 and U.S.$2 a day, 1979–81 to 2001–06	21
3.1	WFP annual contributions, 1998–2007	81
3.2	IFAD resources	87
3.3	IFAD operational activities (1976–2007)	88
3.4	CGIAR funding by type of center, 1972–2005	94
4.1	FAO Investment Centre prepared projects approved, 1964–2004	108
4.2	Geographical distribution of FAO Technical Cooperation Program, 2004–5	110
4.3	World Bank (IBRD+IDA) commitments to agriculture, 2000–7	121
4.4	WFP: from development to emergencies	122
4.5	Beneficiaries of WFP assistance, 1998–2006	127
4.6	WFP primary school feeding programs, 2000–5	129
4.7	IFAD assistance by type of project, 1978–2007	142
4.8	IFAD assistance by region, 1978–2007	143
4.9	Investments in the CGIAR Challenge Programs	169
5.1	United Nations bodies with an interest in food and nutrition security	209

Figures

3.1	FAO financial profile: total biennial resources available 1994–2007	70
3.2	CGIAR's evolving research agenda	89
4.1	World Bank (IBRD/IDA) assistance to agriculture 1970–2001	112
4.2	The CGIAR centers	154

Box

I.1	Millennium development goals and targets	4

Foreword

The current volume is the thirty-first in a dynamic series on "global institutions." The series strives (and, based on the volumes published to date, succeeds) to provide readers with definitive guides to the most visible aspects of what many of us know as "global governance." Remarkable as it may seem, there exist relatively few books that offer in-depth treatments of prominent global bodies, processes, and associated issues, much less an entire series of concise and complementary volumes. Those that do exist are either out of date, inaccessible to the non-specialist reader, or seek to develop a specialized understanding of particular aspects of an institution or process rather than offer an overall account of its functioning. Similarly, existing books have often been written in highly technical language or have been crafted "in-house" and are notoriously self-serving and narrow.

The advent of electronic media has undoubtedly helped research and teaching by making data and primary documents of international organizations more widely available, but it has also complicated matters. The growing reliance on the Internet and other electronic methods of finding information about key international organizations and processes has served, ironically, to limit the educational and analytical materials to which most readers have ready access—namely, books. Public relations documents, raw data, and loosely refereed web sites do not make for intelligent analysis. Official publications compete with a vast amount of electronically available information, much of which is suspect because of its ideological or self-promoting slant. Paradoxically, a growing range of purportedly independent web sites offering analyses of the activities of particular organizations has emerged, but one inadvertent consequence has been to frustrate access to basic, authoritative, readable, critical, and well researched texts. The market for such has actually been reduced by the ready availability of varying quality electronic materials.

For those of us who teach, research, and practice in the area, such limited access to information has been particularly frustrating. We were delighted when Routledge saw the value of a series that bucks this trend and provides key reference points to the most significant global institutions and issues. They are betting that serious students and professionals will want serious analyses. We have assembled a first-rate line-up of authors to address that market. Our intention, then, is to provide one-stop shopping for all readers—students (both undergraduate and postgraduate), negotiators, diplomats, practitioners from non-governmental and intergovernmental organizations, and interested parties alike—seeking information about the most prominent institutional aspects of global governance.

Global food and agricultural institutions

Nothing is more basic to human survival than food. Global concern over the earth's ability to provide for and sustain the world's rapidly increasing human population dates back at least to 1798 when Thomas R. Malthus first predicted that population growth would outstrip the world's food supply.[1] Technological advance during the Industrial Revolution proved Malthus wrong, but the need to balance food production with population growth today remains extremely pertinent. The framing has evolved into a pressing humanitarian and equality issue in terms of how food is distributed and who has access to it.

Even as this volume goes to press, the issue has received a new analytical twist and urgency as record food and oil prices and the relatively new priority given to subsidies for bio-fuels in both industrialized countries as well as in Brazil have led to both higher food prices and lower stocks that are at the root of riots, political instability, and food shortages in poor countries ranging from Haiti to Egypt. In mid-April 2008, the perilous trade-offs between policy choices about the environment and food availability came from 400 experts who were behind the report of the International Assessment of Agricultural Science and Technology for Development (IAASTD).[2]

The IAASTD assessment was the result of a three-year collaborative effort (2005–7) by seven UN agencies;[3] it concludes that while agricultural science and technology have made it possible to greatly increase productivity in the last 50 years, sharing of the benefits has been far from equitable, and progress has been achieved at high social and environmental costs. While many of our readers take food for granted, this is not the case elsewhere. For example, the poorest 20 percent of US households devote about 15 percent of their family budgets to food, whereas Nigerians spend almost 75 percent. Indeed, World Bank president Robert Zoellick pointed to the growing concern for poor people everywhere: "For countries where food comprises from half to three-quarters of consumption, there is no margin for survival."[4]

Other volumes in the series have touched upon the topic of food in relation to human rights,[5] the environment,[6] and humanitarian action for internally displaced persons and for refugees,[7] and so we are delighted to add to our series this informative and well argued volume that deals directly with the nuts and bolts of the essential global institutions dealing with food and agriculture. Over the years, states have created numerous institutions to deal with evolving issues. For instance, the Food and Agriculture Organization (FAO) of the United Nations was created in October 1945—a week before the United Nations Charter went into effect—but intergovernmental discussions regarding the need for a permanent global organization for food and agriculture date back to 1943, two years prior to the UN's founding. In 1961, the FAO and UN General Assembly created the World Food Programme (WFP), and in 1974 the International Fund for Agricultural Development (IFAD) and World Food Council (WFC) were added to the international panoply of UN institutions.

Given the complex history of global food and agricultural institutions, we needed someone with extensive experience and knowledge of the issues to write this volume. We are delighted that John Shaw took up our challenge. John is extremely well positioned to write this book, having served for over 30 years with WFP at its headquarters in Rome, Italy, latterly as its economic adviser and chief of WFP's Policy Affairs Service. He has a long and distinguished career in policymaking, having also worked as a consultant for the FAO, the World Bank, and the Commonwealth Secretariat.

As a senior lecturer in rural economy at the University of Khartoum in Sudan and then a fellow in agricultural economics and founding member of the Institute of Development Studies at the University of Sussex, UK, he has also written extensively on food security and has broadened his interest to include other issues in the development conundrum. Some of his most notable works include *World Food Security: A History Since 1945*, *Sir Hans Singer: The Life and Work of a Development Economist* and *The UN World Food Progamme and the Development of Food Aid*.[8]

As always, we look forward to comments from first-time or veteran readers of the Global Institutions series.

Thomas G. Weiss, the CUNY Graduate Center, New York, USA
Rorden Wilkinson, University of Manchester, UK
August 2008

Acknowledgments

This book has involved consulting the considerable documentation and publications relating to the histories and current activities of the selected global food and agricultural institutions, and interviewing and corresponding with their staff members and others knowledgeable of their past and present work. Without their cooperation, it would not have been possible to give the many details contained in this book. I hope that I have adequately conveyed a sense of indebtedness to them and, particularly, that they feel that the final product repays with gratitude all the help they gave me.

I enjoyed full support and cooperation from all the institutions concerned. I therefore begin my debts of gratitude with the staff members of the institutions. First, I would particularly like to thank those who were designated as contact points. They arranged my timetables of interviews for my visits to Rome, Italy and Washington, D.C., provided me with much material, and responded to my many questions: at FAO, Nick Parsons and Alison Small; at the World Bank's Agricultural and Rural Development Division, Chris Delgado; at WFP, Paul Howe, Marco Cavalcante and Sylvie Trulli; at IFAD, Taysir al-Ghanem; and at the CGIAR secretariat, Nathan Russell.

During my visit to Rome, I met a cross-section of staff at the three UN organizations located there. At FAO, I interviewed Peter Kenmore, Kostas Stamoulis, Doug Kneeland, Deodoro Roca, Michael Wales, Prabhu Pingali, Jorge Csirke-Barcelli, and Abdul Kobakiwal. At IFAD, I spoke with Gary Howe, Sean Kennedy, Eleanor Alesi, Helen Terry, Christian Mersmann, Matthew Wyatt, Bruce Moore, Gunilla Olsson, Kevin Cleaver, Uday Abhyankar, and Khalida Bouzar. At WFP, I met with George Simon, John Aylieff, Jean-Jacques Graisse, Jamie Wickens, Suresh Sharma, Deborah Hines, Joseph Scalise, Robin Jackson, Francis Mwanza, Lisa Doughten, Tina Van Den Briel, Edith Heines, Sarah Laughton, Adama Faye, Ugo Gentilini, Henk Jan

Brinkman, Haladou Salha, and Francisco Espejo. John Powell provided me with documentation and an explanation relating to WFP's financial position. During my visit to Washington, D.C., at the World Bank, I spoke with Gershon Feder, Chirs Delgado, Eric Schesinger, Ranjiva Cooke, and Chris Gerrard. At the CGIAR secretariat, I met with Selcuk Ozgediz, and at IFPRI with Rajul Pandya-Lorch, Regina Birner, Marc Cohen and Djhoanna Cruz.

All the UN organizations and the CGIAR secretariat gave permission to quote from their documentation and publications and to use the tables and figures reproduced in this book. The U.S. Department of Agriculture gave permission to reproduce Table 1.1.Shaohua Chen and Martin Ravallion of the World Bank gave permission to publish Table 1.4. The Brookings Institution gave permission to draw from the histories of the World Bank that they published, Edward S. Mason and Robert E. Asher, *The World Bank since Bretton Woods* (1973) and Devish Kapur, John P. Lewis, and Richard Webb, *The World Bank. Its First Fifty Years. Vol. 1. History* (1997), in describing the origins of the IBRD and IDA and their governance and management, and the work of the Bank's Agricultural and Rural Department during its first 50 years. Gordon Gonway gave permission to quote from his book on *The Doubly Green Revolution* (1997). Cambridge University Press gave permission to refer to the book by Nicolas Stern on *The Economics of Climate Change* (2006). Blackwell Publishing and the Production Manager gave permission to use my articles and book reviews that have appeared in the journals *Development Policy Review* and the *Canadian Journal of Development Studies* respectively. Oxford University Press gave permission to quote from the book by Paul Collier on *The Bottom Billion* (2007). The UNDP gave permission to quote from the report of the *Millennium Project* (2005). Simon & Schuster gave permission to quote from the book by George McGovern on *The Third Freedom. Ending Hunger in Our Time* (2001). The Center for Global Development gave permission to quote from its publication, *Rescuing the World Bank* (2006). James Ingram gave permission to quote from his book *Bread and Stones* (2007). Bo M. I. Bengtsson gave permission to quote from his book *Agricultural Research at the Crossroads* (2007). The Earth Policy Institute gave permission to quote from the books by Lester Brown on *Outgrowing the Earth* (2004) and *Plan B 3.0* (2008). Palgrave Macmillan gave permission to draw in part from my book *World Food Security. A History since 1945* (2007) in Chapter 1, "Background," and in Chapter 5, "Future Directions" concerning the work and demise of the World Food Council.

Simon Maxwell has been a continuous source of encouragement and inspiration. Sartaj Aziz gave me copies of the position papers he prepared for the 1974 World Food Conference when he was director of FAO's Commodities and Trade Division and one of the deputy secretaries-general of the conference that had important bearings on the proposals presented to the conference on IFAD and the WFC and the related outcomes. The WFC secretariat gave me a complete set of the council's documents and papers when it was disbanded in 1993. Uwe Kracht, who served in the WFC secretariat as senior economist (1976–86) and chief of policy development and analysis (1986–93) reviewed the section on WFC and its work. He also gave permission for reference to be made to the book he edited with Wenche Barth Eide on *Food and Human Rights* (2007), and the book he edited with Manfred Schulz on *Food Aid and Nutrition in the Process of Globalization and Urbanization* (2005). Panos Konandreas of the FAO office in Geneva, Switzerland provided me with information concerning the ongoing debate in the WTO on food aid. I am grateful to Kevin Cleaver for his permission to quote from his paper on "Contemporary issues of agriculture and rural development in developing countries" (2007), to Prabhu Pingali and Tim Kelley for their article on "The role of international agricultural research in contributing to global food security and poverty alleviation: The case of the CGIAR" (2007), and to Chris Gerrard for his paper on "Global governance without global government: the growth and implications of Global Partnership Programs" (2008). Karen Rosskopf provided me with material relating to the CGIAR initiative on the Global Open Food and Agricultural University (GO-FAU). I am indebted to Peter Greaves for the quote from a speech by Lord Richie Calder.

I am grateful to my son, Dr. David Christian Shaw, who prepared the tables and figures that appear in this book.

Last, but far from being least, I owe much to my wife, Ileana, and my son and daughter, David and Elizabeth, for their support and encouragement.

I would like to thank the editors of the Routledge Global Institutions series, Thomas G. Weiss and Rorden Wilkinson, and the publisher, Routledge, for the opportunity to write this book, which is the first occasion that the global food and agricultural institutions have been reviewed and analyzed together. A draft manuscript of the book was shown to the series editors and to the five institutions concerned for comment. The comments received were taken into consideration in finalizing the manuscript.

D. John Shaw

Abbreviations

ACC	Administrative Committee on Coordination (UN)
BMI	body mass index
CDC	Centers for Disease Control and Prevention (U.S.)
CGIAR	Concultative Group on International Agriculture Reward
CHS	United Nations Commission on Human Security
ECOSOC	Economic and Social Council of the United Nations
EU	European Union
FAO	Food and Agriculture Organization of the United Nations
FDA	Federal Drug Administration (U.S.)
FTI	Fast Track Initiative (aid for education)
FY	financial year
GDP	gross domestic product
GEF	Global Environment Facility
GNI	gross national income
GNP	gross national product
G8	Group of eight leading industrialized countries (Canada, France, Germany, Italy, Japan, Russian Federation, United Kingdom, United States)
G77	Group of non-aligned developing countries (currently 131 countries)
IAEA	International Atomic Energy Agency
IBRD	International Bank for Reconstruction and Development (World Bank)
IDA	International Development Association (World Bank)
IFAD	International Fund for Agricultural Development
IFC	International Finance Corporation (World Bank)
IFI	International Financial Institution
IFPRI	International Food Policy Research Institute

ILO	International Labour Organization
IMF	International Monetary Fund
INSTRAW	International Institute for Training and Research on Women
IPCC	Intergovernmental Panel on Climate Change
MDG	Millennium Development Goal
NGO	non-governmental organization
ODA	official development assistance
OECD	Organization for Economic Development and Cooperative
OPEC	Organization of Petroleum Exporting Countries
SCN	United Nations Standing Committee on Nutrition
SLM	sustainable land management
UN	United Nations
UNCTAD	United Nations Conference on Trade and Development
UNCTC	United Nations Committee on Transnational Corporations
UNDHA	United Nations Department for Humanitarian Affairs
UNDP	United Nations Development Programme
UNEP	United National Environment Programme
UNESCO	United Nations Educational, Scientific and Cultural Organization
UNFPA	United Nations Population Fund
UNHCR	United Nations High Commissioner for Refugees
UNICEF	United Nations Children's Fund
UNIDO	United Nations Industrial Organization
UNITAR	United Nations Institute for Training and Research
UNU	United Nations University
UNRWA	United Nations Relief and Works Administration for Palestinian refugees
UNRISD	United Nations Research Institute for Social Development
WFC	World Food Council
WFP	United Nations World Food Programme
WHO	World Health Organization
WMO	World Meteorological Organization
WTO	World Trade Organization

Introduction

The five global food and agricultural institutions covered in this book (see Table 1.1)—the Food and Agriculture Organization of the United Nations (FAO), the Agriculture and Rural Development Department (ARD) of the World Bank, the International Fund for Agricultural Development (IFAD), the UN World Food Programme (WFP) and the Consultative Group on International Agricultural Research (CGIAR)—share a number of common features. They all work for or with food. They seek to end hunger and alleviate poverty. They subscribe to contributing to the achievement of the Millennium Development Goals (MDGs) established by world leaders at the UN Millennium Summit in 2000. And they share common member countries. All are committed to working closely with other aid agencies, and non-governmental and civil society organizations, and are endeavoring to strengthen ties with the private sector. But they retain their own separate identities, governing bodies, management structures, financing arrangements, and programs of assistance. Calls have been made for them to work closer together, especially in common programs and projects in the developing countries. In a wider context, there is increasing pressure for them to work in concert with other aid bodies both within and outside the food and agricultural sector against the background of attempts to reform the United Nations system and measures to improve aid effectiveness.

Three of the five institutions (FAO, IFAD and WFP) are located in Rome, Italy and two (ARD and the CGIAR) in Washington, D.C. (see Table I.1). While FAO and the World Bank started operations over 60 years ago, the youngest, IFAD, has been in operation for half that time. It is difficult to compare the level of aid provided by the different institutions owing to differences in computing. But clearly there are considerable differences, with WFP providing some $2.9 billion of assistance in 2006, mostly to meet emergencies, and the World Bank's

2 Introduction

Table I.1 The five global food and agricultural institutions covered in this book

Institution	Location	Start of operation	Staffing	Funding (US$ millions)	Total prof. (US$ millions)	Mission
FAO	Rome, Italy	1946	3,526	867.6[a]	1,577	Helping to build a world without hunger.
ARD+	Washington, D.C.	1946	465	1,807.0[b]	235	To fight poverty.
WFP	Rome, Italy	1963	2,561[d]	2,900.0[c]	1,295	To save lives and end hunger.
IFAD	Rome, Italy	1978	485	566.8[e]	242	To enable the rural poor to overcome poverty.
CGIAR	Washington, D.C.	1971	8,154[g]	426.0[f]	1,115	To achieve sustainable food security and reduce poverty.

+ Agricultural and Rural Development Department of the World Bank
[a] Regular program 2008–9, ex-extra-budgetary funding
[b] FY 2007 commitment to agriculture
[c] operational expenditure 2006
[d] with locally recruited staff, total WFP is about 12,000
[e] total assistance 2007
[f] total funding 2006
[g] includes staffing at 15 CGIAR centers
Source: Institutions' documentation.

commitments to agriculture in financial year (FY) 2007 of $1.8 billion. Staff complements also differ markedly, showing wide staff/aid ratios. But the mission statements of all institutions show a close similarity.

A primary aim of this book is to convey to the general public a clear idea of what these institutions do, how they "tick" in terms of their governance, management, and operations, and what kinds of problems confront them. It is increasingly important that the general public are aware of what these institutions are doing so that they can more effectively take part in their resourcing, activities, and the effectiveness of the aid they provide.

The first chapter gives the status of the various dimensions of poverty and hunger as a background against which the work of these institutions should be seen and assessed. The second chapter describes the different origins of each institution and the ways in which they were created. The third chapter describes their missions, governance, management, staffing and financial positions. The fourth chapter gives details of their policies, programs and projects of assistance to the extent that space allows. The final chapter discusses the problems they face, and solutions proposed, in the light of independent external evaluations that have been carried out and views and opinions expressed.

The indications are that the work of these institutions will be of increasing importance in the years ahead as the problems and crises caused by such factors as climate change and global warming, rising food price, the wider application of genetically modified crops and food, and a process of globalization that is tending to exacerbate rather than eradicate hunger and poverty, take hold. The ways in which these institutions are reformed to take account of major developments in a changing world, and how they cooperate among themselves and with other institutions to solve global problems, will require careful governance, management, and leadership.

1 Background

This chapter provides details of the current dimensions of poverty and hunger, and emerging global crises related to the spread of genetically modified crops and food, sharp and dramatic food and oil price rises, climate change and global warming, and a process of globalization that is exacerbating poverty and hunger, as background for assessing the work and impact of the global food and agricultural institutions included in this book. In addition, their work should be judged against national and international efforts to meet the Millennium Development Goals (MDGs) approved by world leaders at the UN Millennium Summit in 2000. The goals offer a comprehensive and multidimensional development framework and set clear quantifiable targets to be achieved by 2015, including halving the proportion of the world's population whose income is less than a dollar a day and who suffer from hunger (see Box 1.1).

It is a remarkable achievement that, despite a doubling of the world population to more than 6 billion people over the past 30 years, on

---

***Box 1.1* Millennium development goals and targets**

1 Eradicating extreme poverty and hunger

- Halve, between 1990 and 2015, the proportion of the world's population whose income is less that one dollar a day.
- Halve, between 1990 and 2015, the proportion of people who suffer from hunger.

2 Achieve universal primary education

- Ensure that, by 2015, children everywhere, boys and girls alike, will be able to complete a full course of primary education.

3 Promote gender equality and empower women

- Eliminate gender disparity in primary and secondary education, preferably by 2005, and in all levels of education no later than 2015.

4 Reduce child mortality

- Reduce by two-thirds, between 1990 and 2015, under-five child mortality.

5 Improve maternal health

- Reduce by three-quarters, between 1990 and 2015, the maternal mortality ratio.

6 Combat HIV/AIDS, Malaria and other illnesses

- Halt by 2015 and begin to reverse the spread of HIV/AIDS.
- Halt by 2015 and begin to reverse the incidence of malaria and other major diseases.

7 Ensure environmental sustainability

- Integrate the principles of sustainable development into country policies and programmes and reverse the loss of environmental resources.
- Halve, by 2015, the proportion of people without sustainable access to safe drinking water and basic sanitation.
- Achieve, by 2020, a significant improvement in the lives of at least 100 million slum-dwellers.

8 Develop a global partnership for development

- Develop further an open, rules-based, predictable, non-discriminatory trading and financial system (including a commitment to good governance, development, and poverty reduction, nationally and internationally).
- Address the special needs of the least developed countries (includes tariff and quota-free access for least developed countries exports; enhanced programme of debt relief for

> heavily indebted poor countries and cancellation of official bilateral debts; and more generous ODA for countries committed to poverty reduction).
> - Address the special needs of landlocked countries and small island developing states (through the Programme of Action for the Sustainable Development of Small Island Developing States and the outcome of the twenty-second special session of the General Assembly).
> - Deal comprehensively with the debt problems of developing countries through national and international measures in order to make debt sustainable in the long term.
> - In cooperation with developing countries, develop and implement strategies for decent and productive work for youth.
> - In co-operation with pharmaceutical companies, provide access to affordable, essential drugs in developing countries.
> - In cooperation with the private sector, make available the benefits of technologies, especially information and communications.
>
> Source: *United Nations Millennium Declaration* (New York: United Nations, 2000)

average its citizens are now better and more nutritiously fed than ever before as agricultural production has outpaced population growth. Much of the credit for this outcome lies with the food and agricultural institutions reviewed in this publication. But there have been downsides to this progress, and the future will present some formidable challenges. Not all developing regions have made equal progress in food production. The poorest developing countries have experienced low agricultural productivity growth. The situation in sub-Saharan Africa is particularly disquieting, where food production has actually declined. In seven of the last eight years, the world has consumed more grain than it produced. And global grain stocks have declined (Table 1.1)

While long-run real food commodity prices have been declining, prices of basic foodstuffs have increased sharply in recent years (Table 1.2). The agricultural trade deficit of the least developing countries, the difference between the value of their agricultural exports and imports, is widening. Investment in agriculture lags where hunger is most prevalent. External assistance to agriculture is far below the levels of the 1980s, and does not target the neediest countries. The outcome is that hunger and poverty continue to be major problems that require high priority and consistent attention, with particular focus on

Table 1.1 World grain production, consumption and stocks (million tons)

Year	Production	Consumption	Stocks	Consumption days
1960	824	815	203	91
1970	1,079	1,108	193	64
1980	1,429	1,440	308	78
1990	1,768	1,707	492	105
2000	1,843	1,857	564	111
2001	1,875	1,902	534	102
2002	1,822	1,909	441	84
2003	1,862	1,934	356	67
2004	2,043	1,990	404	74
2005	2,017	2,019	389	70
2006	1,992	2,043	336	60
2007	2,077	2,091	309	54

Source: U.S. Department of Agriculture.

the low-income, food-deficit countries and their people. These problems are increasingly complex and require greater coordinated and coherent action both within the agricultural sector and with other sectors of the economies of poor countries.

Dimensions of poverty and hunger

Poverty and hunger have many dimensions, including: food and nutrition insecurity, the effects of population growth, the income factor, the importance of education, the link between employment and

Table 1.2 Cereal import bill in low-income, food-deficit countries (July/June, U.S.$ million)

Regions	2002/03	2003/04	2004/05	2005/06	2006/07	2007/08
Total	14,0251	15,804	18,870	18,040	24,460	33,113
Africa	6,501	7,098	8,417	8,400	10,212	15,210
Asia	7,014	8,052	9,767	8,880	13,337	16,658
Oceania	69	76	78	82	99	124
Europe	133	1,981	201	209	260	397
Cereals:						
Wheat	7,762	8,802	10,814	10,581	14,034	20,729
Coarse grains	3,281	3,300	3,394	3,088	4,614	5,490
Rice	2,982	3,702	4,662	4,370	5,812	6,894

Source: FAO.

8 *Background*

productivity, international trade, and human security. UN organizations and other international institutions publish annual and special reports on various aspects and dimensions of poverty that are read in isolation, often only by specialized groups of readers. If read simultaneously, they give a compounded picture of the various dimensions of poverty and hunger, and their interrelationships, and what might be done to reduce and eventually eradicate them. They also provide a framework for understanding the world in which the global food and agricultural institutions work, and the roles they play in contributing to overcoming hunger and poverty.

Food and nutrition insecurity

Food and nutrition security has been recognized as one of the most fundamental of all human rights at a number of past international conferences. At the same time, it has also been recognized that the world possesses enough resources and know-how to eradicate hunger and malnutrition. Achieving food security has been the subject of countless international conventions, declarations, compacts and resolutions. Yet despite significant progress in the 1990s, it is an appalling fact that in this globalizing world of increasing prosperity, in which the richest tenth of the population own 85 percent of the world's assets, 162 million struggle on less than half a dollar a day, just under one billion people subsist on less than one dollar a day, 2.5 billion (almost half of the developing world's population) exist on less than two dollars a day, and 820 million people in the developing world suffer from under-nourishment in dehumanizing, abject poverty (Table 1.3).

Almost 200 million children under five years of age are underweight due to lack of food. Nearly 6 million children die each year from hunger and related causes. Some 2 billion people suffer from various form of micro-nutrient malnutrition, such as vitamin A, iodine and iron deficiency. Hunger and malnutrition kill more people every year than AIDS, malaria and tuberculosis combined, and more people die from hunger than in wars. At the center of this human tragedy is food and nutrition insecurity, inability to access the safe and nutritious food necessary for a healthy and active life. Yet, world leaders and international bodies have, many times, made a commitment to end hunger and poverty, and have acknowledged that sufficient resources and know-how exist to do so.

It has also been recognized that this scourge is not only morally unacceptable but is a serious impediment to equitable and sustainable economic and social development, and to world peace. Hunger,

Table 1.3 Undernutrition in the developing world, 1979–81 to 2001–6

Developing regions and countries	Number of undernourished people (millions)				Proportion of undernourished people in total population (%)			
	1979–81	1990–92	1995–97*	2000–06	1979–81	1990–92	95–97*	2000–06
Developing World	920.0	823.1	796.7	820.2	28	20	18	17
Asia and the Pacific	727.3	569.7	509.5	524.0	32	20	17	16
East Asia	307.3	198.7	155.1	159.5	29	16	12	12
China	303.8	193.6	145.6	150.3	30	16	12	12
South Asia	330.6	290.4	287.3	298.5	37	26	23	22
India	261.5	214.8	194.7	212.0	38	25	21	20
Latin America and the Caribbean	45.9	59.4	54.8	52.4	13	13	11	10
Near East and North Africa	21.5	25.0	34.9	37.7	9	8	10	9
Sub-Saharan Africa	125.4	169.6	197.4	203.5	36	36	36	32
Countries in transition	n.a.	23.4	23.3	24.7	n.a.	6	6	6

* For countries in transition 1993–95
n.a. = not available
Source: FAO, *The State of Food in Security in The World. 2006* (Rome, Italy: FAO, 2006).

malnutrition and poverty are intricately interlinked. Poverty is now generally regarded as the root cause of hunger and malnutrition. What is not always understood, however, is that hunger and malnutrition can be major causes of poverty. They can affect the capabilities and the capacities of individuals attempting to escape from poverty in several ways, including: reducing the capacity for physical work, and hence the productivity of poor and hungry people through their own labor, usually their only asset; impairing physical and metal development; retarding child growth, reducing cognitive ability, and seriously inhibiting school attendance and performance, thus compromising the effectiveness of investment in education; causing serious long-term damage to health, linked to higher rates a disease and premature death; causing inter-generational disadvantages as, for example, hungry mothers give birth to underweight children who start life with a major handicap; and contributing to social and political instability that further undermines government capacity to reduce poverty.

The causes of food shortages are varied and complex. Many countries have been plagued by severe food shortages for a decade or more. Conflict and economic problems have been cited as the main causes of more than 35 percent of food emergencies during the period 1992–2003. Thirty-three countries, particularly in sub-Saharan Africa, have been described as food emergency "hotspots." They have experienced food emergencies during more than half of the 17-year period between 1986 and 2003. Many conflict-induced complex emergencies, which may also coincide with drought, are persistent and turn into long-term crises. Eight countries suffered emergencies in 15 or more years between 1986 and 2003, with war or civil strife as a major cause.

As the only region in the world currently facing widespread chronic food insecurity as well as persistent threats of famine, sub-Saharan Africa deserves to be given special attention by the international community, as it has been at a number of international conferences. It has been correctly argued that Africa's persistent vulnerability to food in security is due as much to a failure of understanding the causes as to a failure of interventions. As food assistance will be required for a number of years to come in many African countries in order to achieve food security, it has been proposed that an international conference be held to determine common policies and coordinated programs for future food assistance to the region.

But who are the hungry poor, where are they concentrated, and why are they hungry and malnourished? Understanding what has been called the "anatomy" of hunger and food insecurity, and its determinants, is crucial for effective local, national and global strategies and action for their elimination. Hunger and poverty are still predominantly rural phenomena, and are likely to remain so for the next decade at least, although hunger in urban areas is increasing fast. Some 75 percent of the hungry poor live and work in rural areas. Projections suggest that over 60 percent will continue to do so in 2025 as urbanization takes place and urban poverty increases. Some people and places are more vulnerable to poverty and food insecurity than others. Smallholders living in dry lands face a much higher risk than those living and working in irrigated areas. Pastoralists who depend on livestock for much of their subsistence are another high-risk group. These estimated 675 million rural people are highly vulnerable to drought and flood, resource degradation, outbreaks of disease, and increasing pressure as human population increases and grazing areas shrink. Another high-risk group are artisan fishermen who have to supplement and diversify their incomes in many ways.

Wage laborers, especially landless or casually employed farm workers, are almost everywhere among those most likely to be poor and hungry, although the substantial array of marginal populations living in urban areas is also growing. So too are indigenous people and scheduled castes and tribes in the regions of Latin America and the Caribbean, the Near East and North Africa, and Asia and the Pacific. Female single-headed households are also among the most vulnerable to poverty and hunger, as are HIV/AIDS–affected people and communities. The interaction between food insecurity and HIV/AIDS is particularly pronounced. Since the HIV/AIDS pandemic began, 25 million people have died of the disease and another 42 million have become infected. During the present decade, AIDS is expected to claim more lives than all the wars and disasters of the past 50 years. The disease causes and exacerbates food insecurity in many ways, particularly by drastically debilitating and reducing the most productive part of the agricultural labor force. While this classification provides a broad indication of who, and where, the hungry poor are on a global scale, it is of limited value in operational terms. Systems have therefore been developed to map and analyze where the most vulnerable live and work, and why they are poor and food insecure, to help target intervention programs.

The perspective of world food insecurity as it affects children, the most vulnerable group, has been portrayed through the annual publications of the United Nations Children's Fund's (UNICEF) *State of the World's Children*. The publication for 2005[1] gives a relentless account of how nearly half of the 2 billion children throughout the

12 Background

world have been robbed of their childhood through the triple, and often interrelated, realities of poverty, armed conflict, and HIV/AIDS. Every year, more than 20 million low birth-weight babies are born in the developing world. From the moment of their birth, the scales are tipped against them in a vicious cycle of deprivation. The risk of neonatal death is four times higher in infants weighing less than 2.5 kg and 18 times higher for those weighing less than 2.0 kg. Almost a third of children in developing countries are stunted. The damage to physical and cognitive development is usually irreversible. The costs in blighted health and opportunities extend not only through the victim's life but also into the next generation as mothers give birth to low-weight babies. WHO estimates that more than 3.7 million deaths in 2000 could be attributed to underweight. And deficiencies in the three micro-nutrients, iron, vitamin A, and zinc, each caused an additional 750,000–850,000 deaths.

Childhood poverty and malnutrition have been found to portend high costs into adult life. Children who grow up poor and malnourished can cost the country in which they live because as adults they are less productive, earn less, have more health-related expenses, and may resort to crime as members of a marginalized underclass. This indicates that investing resources in poverty reduction is more cost-effective than generally thought. One measure used to quantify the impact of malnutrition on both poor health and increased mortality is called "disability-adjusted life years" (DALYs), the sum of years lost as a result of both premature death and disabilities, adjusted for severity. A *Global Burden of Disease Study*, sponsored by the World Health Organization (WHO) and the World Bank, ranks being underweight as the single most significant risk factor for DALYs worldwide, and for both death and DALYs in the group of high-mortality developing countries. This group includes almost 70 countries with a combined population of more than 2.3 billion people. Overall, childhood and maternal under-nutrition are estimated to cost more than 220 million DALYs in developing countries. When other nutrition-related risk factors are taken into account, the toll rises to almost 340 million DALYs, representing a loss of productivity equivalent to having disaster kill or disable the entire population of a country larger than the U.S.A.

The direct medical expenditure of treatment throughout the developing world is estimated at around $30 billion a year. These direct costs are dwarfed by the indirect costs of low productivity and reduced income caused by premature death, disability, absenteeism, and lower educational and occupational opportunities. Provisional estimates suggest that these indirect costs range in the hundreds of billions of dollars.

Coming at the costs of hunger from another direction, FAO conducted a macro-economic study to estimate the benefits of reducing by half the number of hungry people in the world by 2015. The study estimated the value of increased production that would be unleashed. Based only on increased life expectancy, the total discounted value over the years up to 2015 was estimated at about $3 trillion, which translates into an annuity benefit of $120 billion a year. The study also estimated that an increase of $24 billion a year in public investment, associated with additional private investment, would make it possible to halve the number of hungry people by 2015. This would boost GDP by $120 billion a year as a result of longer and healthier lives.

UNICEF and the World Bank joined forces to provide a perspective on global efforts to address malnutrition and to evaluate how the two organizations could contribute to overcoming it.[2] According to the joint study, nutrition has improved globally in the past decade but "slowly and unevenly." That was why, the joint study concluded, the MDGs could not be reached without significant progress in eliminating malnutrition. And yet, the joint assessment found, the prospects for eliminating malnutrition were "grim." There were several reasons for this finding. Nutrition was improving only slowly in some regions and was stagnant in others. Nutrition was "sidelined" in poverty reduction agendas despite its potential to improve health, development, and productivity.

While there had been broad agreement on key interventions to improve nutrition, and on the factors necessary for successful implementation, this was not reflected in action. Few large-scale nutrition-improvement programs were rigorously monitored and evaluated. Capacity in developing countries to tackle malnutrition as a major factor limiting progress toward poverty reduction was inadequate and spending on nutrition improvement was generally low and poorly targeted. And better collaboration and coordination among the numerous organizations involved in combating malnutrition could strengthen nutrition-improvement action.

In many ways, the UNICEF World Bank relationship represents a microcosm of the institutional incoherence that exists in trying to establish coherent and complementary actions among the numerous organizations and agencies involved in addressing malnutrition and nutritional concerns (see below). While both organizations shared a common vision for nutrition improvement, they differed significantly on processes, institutional approaches and means. It was recommended that both organizations should consider launching a special joint initiative to reach the MDGs in concert with other organizations.

The International Food Policy Research Institute (IFPRI) has made major contributions to both an understanding of the causes of world food insecurity and to their eradication. In 1995, the institute launched a *2020 Vision for Food, Agriculture, and the Environment* to seek consensus about the problems of ensuring adequate future food supplies, while protecting the world's natural resources. It created a vision for the future and recommended immediate action. This vision was complemented by the institute's *Reaching Sustainable Food Security for All by 2020: Getting the Priorities and Responsibilities Right*,[3] which identified nine "driving forces" regarded as critical in efforts to achieve the *2020 Vision*: accelerating globalization and further trade liberalization; sweeping technological changes; halting degradation of natural resources and increasing water scarcity; health and nutrition crises; addressing rapid urbanization; recognizing the changing nature of farming in developing countries with small-scale family farms under threat; facing continued conflict; reversing climate change; and recognizing the changing roles and responsibilities of key actors, especially local governments, business and industry, and NGOs, as national governments played new and diminished roles. IFPRI emphasized that rapid economic growth is essential to achieve food security for all by 2020, but the challenge is to achieve that growth in ways that benefited the poor through what is called "pro-poor economic growth."

In a book published by IFPRI in 2003 on *Ending Hunger in our Lifetime*,[4] the themes from IFPRI's *2020 Vision* were extended and deepened. In their foreword to the book, IFPRI's director general, Joachim von Braun, and the president of the non-denominational NGO, Bread for the World, David Beckmann, wrote:

> Hunger, and the misery that accompanies it, have been scourges for millennia. But in a global society, increasing interconnected communities can no longer conjure [up] excuses for failing to banish the chronic, recurring, hunger-related crises affecting their neighbors. In fact, the global community stands indicted for knowing much about how to reduce hunger, but not doing so. In this context, "business as usual" takes on a distinctly unethical meaning, describing as it does a global effort falling far short of ending hunger anytime soon, even by 2050. ... No one can pretend that ending hunger will be easy, but it *must* and *can* be done.
>
> (original emphasis)

The book presents a wide-ranging array of ideas, arguments, and facts and figures, on ending hunger. One of its main themes is that global peace and stability can only be achieved by ending the deprivation of the world's poor. The authors predict that the goal of halving the world's hungry by 2015 "will almost certainly not be reached." However, their analysis shows that global hunger could be substantially reduced by 2025 and chronic mass hunger ended by 2050. They regard this achievement as no more ambitious than that of the near-elimination of the many infectious diseases that stalked the world a century ago. But they recognize that unlike vaccination against disease, food insecurity will need a larger set of changes if it is to be eradicated, including: institutional reforms in trade policies; the rehabilitation and renewed commitment to multilateral aid; significant reforms in natural resource management; and major new investment in agricultural science and technology. They believe that while national governments will play a central role in facilitating these changes, part of the burden will fall on the private sector, non-governmental organizations (NGOs) and civil society, and that broad international cooperation among rich and poor countries will be essential if the fight against hunger, misery and discontent is to succeed. The authors acknowledge that without major changes in more countries, progress against poverty and hunger will be "too slow to win the fight."

The authors observe that the ways of improving poverty, health and food security are closely interconnected, and require a strengthening of cooperation among the various international agencies involved. They call for: reform of the World Bank to support pro-poor growth and to shift its resources toward grants for the poorest countries and poorest segments of the populations of middle-income countries; expanded roles for FAO and WHO; an effective organization to address international environmental issues; the same standards of accountability, transparency and legitimacy for NGOs that they seek to impose on international organizations; an increase in the efficiency of the global food distribution system; a fair and just involvement of developing countries in the international market economy; and much greater foreign assistance. The book ends with a quotation from Amartya Sen, who was awarded the Nobel Prize in Economics in 1998:

> The contemporary age is not short of terrible and nasty happenings, but the persistence of extensive hunger in a world of unprecedented prosperity is surely one of the worst. ... massive endemic hunger causes misery in many parts of the world—debilitating

16 *Background*

hundreds of millions and killing a sizable proportion of them with statistical regularity. What makes this widespread hunger even more of a tragedy is the way we have come to accept and tolerate it as an integral part of the modern world, as if it is a tragedy that is essentially unpreventable. [5]

An alternative, controversial and less optimistic view of the state of world food and nutrition security than that of the global food and agricultural institutions covered in this book is given by Lester Brown, president of the Earth Policy Institute, which he founded in 2001. He presents the case for redefining world food security by pointing out that for the past 40 years international trade negotiations have been dominated by the main grain-exporting countries seeking markets. But now the world may be moving into a period dominated not by food surpluses but by shortages.[6] If this were to happen, the issue becomes not exporters' access to markets but importers' access to supplies, in what Brown calls "the politics of food scarcity." He considers that the big test for the international community's capacity to manage food scarcity may come if China imports large amounts of grain every year on a scale that could quickly overwhelm world gain markets and raise prices, with serious consequences for poor, food importing, developing countries, and for world food security. Opposite and more optimistic views have been presented that China will effectively manage its food economy, including by producing food abroad in countries with land capacity, such as Brazil and Sudan.

Brown reasons that as food surpluses are replaced by scarcity, more attention will need to be paid to the international management of carryover grain stocks, and on stabilizing four critical agricultural resources: cropland, water, rangeland, and the earth's climate. He considers that future food security cannot be left to ministries of agriculture alone but will depend on an integrated effort of several government departments and strong national political leadership. Similarly, he calls for better integration among the international agencies concerned with global food security. He concludes that in a world that is increasingly integrated economically, food security is now a global issue that gets little attention in the UN Security Council or at G8 summit meetings. He warns that unless we recognize the nature of the era we are now entering, and adopt new policies and priorities, world food security could begin to deteriorate and quickly eclipse international terrorism as an overriding concern. Many will take issue with Brown's views and perspective, but they amount to a wakeup call that should not be ignored.

Obesity

Another phenomenon has appeared that shows the paradox of hunger in a world of plenty in a new and stark light. Obesity, not hunger, has emerged as a killer in the rich industrialized countries, and is threatening to invade the Third World as well. The WHO International Task Force on Obesity estimates that 1.3 billion people globally are overweight or obese. (A person is classified as obese if the body mass index (BMI) is 30 or higher, taking into account both weight and height.) A WHO/FAO Expert Consultation on Diet, Nutrition and the Prevention of Chronic Diseases has proposed a strategy for dietary changes, including limits on sugar consumption, as well as policies that might make it easier for people to eat healthily. Stricter labeling requirements have been proposed, which is meant to prevent biotechnology hazards by giving countries enough information about gene-altered products to help them decide whether or not to reject imports. Governments, both national and regional, have a role to play. The unbridled activities of the food industry must be curbed in the interest of consumers, with a distinct separation of government responsibility for the promotion of food production from that of its protection of food consumers. Governments should insist on clearer labeling so that consumers can make informed choices. And they have a duty to protect children. Equally, individuals and parents must assume personal responsibility in eating wisely.

The world food system has evolved dramatically since the end of the Second World War (1939–45). From a situation of food shortages in the developing countries, and the use of the so-called food surpluses of the developed countries, the focus switched to the importance of ensuring access of poor people to the food they need through increasing their employment and purchasing power. At the same time, powerful forces entered the world food system, including the emergence of large multinational food corporations, which has led to increasing commercialization and their control of the food chain. Population growth and urbanization has resulted in a considerable expansion of world food trade. Another significant development has been the changing pattern of food consumption through the emergence of the fast food industry and supermarkets. The industrialization of food is systematically destroying traditional food cultures and eating habits.

The prospects for reducing poverty, and hence malnutrition and hunger, around the world are also being shaped by changes in the international economy caused by such factors as modifications in the international rules and institutions governing trade and finance, the flow of private capital as well as Official Development Assistance (ODA), and the global impact of growth in the major developing countries, particularly China and India. This has led to the accusation of an "international organization of hunger" through the interdependence and hegemony of countries and regimes and the powerful domination of a small number of developed nations on the one hand.[7]

It is increasingly being realized that like hunger, obesity must be addressed holistically and not bit by bit like pieces of a jigsaw puzzle that lie scattered and unconnected. Both have personal, national and global consequences that go well beyond their nutritional significance. It would be grotesquely perverse if attention to world hunger and food insecurity were to be diverted by a focus on the obesity epidemic. Both crises must be overcome.

The population dimension

No discussion of world poverty and food insecurity is complete without consideration of their population dimension.[8] The race between the relentless rise of the world's population and the growth of food production can be traced back to biblical times. It is now generally accepted that the problem of food insecurity can be overcome. The division of opinion between the optimists and pessimists remains, but with an important difference. The division now seems to be over not whether it *can* be done but whether it *will* be done: between the optimists of the one-world school and the pessimists of the Malthusian persuasion.

The UN Population Division has shown the astonishing growth in the world's population in recent times, from the first billion reached in 1804, to 2 billion in 1927, 3 billion in 1960, 4 billion in 1974, 5 billion in 1987, and 6 billion in 1999.[9] The UN projections of future population growth give three possible scenarios. Under what is called the "low-fertility" scenario, world population is expected to peak at 7.5 billion by 2040 and then fall to 7.4 billion in 2050. A "medium-growth" scenario would result in the world population reaching 8.9 billion by 2050 and 9.2 billion by 2075. Under the "high-growth" variant, world population would rise to 10.6 billion by 2050 and to 14 billion by 2099.

The latest UN population projections show somewhat lower population growth than previously expected, reflecting lower fertility and higher mortality related to AIDS. The world's population grew by 76 million people in 2004, 73 million of them in developing countries.[10] Some 5.2 billion live in the least-developed countries where the

Background 19

population grew 16 times as fast as in the industrialized countries. Six countries accounted for about half the world's population increase: India, with 21 percent of the world's population growth; China, 12 percent; Pakistan, 5 percent; and Bangladesh, Nigeria and the United States 4 percent each. According to the latest UN population projections, the population of India will overtake that of China before 2030, earlier than expected. The combined population of developed countries is expected to remain virtually unchanged between 2005 and 2050, at about 1.2 billion, less than the populations of either China or India. In contrast, the total population of the least developed countries is projected to more than double.

The International Conference on Population and Development (ICPD) held in Cairo, Egypt in 1994 adopted a wide-ranging 20-year action plan. It agreed to work toward universal access to family planning and reproductive health by 2015 and targets that were incorporated into the MDGs (see Box 1.1). The central premise of the ICPD was that population size, growth, age structure, and rural urban population distribution have a critical impact on development prospects and specifically on prospects for raising the living standards of the poor, including improving their food security. Reflecting this understanding, the ICPD called on countries to "fully integrate population concerns into development strategies, planning, and decision making and resource allocation at all levels." Participants pledged to invest a combined $17 billion a year by the turn of the century, rising to $22 billion by 2015, in basic reproductive health services and related activities in developing countries. Developing countries undertook to provide two-thirds of total investment with the remaining one-third coming from external sources. Over halfway to 2015, developing countries were said to have met at least 80 percent of their promised contributions while the wealthier donor countries had only provided half their pledges.[11]

In 2004, over 350 million couples still lacked access to the full range of reproductive health and family planning services. Some 8 million women a year suffered from life-threatening pregnancy-related complications. Over 529,000 died as a consequence, mainly in developing countries. One third of all pregnant women received no health care during pregnancy. Meeting the needs of 201 million women without access to effective family planning services was estimated to cost $3.9 billion a year. This could avert 52 million pregnancies, of which about 22 million were ended by induced abortions. In 2003, some 3 million people died of AIDS: 2.5 million adults and 500,000 children under 15 years of age. Five million new cases of HIV infection occurred during

20 *Background*

2003, an average of 14,000 a day, 40 percent of whom were women and nearly 20 percent children. At the same time, the population was ageing, especially in developed countries. Between 2005 and 2050, it was projected that the proportion of the world's population aged 65 years or older would double in most developed countries.

The income factor

The level of income has been recognized as a key factor in determining access to adequate basic needs, including food. A pivotal MDG is to halve the proportion of the world's population living on less than a dollar a day by 2015 (Box 1.1). The World Bank estimated that at the start of the new millennium in 2000, of the world's 6 billion people, 1.2 billion—one-fifth—subsisted on less than one dollar a day, and 2.8 million—almost half—existed on less than two dollars a day (see Table 1.4).[12] In 2002, the World Bank estimated that by this standard there were 200 million fewer poor in the world in 1998 than in 1980.[13] This figure was contested, hence two new studies were conducted by the bank's Development Research Group in 2004 and 2007. This involved constructing a new, internally consistent, data series for the 1980s and 1990s.

The latest estimates, published in April 2007, put the number of people in 2004 living on a dollar a day at below one billion for the first time, 18 percent of the population of the developing world, compared with just below 1.5 billion in 1981.[14] At the same time, it was estimated that 2.5 billion, or 48 percent of the total population of developing countries, live on less than $2 a day, almost the same number as in 1981. This reflected the rising number of people living on between $1 and $2 a day. There is clear indication of rising poverty in sub-Saharan Africa and, as urbanization increased, the rate of rural poverty has fallen much more than the urban rate. In some countries, inequality has worsened as poor people have not benefited from the economic expansion that has occurred because of lack of job opportunities, limited education, and bad health. At the current rate of decline, it is projected that there would still be over 800 million people living on under a dollar a day in 2015, thereby missing the MDG of halving the proportion of people living at that level by that date, and 2.8 billion people living on less than two dollars a day, reflecting the rising number of people living on between $1 and $2 a day.

IFPRI has taken the analysis of the world's "bottom billion" even further in preparing for its conference on Taking Action for the World's Poor and Hungry People in Beijing, China in 2007.[15] Of the

Table 1.4 Number of people living below US$1 and US$2 a day, 1981–2004 (millions)

Region	1981	1984	1987	1990	1993	1996	1999	2002	2004
Below $1 a day									
East Asia and Pacific	796.40	564.30	428.76	476.22	420.22	279.09	276.54	226.77	169.13
Of which China	633.66	425.27	310.43	374.33	334.21	211.44	222.78	176.61	128.36
Eastern Europe and Central Asia	3.00	2.27	1.61	2.16	16.94	20.87	17.90	6.01	4.42
Latin America and Caribbean	39.35	50.90	50.00	44.60	38.83	42.96	49.03	48.13	47.02
Middle East and North Africa	8.81	7.26	6.41	5.26	4.53	4.38	5.67	4.88	4.40
South Asia	455.18	445.05	471.14	479.10	436.74	452.91	463.40	469.55	446.20
Of which India	363.72	359.41	368.60	376.44	376.14	378.91	376.25	377.84	370.67
Sub-Saharan Africa	167.53	199.78	222.80	240.34	252.26	286.21	296.07	296.11	298.30
Total	1,470.28	1,269.56	1,180.73	1,247.68	1,170.17	1,087.81	1,108.61	1,051.46	969.48
Total excl. China	836.62	844.29	870.30	873.35	835.96	876.37	885.83	874.85	841.12
Below $2 a day									
East Asia and Pacific	1,169.74	1,115.97	1,040.71	1,112.93	1,083.21	907.83	882.70	766.26	683.83
Of which China	875.77	819.11	744.07	819.11	802.86	649.47	627.55	524.24	452.25
Eastern Europe and Central Asia	19.78	17.38	14.03	20.07	77.83	84.88	87.94	60.75	46.25
Latin America and Caribbean	103.90	125.58	122.30	114.85	111.08	122.30	128.44	131.14	120.62
Middle East and North Africa	50.56	48.62	50.24	48.91	51.80	55.40	64.50	60.92	59.13
South Asia	813.04	852.39	904.21	953.00	973.99	1,031.48	1,067.15	1,115.54	1,115.77
Of which India	624.92	658.92	694.71	733.13	767.39	798.07	825.93	853.32	867.62
Sub-Saharan Africa	295.46	332.87	365.02	396.32	422.11	458.37	490.58	512.62	522.34
Total	2,452.47	2,492.81	2,496.50	2,646.09	2,721.72	2,665.66	2,721.31	2,647.22	2,547.94
Total excl. China	1,576.70	1,673.70	1,752.42	1,826.98	1,918.86	2,016.19	2,093.75	2,122.98	2,095.69

Source: Shaohua Chen and Martin Ravallion, *Absolute Poverty Measures for the Developing World 1981–2004* (Washington, D.C.: Word Bank, 2017).

almost 1 billion people living on less than a dollar a day, the IFPRI study found that 485 million live on between 75 cents and a dollar a day, 323 million exist on between 50 and 75 cents a day, and 162 million, the "ultra poor", whose lives and livelihoods are dominated by a struggle for survival, and for whom hunger is a continuous reality, subsist on less than 50 cents a day.

Three-quarters of the world's ultra poor live in sub-Saharan Africa. While some developing regions have made remarkable progress against poverty and hunger, this region has seen actual increases in the number of abjectly poor people, calling into question the assumptions behind economic growth models that predict a convergence between growth and poverty reduction. The IFPRI study found the following characteristics in the world's hungry poor. Despite a global trend of poverty shifting toward urban areas, the incidence of poverty is still higher in rural areas. The poorest and most undernourished households are located furthest from roads, markets, schools and health centers. Adults in ultra poverty are significantly less likely to be educated, be they male or female. Children from poorer families are less likely to go to school, though the relationship varied among the developing regions. Each of the countries studied had minority and other subgroups that have consistently higher prevalence of poverty and hunger.

It was found that the location of a household has a large impact on potential household welfare. The coincidence of severe and persistent poverty and hunger indicated the presence of "poverty traps," conditions from which individuals or groups cannot emerge without the help of others. Three commonly found causes of poverty traps were: inability of poor households to invest in the education of their children; limited access to credit for those with few assets; and lack of productive labor of the hungry. Within the poverty traps, poverty brought hunger and hunger brought poverty. In addition, the systematic exclusion of certain groups from access to resources and markets increased their propensity to be poor.

The study suggested five interventions for helping the poorest move out of poverty: improving access to markets and basic services for those in the most remote rural areas; providing insurance to help households deal with health crises; preventing child malnutrition; enabling investment in education and physical capital for those with few assets; and addressing the exclusion of disadvantaged groups. These findings also highlight the importance of improving knowledge and understanding of the world's hungry poor by careful data collection necessary for the design, monitoring, and evaluation of policies and interventions for improving the welfare of the most deprived.

The Beijing conference identified five priority areas of action to accelerate poverty and hunger reduction: (1) focusing on inclusive growth; (2) improving access to assets and markets; (3) phasing in social protection more quickly and comprehensively; (4) accelerating investment in health and nutrition programs; and (5) including the excluded. It also noted that effective action required political and institutional change in: (a) political core issues; (b) scaling up of successful and model projects; (c) political processes to create board-based support for action; (d) building community organizations and political institutions for and with the poor in order to strengthen local action; and (e) improved capacity to implement.[16]

Another illuminating study of the "bottom billion" has diagnosed their predicament in terms of a number of development traps from which they cannot escape.[17] This may be a "conflict trap," a pattern of violent internal challenges to government that may be prolonged, as in a civil war, or over swiftly, through a coup d'état, that can trap a country in poverty. It may be a "natural resource trap," where a country rich in natural resources and minerals can have internal conflict and a waste of revenues, or underinvestment in natural resources, for what should have been a positive advantage. Another trap may be that a country is "landlocked with bad neighbors." Yet another trap is caused by bad governance and economic policies, particularly in small countries. These traps have led to the marginalization of the bottom billion in the world economy and prevented them from sharing in the benefits of globalization. Understanding the nature of these traps, and their effects on abjectly poor people, can lead to more effective interventions to help them.

Education for all

Education has been recognized as the gateway to development in the broadest sense, and gender parity in education as particularly important for ensuring equitable and sustainable development, including food security. These basic truths are recognized in the two MDGs that set targets for all children to have access to primary education by 2015, and call for gender disparity in primary and secondary education to be eliminated by 2005, and in all levels of education no later than 2015 (Box 1.1). The United Nations Educational, Scientific and Cultural Organization (UNESCO) has instituted an annual series of Education for All (EFA) *Global Monitoring Reports* starting in 2002.[18] These reports are written by an independent international team based in UNESCO, supported by UNESCO staff, and drawing from

UNESCO's Institute of Statistics and commissioned studies by researchers and institutes around the world.

According to these reports, "steady progress" has been made since 1998, especially toward universal primary education (UPE) and gender parity in education among the poorest countries. But the overall conclusion is that "the pace is insufficient" for the educational MDGs to be met by 2015. Projections suggest that without accelerated efforts: 58 of the 86 countries that have not yet reached universal primary school enrolment will not achieve it by 2015; 72 out of the 101 countries will not have succeeded in halving their adult literacy rates by 2015; and only 18 of the 113 countries that missed the gender parity goal at primary and secondary school level in 2005 stand a chance of achieving it by 2015.

Major challenges remain for achieving education for all (EFA). About 100 million children are estimated not to be enrolled in primary schools, 55 percent of them girls. Primary school fees, a major barrier to access, are still collected in 80 of the 103 countries surveyed. And high fertility rates, HIV/AIDS, and armed conflict continue to exert pressure on, and disrupt, the education systems in many countries with the greatest EFA challenges. The MDG 2005 gender parity target was missed by 94 of the 194 countries for which data are available. Quality of education was assessed as being "too low," with too few primary school teachers, many lacking adequate qualifications. Literacy remains neglected, with an estimated 771 million people aged 15 years and above without basic literacy skills, and insufficient priority and funding is being given by governments and aid agencies to youth and adult literacy programs.

The reports published by UNESCO have been complemented by those of UNICEF and the World Bank. UNICEF's annual report on *The State of the World's Children* for 2004 focused on gender disparity in education and its implications for development.[19] In his foreword to the report, the then UN secretary-general, Kofi Annan, paints a tragic picture of the human waste of uneducated, marginalized girls and women "ill-prepared to participate fully in the political, social and economic development of their communities. They, and their children, are at higher risk to poverty, HIV/Aids, sexual exploitation, violence and abuse." Conversely, "to educate a girl is to educate a whole family, and what is true of families is also true of communities and, ultimately, of whole countries." Thus, "there is no tool for development more effective than the education of girls."

The UNICEF report pointed out that despite decades of attention to the importance of education for all, some 121 million children were out of school, 65 million of them girls. To focus attention on improving the quality and availability of girls' education, 13 UN agencies have formed a UN Girls' Education Initiative, with UNICEF as its lead agency. UNICEF has also launched a "25 by 2025" initiative, with a specific focus on 25 countries, 15 in sub-Saharan Africa, considered to be at risk in failing to achieve the MDG of eliminating gender disparity in education. This involved a new concept of partnership, graphically described as "walking the distance with a country—and if necessary going the extra mile," by instituting long-term support with a total resource package, without being unduly obtrusive or trying to dictate, and being constructive with both support and advocacy for change where needed.

Bilateral aid to education was $4.7 billion in 2003, well below the 1990 high of $5.7 billion, of which 60 percent went to post-secondary education. Total aid to basic education accounted for only 2.6 percent of ODA, with adult literacy receiving a miniscule share. It is estimated that aid to education would have to double to reach the $7 billion considered necessary just to achieve the UPE and gender parity MDGs. As with aid to other sectors, the neediest people and countries miss out. A disproportionate amount goes to middle-income countries with relatively high primary school enrollments. Aid for basic education more than doubled between 1999 and 2003. It could rise further to $5 billion a year by 2010 following commitments made by major donors, but would be well below the annual amount of $11 billion estimated to be required to reach the EFA goals.

What is called the Fast Track Initiative (FTI) has emerged as a key coordinating mechanism for aid agencies. The FTI was established by the Development Committee of the International Monetary Fund (IMF) and World Bank in 2002 to accelerate progress toward UPE by 2015. The committee also called for a close monitoring of its impact. For this purpose, the World Bank developed a new database to track progress. This showed that over the 1990s, the average rate of primary school completion in the developing world (on a country-weighted basis) improved only from 72 to 77 percent, far short of the progress needed to reach the MDG education target.[20] On a population-weighted basis, buoyed by China's high reported primary school completion rate, the global situation looked slightly better, rising from 73 to 81 percent. But the global average masked large regional differences. Sub-Saharan Africa had by far the lowest completion rate with barely half of all school-age children completing primary school, followed by South Asia with an average completion rate of 70 percent, compared with Europe and Central Asia with a completion rate of 92 percent. Of the 70 countries lagging behind, 51 were in the low-income category. But, overall, the trends indicated that where political will was strong, effective reforms adopted, and international support adequate, "dramatic progress" in increasing primary school completion rates was possible.

It was estimated that for all developing countries, between $33 billion and $38 billion a year in additional spending would be needed if the MDG education target was to be met, of which $5–7 billion, a small fraction of the annual global military budget of $1.2 trillion, would need to come through external aid. The IMF/World Development Committee endorsed a new compact for primary education in April 2002, called the EFA FTI, to which a first set of 18 low-income countries and a second set of high-priority countries (Bangladesh, Democratic Republic of Congo, India, Nigeria, and Pakistan) were invited to join. The World Bank study concluded that universal completion of primary education was crucial for national economic and social advancement, a goal to which all developing countries should be committed. But this goal would not be achieved without significant acceleration in current progress, which would require bridging substantial gaps in policy, capacity, financing and data.

Employment and hunger and poverty reduction

While the importance of employment in reducing poverty and food insecurity had been appreciated for some time, the 1976 International Labour Organization (ILO) World Employment Conference,[21] and the work of Amartya Sen on the dynamics of famines and food "entitlements,"[22] among others, served to re-emphasize the imperative of ensuring productive and remunerative work for the hungry poor as an essential part of a strategy to satisfy people's basic needs. But it was not until the 1990s that it was fully recognized that:

> Today, understanding the labour market is as important for addressing the food security problems of the rural and urban poor in developing countries as understanding the food market. It is now widely accepted that food security is at least as much a matter of poverty—limited access to food—as it is a matter of supply—limited availability of food. [23]

The ILO's *World Employment Report 2004–05* explored the evidence regarding the impact of productivity performance on both employment growth and poverty reduction. Increased focus on the generating of what was called "decent work" opportunities was regarded as central to achieving the MDGs. Much work was so poorly remunerated as to prevent those classified as employed from earning more than a dollar a day. Better as well as more jobs were therefore needed. The ILO report also focused on poverty among the world's workers or on what was described as "working poverty." This concept of the working poor in the developing world added a new dimension to the study of labor markets by placing decent and productive employment at the forefront of the poverty discussion. It was estimated that in 2003, 1.39 billion people were unable to lift themselves and their families above the 2 dollar a day poverty line. Among them, 550 million and their families could not rise above the dollar a day threshold. This meant that almost half (49.7 percent) of the world's workers and over half (58.7 percent) of the developing world's workers did not earn enough to lift themselves and their families out of poverty. Almost one-fifth (19.7 percent) of the world's employed people, and approaching one-quarter (23.3 percent) of the developing world's workers, were living in dehumanizing, abject poverty on less than a dollar a day. In addition, it was estimated that there were 185.9 million unemployed people in the world.

The ILO report concluded that given the persistently high number of "working poor," together with the high number of unemployed, and the uncertain number of people who remained outside the labor force for involuntary reasons, there was a large and persistent deficit of decent work in the world. This constituted a great challenge in the fight against poverty. It argued that the focus needed to be on parts of the economy where the majority of people worked, such as agriculture, small-scale activities in the urban and rural informal sector, and services, as well as manufacturing.

International agricultural trade

The importance of world agricultural trade for achieving food security and economic development in the developing countries was recognized at a number of international conferences throughout the 1990s. The conclusion of the General Agreement on Tariffs and Trade (GATT) Uruguay Round of multilateral trade negotiations and the setting up of the World Trade Organization (WTO) in 1995 provided a major opportunity for reaching agreement on free and fair world trade within a liberalizing world economy. But progress toward that aim proved elusive at the first three WTO ministerial meetings. Promise of a breakthrough came at the fourth WTO ministerial meeting at Doha, Qatar in 2001.

The Ministerial Declaration that emerged from the meeting provided a framework for significant progress.[24] In it, ministers declared their determination "to maintain the process of reform and liberalization of trade policies" and pledged "to reject the use of protectionism." They recognized that international trade "can play a major role in the promotion of economic development and the alleviation of poverty." The special problems of the least-developed countries were recognized. A commitment was made to address their marginalization in international trade and to improve their effective participation in the multilateral trading system. A "broad and balanced" work program was agreed upon, which sought to place the interests of developing countries at its heart.

Concerning agricultural trade, the work program recalled the long-term objective of the WTO Agreement on Agriculture to establish a fair and market-oriented trading system and prevent restrictions and distortions in world agricultural markets. A commitment was made to comprehensive negotiations aimed at: substantial improvements in market access; reduction and eventual phasing out of all forms of export subsidies; and substantial reductions in trade-distorting domestic support programs. Special and differential treatment for developing countries was recognized to take account of their development needs, including food security and rural development. Non-trade concerns would also be taken into account and modalities for further commitments established by the end of March 2003.

Doha set a development agenda of considerable promise based on agreement to substantially reduce trade barriers in agriculture. But progress on the commitments made at Doha has proved to be difficult and tardy. Agriculture in many developed countries remains a highly sensitive and protected sector. Changes in agricultural policies in the European Union (EU) and the United States (U.S.), two major players in world agricultural trade, have tended to exacerbate rather than reduce agricultural protection. Many developing countries also have considerable agricultural protection and are reluctant to make reciprocal concessions to further Doha negotiations. The G77 and China expressed the view that the benefits of the existing multilateral trading system continue to elude the developing countries, and expressed disappointment at the lack of any meaningful progress on implementation of the agreements reached at Doha.

The WTO ministerial meeting in Hong Kong in 2005 renewed resolve to complete the Doha work program in 2006. At the meeting, the EU, U.S. and Japan pledged to phase out all their direct subsidies on food exports. Developing countries, including Brazil and India, called for easier access to developed country markets for prepared foods and cuts in overall farm subsidies. They claimed that developed countries spent six times as much on farm subsidies as the total world aid budget. An emergency meeting held in Geneva, Switzerland in July 2006 of the six "core negotiators" of the Doha round of multilateral trade negotiations, Australia, Brazil, EU, India, Japan and the U.S.A., collapsed over irreconcilable difference concerning the liberalization of world agricultural trade. The U.S. continued to argue for big cuts in farm import tariffs to open markets for its farmers, which was rejected by the EU, India and Japan. They said that the U.S. should first go further in cutting its agricultural subsidies. The Doha round has now entered a period of indefinite suspension. Consensus in the WTO's 149 member countries must be found to revive it. This throws into doubt the future of the WTO itself as an effective forum for reaching agreement in multilateral trade negotiations.

Why has the early promise of the WTO turned so sour?[25] The WTO differs substantially from the International Trade Organization (ITO), the creation of the famous British economist John Maynard Keynes, modified by the U.S., that was approved in the 1948 Havana Charter on Trade and Employment, but not ratified by the United States Congress, and the UN body concerned with trade and development, the United Nations Conference on Trade and Development (UNCTAD). The major industrialized countries, particularly the United States and the EU, did not want the WTO to be part of the UN system. While UNCTAD explicitly links trade and development, WTO is only concerned with trade issues. Unlike the proposed ITO, WTO is not concerned with the stabilization of commodity prices and with controlling the activities of the multinational corporations, which account for up to 70 percent of international trade. WTO serves to facilitate export orientation, an essential component of multinational corporate expansion. Its mandate to cooperate closely with the IMF and the World Bank "with a view to achieving greater coherence in global economic policy making" is seen by many developing countries as another strike against their interests.

UNCTAD has had a different history and record. The first UN Conference on Trade and Development was held in 1964 with the specific aim of promoting the integration of developing countries into the world economy. Within UNCTAD, set up with a permanent secretariat in Geneva, Switzerland, the Group of 77 (G77) developing countries (now comprising 131 countries) was established to voice their concerns for market reforms that were seen by them to add economic advantage to the richer countries and threaten their industries. They consider that the market-based liberalization foisted on developing countries since the 1980s has led to unsatisfactory outcomes. Criticisms of market economics and deregulation mutedly voiced during the 1980s and 1990s are now being made more openly in UNCTAD publications, especially as recriminations following the collapse of the Doha round of multilateral trade negotiations have taken the gloss off the free traders and halted the momentum for trade liberalization.

UNCTAD's annual report for 2006, while rejecting the protectionism of the major developed countries, argued that countries such as the Asian "tiger economies" were able to strengthen the creative power of their markets through proactive industrial policies that provided some temporary protection, which should be considered a key element of a policy aimed at "strategic trade integration."[26] The call for subsidies, however temporary, comes at a fragile time for efforts to bring down the tariff barriers of developed countries and open their markets to developing countries.

The UNCTAD secretary-general explained that his organization was not recommending any anti-trade stance but to point to the need to strengthen the creative forces of the market. Free-market campaigners have attacked the UNCTAD report on grounds that its advice could lead to lower living standards and the creation of inefficient industries that would ill-serve consumers in developing countries. UNCTAD insists that it has close working links with the WTO, with which it has signed a memorandum in 2003 providing for cooperation and joint studies. UNCTAD has called for a level playing field in trade and development but its powers of persuasion have been muted by the work of other UN bodies, particularly the IMF and World Bank, and by the creation of the WTO.

Human security

In addition to the concerns described above, the issue of human security has now assumed major importance. Human security was on the international agenda well before al-Qaeda terrorists flew passenger planes into the twin towers of the World Trade Center in New York and the Pentagon in Washington, D.C. on 11 September 2001. Described as a "defining moment" in the history of the modern world, it triggered the war against international terrorism. It also carried further the debate on redefining the concepts and the relationship between human security and food security. Up to the late 1980s, the concept of human security was more narrowly interpreted as security of territory from external aggression or global security from the threat of nuclear holocaust.[27] With the end of the Cold War and the break-up of the imposed political structure of the former Soviet Union, a broadening of the concept occurred as the number of conflicts increased within, not between, states.

A new concept of global security was called for in 1990 that focused not on military security but on "the overall security of individuals from social violence, economic distress and environmental degradation" and sought to focus attention on the obstacles to "realization of the full potential of individuals."[28] This transformation was captured and redefined further in the UNDP annual *Human Development Report* (HDR) for 1994, which identified two, interrelated, elements: safety from chronic threats such as hunger, disease, and repression; and protection from sudden and hurtful disruption in the pattern of daily life.[29]

This concept explicitly linked human security with the development process. It allowed people to exercise their expanded choices and develop their capabilities. Conversely, the absence of such security undermined the process of development and led to social disintegration and humanitarian catastrophes. Under this broadened concept, the threats to human security are wide, including: food, health, economic, environmental, and personal and community, and political security. Human security is also seen as having four characteristics: universal concern; a number of components, including food security, that are interdependent; preventive, protection, and, most recently, pre-emptive measures; and a people-centered concern and solution.

A Human Security Network was founded in 1999 to define concrete policies in the area of human security as a basis for coordinated action and to serve as a catalyst to raise awareness of new issues as they arose. The network considered it necessary to go beyond its original "freedom from fear" focus to incorporate the "freedom from want" issues emphasized in the 1994 HDR. In May 2003, the UN Commission on Human Security (CHS) presented a report to the UN secretary-general in which human security was defined in the following terms:

> In essence, human security means safety for people from both violent and non-violent threats. It is a condition or state of being characterized by freedom from pervasive threats to people's rights, their safety, or even their lives. From a foreign policy perspective, human security is perhaps best understood as a shift in perceptions or orientation. It is an alternative way of seeing the world, taking people as its point of reference, rather than focusing exclusively on the security of territory or governments.[30]

The CHS was established in 2000 with the remit of promoting public understanding of human security and developing the concept as an operational tool for policy formulation and implementation, and to propose a concrete program of action. The CHS report took a broad approach, bringing together physical protection, human rights and development. According to the commission, human security necessitated policies that went beyond ensuring people's survival to policies that focused on people's livelihoods and dignity in good times as well as bad.

The UN secretary-general convened a High-Level Panel on Threats, Challenges and Change to consider the best ways of implementing the recommendations of the CHS report.[31] The panel made the case for a more comprehensive concept of collective security and a strategy against terrorism, organized crime, control of weapons of mass destruction, peacekeeping and peace-building, and strengthening the role of the UN Security Council. At the same time, democracy should be promoted, the rule of law strengthened, and all internationally recognized human rights and fundamental freedoms respected. To achieve these aims, the UN Office of the High Commissioner for Human Rights was strengthened and the UN Commission for Human Rights was replaced by a UN Human Rights Council. The UN secretary-general also called for a strengthening of the major components of the UN and for improving coherence and cooperation among the UN bodies.

The Worldwatch Institute devoted its annual publication on the *State of the World* for 2005 to "redefining global security."[32] In his foreword to the publication, Mikhail Gorbachev, former president of the Soviet Union, Nobel Peace Prize laureate, and now chairman of Green Cross International, identified three interrelated global challenges: security, including the risks associated with weapons of mass destruction and terrorism; poverty and underdevelopment; and environmental sustainability. He stated: "We are the guests, not masters, of nature and must develop a new paradigm for development and conflict resolution, based on the costs and benefits to all people and bound by the limits of nature herself rather than the limits of technology and consumerism."

Worldwatch emphasized that the need for international cooperation had grown stronger as the rifts and divides among nations widened. Four "core insights" were identified in examining the roots of global insecurity. Weapons did not necessarily provide security. Real security in a globalizing world could not be provided on a purely national basis. The traditional focus on state or regime security needed to encompass the safety and well-being of the population. And non-military dimensions had an important influence on security and stability. Throughout history, big powers had repeatedly intervened in well-endowed countries in order to control lucrative natural resources. The vast reservoir of unemployed young people in many developing countries was in some ways more worrisome. Demographic forces could exert strong pressures on a society and its institutions and have important implications for domestic stability and international security.

Worldwatch pointed out that countries from every major political and religious background, and in virtually every region, had experienced momentous changes in the size and structure of their populations. Yet the transformation from large families and short lives to smaller families and longer lives remained incomplete. Roughly one-third of all countries were still in the early stages of transition, with fertility rates at about four children per woman. Studies had shown that these countries bear the highest risks of becoming embroiled in armed conflict. Many were bogged down by a debilitating demographic situation: a large and growing young population; low per capita availability of cropland and fresh water; a rising pandemic of HIV/AIDS; scarce economic opportunities; social challenges; and political hazards. According to UN data, over 100 countries had what was called a "youth bulge" in 2000, where people aged 15–29 years accounted for over 40 percent of all adults.

Prior to the dramatic events of 11 September 2001, poverty, instability and warfare in poor countries were widely regarded as marginal to the interests and welfare of the rich countries. After that date, it was quickly realized that conditions of political turmoil and social misery could not be confined to the periphery. But the war on international terrorism ran the risk of sidelining the struggle against hunger, poverty, health epidemics, and environmental degradation. Three "core principles" were identified for a more secure world. First, a new security policy needed to be "transformative" in nature, strengthening the civil institutions that can address the root causes of human insecurity. Second, it must be above all "preventive" in nature, based on a clear understanding of the root causes of conflict and insecurity, which implied a far broader and earlier applicability, not merely a reaction that addressed symptoms. Lastly, it needed to be "cross-cutting and integrative," bring together insights from a broad range of disciplines. As the Worldwatch report demonstrated, there are many social, economic and environmental policies that can help create a more just and sustainable world. It concluded that such policies "offer the added bonus of creating real security in a way that force of arms never can."

Practical proposals

Two specific proposals have been made to end hunger and achieve the MDGs established at the UN Millennium Summit in 2000.

The Third Freedom: to end world hunger

George McGovern, U.S. congressman and senator, the first director of the U.S. Food for Peace program in the Kennedy administration, and the Democrats' presidential candidate in 1972, has made a number of proposals to end world hunger and took the personal initiative that led to the establishment of the UN World Food Programme in 1961.[33] More recently, while U.S. ambassador to the UN food and agricultural agencies in Rome, Italy, he advocated another way to overcome world hunger.[34] His strategy consists of a five-point initiative: a school lunch program to reach every child in the world; a worldwide special nutrition program for mothers, infants and children; the establishment of global food reserves; an assistance program to help developing countries improve their own food production, processing and distribution; and the dissemination of the results of high-yielding scientific agriculture, including genetically modified crops.

McGovern estimates that the cost of his strategy to be $5 billion a year, of which, he suggests, $1.2 billion could come from the United States. If correct, the cost would be well within the financial means of developing countries and the international community. He considers that if this annual allocation continued to 2015, the number of chronically undernourished people in the world would be cut by half. Hunger among the remaining malnourished would disappear if roughly the same amount were invested annually until 2030. The U.S. Agency for International Development (USAID) put the cost of his scheme at $2.6 billion annually, and FAO at $6.0 billion a year. McGovern correctly points out that the cost of not ending world hunger would be much higher. The World Bank, for example, estimates that each year, malnutrition robs the world of 46 million years of productive living at a cost of $16 billion. McGovern recognizes that the cost of hunger should not be evaluated solely in dollar terms. He asks: "what is the value of a human life?" In the last half of the twentieth century, he estimates 450 million people may have died from malnutrition and related causes. And the vicious circle of hunger, conflict and more hunger will continue unless decisive steps are taken to end it.

The UN Millennium Project

The UN Millennium Project is an independent advisory body commissioned by the then UN secretary-general, Kofi Annan, to propose the best strategy for achieving the MDGs.[35] In its report, *Investing in Development: A Practical Plan to Achieve the Millennium Development Goals*, the MDGs are described as "the most broadly supported, comprehensive, and specific poverty reduction targets the world has ever established." For the international political system, they are regarded as the "fulcrum" on which development policy should be based. For people living in extreme poverty, they represent "the means for a productive life." And for everyone else, they are described as the "linchpin" to the quest for a more secure and peaceful world. The report notes that there has been "significant progress" in achieving many of the MDGs, but that progress has been "far from uniform" across the world, or across the MDGs. There remained "huge disparities" in achieving many of the MDGs. Within developing countries, poverty was greatest in rural areas, although urban poverty was also "extensive, growing and underreported." Sub-Saharan Africa was described as the "epicentre of crisis," with a widespread shortfall in most MDGs. Asia was the region with the "fastest progress; other regions had "mixed records."

But why has progress been so variegated? The report noted that in the process of economic growth, the MDGs played two roles: as ends in themselves; and as inputs to economic growth and further development. When the most basic infrastructure, health services and education were lacking, market forces alone could accomplish little. People, and whole economies, remained trapped in poverty, and failed to reap the benefits of globalization—and may even suffer from it through the adverse effects of the brain drain, environmental degradation, biodiversity loss, capital flight, and terms-of-trade declines. The report identified four main reasons for shortfalls in achieving the MDGs: failures of governance; poverty traps, considerable variations in household incomes; and areas of specific policy neglect. Some MDGs were not being met because policy-makers are neither aware of the challenges, or of what to do, or neglectful of core policy issues.

The report made ten major recommendations to reach the MDGs. (1) All countries should have what are called "MDG-based poverty reduction strategies" by 2006. (2) These strategies should provide the "anchor" and "framework" for cohesive action concerning public investment, capacity building, domestic resource mobilization, and ODA, and for strengthening governance, promoting human rights, engaging civil society, and promoting the private sector. (3) Developing country governments should "craft and implement" these strategies closely, and in transparent and inclusive ways, with civil society organizations, the domestic private sector, and international partners. (4) International donors should identify at least a dozen MDG "fast-track" countries for a rapid scale-up of ODA. (5) Developing and developed countries should jointly launch "quick win actions" and "massive training programs" for community-based workers to save and improve millions of lives and promote economic growth. (6) Developing country governments should align national strategies to regional initiatives, groups and projects. (7) High-income countries should increase ODA from 0.25 percent of donor GNP in 2003 to around 0.54 percent in 2015 to support the MDGs, particularly in low-income countries, with improved ODA quality that was harmonized, predictable and largely in grant form, and with debt relief more extensive and generous. (8) High-income countries should open their markets to developing country exports and help the least developed countries raise their export competitiveness through investments in critical trade infrastructure; the *Doha Development Agenda* should be fulfilled and the Doha round of multilateral trade negotiations completed. (9) International donors should mobilize support for global scientific development to address the special needs of the poor in the areas of health, agriculture, natural resources and environmental management, and climate control, for which about $7 billion would be needed by 2015. (10) The UN secretary-general and the UN Development Group should improve the coordination of UN agencies, funds and programs, and UN country teams should be strengthened and work closely with the international financial institutions to achieve the MDGs.

The costs of meeting the MDGs in all developing countries were estimated to be of the order of $121 billion in 2006, rising to $189 billion in 2015, taking into account co-financing increases at the country level. This was considered to be well within the promises made by donors at the International Conference on Financing for Development at Monterrey, Mexico in 2002 to increase their aid. The requested doubling of annual ODA to $135 billion in 2006, rising to $195 billion in 2015 (0.44 percent and 0.54 percent of donor GNP respectively) "paled" when compared with the wealth of the high-income countries and the world's military budget of $1.2 billion a year. It has been estimated that the United States has so far spent over $400 billion on the war in Iraq and that the final cost of U.S. involvement in

Iraq could run as high as $2 trillion: another estimate puts the true cost of the war at $3 trillion.[36] And the increase in development assistance requested and committed would make up only half of one percent of the rich countries' combined incomes.

As might be expected, these concrete proposals have their supporters and detractors. Some have called the UN Millennium Project an impressive, even heroic, piece of work, with clear and attainable guidelines. Others are more skeptical, regarding the proliferation of goals and recommendations as hugely over-ambitious, tending toward a kind of utopian central planning by global bureaucrats that places far too great a strain on the puny resources of dysfunctional administrations in developing countries in the elusive quest for growth.[37] The retort of the project's director, Jeffrey Sachs, is to find where aid can work, spend it generously, and sustain it. Critics point to the difficulties of targeting the poor and involving them in their own development. They see a trade-off between an active pro-poor policy and higher economic growth, although the evidence of such a trade-off, if it exists, is unlikely to be very significant.

Uneven progress has been made in achieving the MDGs. A number of countries, especially in sub-Saharan Africa, now seem unlikely to reach the targets set for 2015, unless there is a major increase in the efforts of poor and rich countries alike. But the MDGs are the most broadly supported, comprehensive and specific, poverty reduction targets ever established, and they can now be closely monitored. Most seem to agree that they call for a sea change in the attitude and determination of national governments, and sustained and adequate support from the international community.

Other major issues

There remain four major issues that could have a profound effect on future world food security, and economic and social advancement generally, on which opinion, particularly between Europe and the United States, remains dangerously divided: genetically modified (GM) crops and food; rising food prices; climate change and its potential effects; and globalization of the world economy.

GM crops and food

As the world population continues to grow, pressure on the earth's finite resources to produce more food has increased. In the past, agricultural production was able to keep ahead of increasing demand through advances in plant breeding, technological innovations, and the expansion of arable land. The search for new technologies has intensified as the limits of these options and possibilities were seen to be rapidly approaching. Since the 1970s, a major breakthrough was seen to lie through advances in genetic engineering that made it possible to modify the genetic information of living organisms in a new way, by transferring one or more gene-sized pieces of DNA directly between them. This genetic modification of crops has been proclaimed by science and the food industry, particularly the large multinational food corporations, as the answer to the future world food problem, but sharp differences remain on the need for GM crops and food, and what benefits and costs they could bring.

GM crops currently occupy a relatively small proportion of the world's croplands. In 2002, they were cultivated on some 59 million hectares, almost entirely in four countries: the United States (66 percent), Argentina (23 percent), Canada (6 percent), and China (4 percent). By 2006, the area cultivated had increased to 114 hectares, mainly in the United States but with rapid growth in Argentina, Brazil, China, and India. Three crops dominate GM cultivation: soybean, maize (corn), and cotton. Traits achieved by GM primarily involve herbicide tolerance and insect pest resistance, or a combination of both in the same crop. The market for agricultural biotechnology grew from about $3 billion in 2001 to over $6 billion in 2006, and is expected to reach $8.4 billion by 2011. One estimate suggests the figure could reach $50 billion by 2050 as the second generation of GM technology, now in the pipeline, reaches the market. The claim is that this new generation will taste better, be healthier, and will produce no trans-fats during cooking.

A wide-ranging regulatory framework has been in place in the EU since 1990, which stipulates that any new GM crop or food must be subject to an approval process that looks in detail at the potential impact on the environment and health. Public attitudes will be important in determining the future of GM crops and foods. Differences in approaches between the EU and some other countries, particularly the United States, are already causing trade tensions. Faced with growing interest and concern over the potential risks and dangers as well as the potential benefits of GM crops and food, the U.K. government initiated a "GM Dialogue" in 2002 that had three strands: a national public debate, a study of the possible costs and benefits of GM, and an independent review of the scientific literature on GM.

The national debate revealed the widespread skepticism, even hostility, that existed. The majority rejected any suggested benefits except to

Background 39

the food companies that promoted GM. The economic study concluded that in the short run, negative consumer attitudes could be expected to limit the demand for GM products. While there might be significant potential benefits from the future development of GM crop technology, the international implications could be significant, and should not be underestimated. The ability of developing countries to choose whether or not to adopt GM crop technology may be affected by considerations about the possible impact on their exports to the EU. And taking a significantly different policy direction from other countries could cause serious trade tensions. The GM scientific review noted that new technologies in whatever field brought uncertainties and generated new gaps in knowledge. It found no scientific case for ruling out all GM crops and their products, nor did it give them blanket approved. It emphasized that GM was not a single homogeneous technology and that its application needed to be considered on a case-by-case basis.

The review pointed to two of the most serious potential negative effects of GM technology: acceleration of the loss of agricultural biodiversity, and what has been termed "biopiracy." During the twentieth century, as much as three-quarters of the genetic diversity of agricultural crops may have been lost.[38] The greatest factor contributing to the loss of crop and livestock genetic diversity was the spread of industrial agriculture and the displacement of more diverse, traditional agricultural systems. New, uniform plant varieties were replacing farmers' traditional varieties and their wild relatives were becoming extinct. Industrial agriculture favoured genetic uniformity, and GM could accelerate that process. But a uniform GM crop could be a breeding ground for disaster, because it would be more vulnerable to epidemics of pests and diseases with no fall-back position that biodiversity provided.

At the same time, the rights of farmers were being eroded as plant and animal resources became subject to monopoly control under evolving intellectual property rights systems. Plant breeders' rights and industrial patents increasingly denied farmers the right to save seed, and prohibited researchers from using proprietary germplasm, thereby restricting access to and exchange of germplasm. This process could be taken further if GM crops and foods came under the monopoly control of multinational food corporations. The Convention on Biological Diversity of 1995, the first legally binding framework for the conservation and sustainable use of biodiversity, recognizes the knowledge, innovation and practices of indigenous and local communities and specifically encourages the equitable sharing of benefits arising from their utilization. FAO has championed the rights of farmers, and through the International Undertaking on Plant Genetic Resources of 1983 (amended in 1989), as well as other measures, has sought to strengthen intergovernmental control over crop germplasm held in trust under the auspices of the United Nations and to prohibit intellectual property claims on this material.

FAO issued a statement on biotechnology in March 2000 in which it stated that this provided a potentially powerful tool for the sustainable development of agriculture and the food industry.[39] When appropriately integrated with other technologies for the production of food, it could be of significant assistance in meeting the needs of an expanding, and increasing urban, population. But FAO also recognized that genetically modified organisms (GMOs) had become the target of very intensive, and at times emotionally charged, debate. It was aware of the concern about the potential risks posed by certain aspects of biotechnology on human and animal health and the environment. It therefore supported a science-based evaluation system that could objectively determine the benefits and risks involved.

The subject was addressed again in 2002 when several governments in Southern Africa expressed reservations about accepting food aid containing GMOs and sought UN advice.[40] It was noted that no international agreements were in force regarding trade in food or food aid containing GMOs. It was UN policy that the decision rested with the recipient country. It was WFP policy that all donated food met the food safety standards of both donor and recipient countries, and all applicable international standards, guidelines, and recommendations. The UN believed that governments must consider carefully the severe and immediate consequences of limiting the food aid available for its citizens so desperately in need. Based on information available from a variety of sources and current scientific knowledge, FAO, WFP, and WHO held the view that the consumption of food containing GMOs was not likely to present human health risks. In 1999, the FAO/WHO Codex Alimentarius Commission established an ad hoc Intergovernmental Task Force on Foods Derived from Biotechnology to consider their health and nutrition implications. It was concluded that any potential risks to biological diversity and sustainable agriculture should be judged and managed by countries on a case-by-case basis.

FAO returned to the subject of agricultural biotechnology and its potential for meeting the needs of the poor in its annual flagship publication *The State of Food and Agriculture* for 2003–4.[41] It noted that agriculture faced serious challenges, including feeding an additional 2 billion people by 2030 from an increasingly fragile natural resource base. The effective transfer of existing technologies to poor rural communities, and the development of new and safe biotechnologies, could greatly improve agricultural productivity. But technology alone could not solve the problems of the poor, and some aspects of biotechnology, particularly its socio-economic impact and environmental implications, needed to be carefully assessed. While the Green Revolution came about through an international program of agricultural research specifically aimed at creating and transferring technologies to developing countries as free public goods, the "Gene Revolution" was being driven by the private sector, focused on developing products for large commercial markets, which raised questions about the type of research undertaken and the likelihood that the poor would benefit. FAO therefore recognized the need for a balanced and comprehensive approach to biotechnological development, which took into consideration both the opportunities and risks involved.

The controversy over GM crops and foods has been exacerbated by the criticism that in drawing up its 1992 policy, which remains in effect, the U.S. Food and Drug Administration (FDA) "responded to political pressure for a permissive regulatory approach by exploiting gaps in scientific knowledge, creatively interpreting existing food law and limiting public involvement in the policy's development."[42] This has led to a situation which has been characterized as one of "great uncertainty." Despite repeated recommendations that the issue be the subject of a major public research effort, no action has so far been taken. Thus, while FDA's policy settles questions as a legal matter, questions remain unsettled as a scientific matter.

Equally disturbing are the implications for farmers in the developing world. Focusing on GM crop improvements and the development of seven GM crops (six food staples and cotton) over the past 15 years in Africa, case studies have revealed a number of unexpected scientific, legal, economic and political barriers to the development of GM crops, and long delays in developing and implementing national biosafety regulations and guidelines.[43] It was concluded that most GM crops are at least 10–15 years or longer from reaching smallholder farmers in Africa. It was proposed that during this time, special attention should be given to strengthening conventional plant breeding programs into which biotechnological approaches could be integrated. Special attention should also be given to raising public awareness of biotechnology, mobilizing political support and commitment to strengthening African capacity in biotechnology, biosafety, food safety, and intellectual property rights, and mounting long-term training programs for the next generation of African plant breeders and GM crop specialists.

Rising food prices

Since the last serious world food crisis of the early 1970s, when the prices of both food and oil rose sharply, leading to the World Food Conference of 1974, food prices have been remarkably low and stable. For as long as most people can remember, food has been getting cheaper. Between 1974 and 2005, food prices on world markets fell by three-quarters in real terms. But 2005 saw the start of an unforeseen and unprecedented rise in basic food prices driven by historically low food stocks, drought, and floods linked to climate change. At the same time, high oil prices have increased the price of fertilizers and transport, and the demand for biofuel. Between 2005 and December 2007, real food prices increased by 75 percent (Table 1.2).[44]

What is unusual is that rapidly increasing food prices are occurring at a time not of scarcity, as happened in the early 1970s, but when the world's cereals harvest is the largest on record. This is particularly affecting the hungry poor who spend most of their meager incomes on food, like small-scale farmers, the rural landless, pastoralists, and single-headed households. The price rises are producing what is now called the "new face of hunger," particularly among the urban poor who suddenly can no longer afford the food they see in stores because prices have soared beyond their reach. It is not a matter of availability, as in a drought situation, but is about accessibility, and is particularly hitting the urban populations who rely on markets for their food. Unlike their rural counterparts, they will not suffer in silence, largely out of sight of the media, and will demand that their condition be addressed quickly and adequately.

Two reasons have been identified for this new phenomenon. One is not only the continuing rise in the world's population but the steady, incremental change in the diet of countries like China and India as incomes and purchasing power have increased. This has translated into an increasing demand for more meat in the diet, which in turn has led to more cereals being used to feed livestock. More cereals are needed to produce meat: 3 kg of cereals to produce 1 kg of pork, 8 kg for a kilogram of beef. Farmers have switched to producing cereals for livestock feed to meet the rising demand.

The other factor, perhaps more accountable for the steep recent rise in food prices, is the demand for biofuel, characterized as providing fuel security for the rich at the expense of food security for the poor. It is now on the political agendas of both political parties in the United States to reduce dependence on imported oil. In 2000, about 15 million tons of the U.S. maize (corn) crop was used to produce ethanol. In

2007, it was 85 million tons. The U.S.A. is the largest exporter of corn. It now uses more of its corn crop for ethanol than it sells abroad. The dramatic rise in demand for corn, stimulated further by government subsidies, has encouraged farmers to switch from other cereals used for food. It has also resulted in reducing food stocks to record low levels. The Energy Independence and Security Act of 2007 calls for the annual production of 36 billion gallons of renewable fuels by 2012, a five-fold increase from current ethanol production levels, leading to a long-term diversion of farm land from food crops to the production of ethanol and other synthetic fuels, and to food price increases. The International Monetary Fund (IMF) estimates that corn ethanol production in the United States accounted for at least half the rise in world corn demand in each of the past three years. It remains to be seen whether the new farm bill in the United States, which will run for the next five years, will make these new dramatic developments a permanent feature.

The net result is that the food import bill of low-income, food-deficit countries has increased significantly. FAO estimates that their food imports in July 2008 will be some 35 percent higher than in the previous year, surpassing $33 billion. It could also affect humanitarian food aid by reducing food aid availability and increasing the cost of providing food aid. At the end of 2007, 37 countries faced food crises due to conflicts and disasters. Increased aid was required in the form of seeds, fertilizer and other inputs to increase local food production.

On the other hand, rising food prices could bring benefits depending on governments' response, particularly in developed countries. It could make it possible to reduce subsidies without hurting farmers' incomes. It could increase the share of public spending going to agriculture in developing countries that has fallen by half since 1980. It would ultimately lead to a return to low food prices. And it could open the markets of developed countries to agricultural imports from developing countries. But the immediate reaction of governments in developing countries is to restrict their exports to ensure food availability

Climate change and global warming

Climate change is now generally regarded as one of the greatest challenges facing humankind. Potentially, it could pose a serious threat not only to food security but to the existence of life on earth. Yet, opinion has been deeply divided both on an assessment of the dimensions of this global threat and on developing a common and united response to address it. International concern about the possible negative interaction between human activity and climate change was voiced at the first World Climate Conference organized by the World Meteorological Organization (WMO) in 1979, which expressed the view that "continued expansion of man's activities on earth may cause significant regional and even global changes in climate" and called for "global cooperation in exploring the possible future course of global climate."

In 1985, a conference on Assessment of the Role of Carbon Dioxide and other Greenhouse Gases on Climate Variations and Associated Inputs, organized by WMO and UNEP, concluded that "as a result of increasing greenhouse gases it is now believed that in the first half of the next century a rise of global mean temperatures could occur which is greater than any in man's history." Recognizing the need for objective, balanced and internationally coordinated assessment of climate change, WMO and UNEP jointly agreed in 1988 to set up an Intergovernmental Panel on Climate Change (IPCC), a worldwide network of 2,500 leading scientists and experts, to review scientific research in three working groups on: the available scientific information on climate change; the environmental and socio-economic impacts; and the formulation of response strategies.

Since 1990, the IPCC has produced four assessment reports with increasing concern about the potential widespread negative effects of global warming caused by climate change. The final report, released in March 2007, declared, for the first time, that warming of the world's climate system was "unequivocal" and caused by human activity. The linear warming trend over the past 50 years was nearly twice that for the last 100 years. Eight of the warmest years on record have all occurred in the last decade. The report painted a pictured of a world of starvation, mass migration of people, rampant diseases, and the extinction of many animal species. If unchecked, climate change could lead to 50 million people becoming refugees by 2010. The worst effects would be felt in regions that were already poor. About 250 million people would face hunger. Diseases, such as malaria, dengue fever, yellow fever, and Nile fever, would spread. Billions of people in Asia would be at risk from flooding. On the other hand, wealthier countries in the higher latitudes could benefit from higher temperatures, leading to increased agricultural production, open Arctic seaways, and fewer deaths from cold. The report warned that the world should begin to adapt now or face a bill of many billions of dollars more and a heavy toll in human suffering within a few decades. It suggested that most of the cost should be met by the private sector and business rather than governments.

A comprehensive review of the economics of climate change commissioned by the U.K. government was published in October 2006.[45] At the launch of the review, the author, Sir Nicholas Stern, head of the U.K. Government Economic Service at the time, and formerly chief economist at the World Bank, said:

> The conclusion of the Review is essentially optimistic. There is still time to avoid the worst impacts of climate change, if we act now and act internationally. Governments, businesses and individuals all need to work together to respond to the challenge. Strong, deliberate policy choices by governments are essential to motivate change. But the task is urgent. Delaying action, even by a decade or two, will take us into dangerous territory. We must not let this window of opportunity close.

In the meantime, intergovernmental action has been increased. A United Nations Framework Convention on Climate Change entered into force in March 1994, ratified by 189 of the 192 UN members. The convention aims "to achieve ... stabilization of greenhouse gas concentrations in the atmosphere at a level which would prevent dangerous anthropogenic interference with the climate system." It sets an overall framework for intergovernmental efforts to tackle the challenges posed by climate change. The convention recognizes that the world's climate system is a shared resource whose stability can be affected by industrial and other emissions of carbon dioxide and other greenhouse gases. Under the convention, developed countries agreed to reduce their emissions to 1990 levels by 2000 and to transfer to developing countries technologies and information to help them respond to the challenges of climate change. The Kyoto Protocol was adopted in 1997, which strengthened the UN convention by committing parties to individual, legally binding, targets to limit or reduce their greenhouse gas emissions. The protocol, which entered into force in February 2005 and runs to 2012, is ratified by 165 countries. Of these, 35 countries and the EU are required to reduce their emissions below levels specified for each country. Total cuts in emissions add up to at least 5 percent from 1990 levels.

A major impediment to coordinated international action to meet the challenges of climate change has been the marked differences between the United States and other countries. The U.S. has neither ratified the UN convention nor the Kyoto Protocol, despite being the world's largest source of global greenhouse gas emissions. With 5 percent of the world's population, the U.S. accounts for 24 percent of global carbon dioxide emissions and for 36 percent of 1990 emissions. Uncertainty or unacceptance of the scientific evidence and predictions of the severity of the problem, and the cost of the proposed solutions, have been quoted as reasons for U.S. reluctance to cooperate. Aspects of domestic politics also play a role. Many attribute the U.S. reluctance to take action on climate change to politically powerful industrial and energy interest groups. These groups argue that imposing cuts in greenhouse gas emissions is a ploy to impose a tax on them, which would handicap their competitiveness in domestic and international markets, and result in losses in economic growth and employment. Another factor is seen as the separation between the executive and legislative branches of the U.S. domestic political process, which requires a super-majority of the Senate plus presidential approval to take on international obligations.

The latest twist is that in the absence of federal leadership to reduce greenhouse gas emissions, a number of the U.S.A.'s states and regions have taken action to address the issue of climate change, almost always with long-term economic well-being in mind. The Energy Independence and Security Act of 2007 has set higher fuel economy standards for cars and light trucks for the first time in 22 years, together with new efficiency requirements for household appliances and government buildings. The U.S. Environmental Protection Agency has prevented states from applying their own standards, requiring automakers to apply higher standards to reduce greenhouse gas emissions by 30 percent by 2016, arguing that "national solutions" (which the federal government has refused to pass) were preferable to a "confusing patchwork of state rules." The former vice president of the United States, Al Gore, has played his part in helping to turn public opinion against the skeptics in the U.S. and elsewhere with his commentary on the film, and his book, on *An Inconvenient Truth*, for which he shared the Nobel Peace Prize in 2007 with the IPCC.

A UN Conference on Climate Change was held in Bali, Indonesia in December 2007. The UN secretary-general, Ban Ki-moon, described it as the "political response" to the scientific reports of the IPCC. He urged all countries to reach agreement by 2009 and to have it in force by the expiry of the Kyoto Protocol in 2012, adding: "We cannot continue with business as usual. The time has come for decisive action on a global scale." The contentious two-week conference revealed the continuing opposition of the U.S. administration to any agreement to take decisive global action to counteract the effects of climate change. A delegate from Papua New Guinea caught the mood of the conference when he rebuked the American delegation: "if for some reason you are not willing to lead, leave it to the rest of us. Please, get out of the way." Al Gore vented the frustration of many delegates when he accused the U.S. administration of blocking efforts to tackle global warming. He advised the conference to look beyond the current U.S. administration whose tenure ends in 2009.

Both sides claimed victory in the final wording of the Bali Action Plan. The U.S. succeeded in omitting any reference to setting specific emission reduction targets, despite an aggressive campaign by the EU to include reduction targets for industrial countries of between 25 and 40 percent below 1990 levels by 2020. But the action plan did contain reference to the IPCC's dire warning that "warming of the climate system is unequivocal, and that delays in reducing emissions significantly constrains opportunities to achieve lower stabilization levels and increases the risk of more severe climate change impacts," and that "deep cuts in global emissions will be required."

Most significantly, the U.S. dropped it opposition to a UN-managed "roadmap," which laid out in detail an agenda and schedule of negotiations to find ways to reduce pollution and help poor countries adapt to climate change by speeding up the transfer of technology and financial assistance by 2009, and to have agreement in place by the time of the ending of the Kyoto Protocol in 2012. And an Adaptation Fund was established to assist developing countries. Yvo de Boer, executive secretary of the UN Framework Convention on Climate Change, said at the end of the conference: "This is a real breakthrough, a real opportunity for the international community to successfully flight climate change." But he was under no illusion that finalizing negotiations by 2009 would be more difficult than reaching agreement on the Bali Action Plan.

Globalization

Globalization is now one of the most prominent and contentious issues, as can be seen from the burgeoning literature on the subject, and public demonstrations at the sites of international meetings. Depending on its definition, intent, and projected outcomes, it has attracted passionate supporters and violent opponents. The process of globalization has been conceived predominantly in economic terms, with little linkage to politics, history, culture, environment, and society, but has important non-economic outcomes. Given such disarray, it is difficult to separate impartial analysis from rhetoric.

Many of the antagonists see the problem not with globalization itself, which some regard as a necessary and inevitable process for one planet with finite resources, but with the way in which globalization has so far been managed.[46] Economic forces have been driving globalization but politics has shaped it. Decisions are made because of ideology, preconceived ideas, and denial, not on the basis of impartial evidence. The rules of the game that govern globalization have been largely set by the advanced industrialized countries, and interest groups in those countries, and international agencies and institutions that they have created and support to further their own interests. They have not sought to create a fair set of rules, let alone those that would promote the well-being of the poorest countries and people. Witness the contrasting views expressed at meetings of the World Economic Forum and the World Social Forum. There is lack of consultation and effective representation in the world's key economic decision-making bodies that were set up by the victorious Second World War powers, resulting in what has been described as a "democratic deficit" in the way globalization has been managed. This has led to the view that globalization, as currently pursued, has caused or sustained hunger and poverty, and inequalities in the distribution of its benefits, rather than helped to remove them[47].

Faced with growing criticism, even resentment, in 2001 the ILO established a World Commission on the Social Dimensions of Globalization.[48] In 2004, the commission produced a highly skeptical report, which began: "The dominant perspective on globalization must shift more from a narrow preoccupation with markets to a broader preoccupation with people." The social dimensions of globalization were not only about jobs, health, and education but about democratic participation and national prosperity. In the view of the commission: "A better globalization is the key to a better and secure life of people everywhere in the 21st century."

The commission's report indicated what was generally felt about globalization at the time:

> The current process of globalization is generating outcomes, both between and within countries. Wealth is being created, but too many countries are not sharing in its benefits. They also have little or no voice in shaping the process. Seen through the eyes of the vast majority of women and men, globalization has not met their simple and legitimate aspirations for decent jobs and a better future for their children. Many of them live in the limbo of the informal economy without formal rights and in a swathe of poor countries that subsist on the margins of the global economy. Even in economically successful countries some workers and communities have been adversely affected by globalization. Meanwhile the

revolution in global communications heightens awareness of these disparities ... [which] are morally unacceptable and politically unsustainable.

The commission's survey of 73 countries produced some startling results. With the exception of the EU, the U.S.A. and South Asia, every region had experienced increasing unemployment rates between 1990 and 2002. By 2004, global unemployment had reached a new high of 185.9 million people. Fifty-nine percent of the world's population was living in countries with growing inequality; only 5 percent in countries with declining inequality. Even in most developed countries, the gap between rich and poor was widening. While there were no simple solutions, the commission called for a focus on people, a democratic and effective state, and sustainable development. The problem was not due to globalization as such but to deficiencies in its governance. Global markets had grown rapidly without the parallel development of economic and social institutions necessary for their smooth and equitable functioning.

At the same time, concern was expressed about the unfairness of key global rules on trade and finance and their asymmetric effects on rich and poor countries, and the failure of international policies to respond adequately to the challenges posed by globalization. Market-opening measures and financial and economic considerations predominated over social ones. ODA fell far short of the minimum amounts required to achieve the MDGs and to tackle growing global problems. The multilateral system responsible for designing and implementing international policies was "under-performing." It lacked policy coherence as a whole and was insufficiently democratic, transparent and accountable. These rules and policies were the outcome of a system of global governance shaped largely by powerful countries and people.

The commission made proposals for making globalization more fair and equitable. At the national level, a number of "essentials" were identified, on which there was already wide international agreement, including: good political governance; an effective state; and a vibrant civil society with strong representative organizations both of workers and employers for fruitful social dialogue. At the international level, parliamentary oversight of the multilateral system should be "progressively expanded." This should include the creation of a "Parliamentary Group" to ensure coherence and consistency between global economic, social and environmental policies and integrated oversight of the major international organization. Developing countries should have increased representation in the decision-making bodies of the IMF and World

Bank and the working methods of the WTO. Coordination between the organizations of the UN system should be strengthened.

The report of the commission was presented to the UN General Assembly in 2004, which passed a resolution requesting that it take note of the report "as a contribution to the international dialogue towards a fully inclusive and equitable globalization." Organizations of the UN system were invited to provide information to the UN General Assembly on their activities towards that goal, and the UN secretary-general was requested to take the commission's report into account when preparing his report on follow-up action five years after the UN Millennium Summit of 2000.

Global economic integration has increased considerably over the past two decades, particularly in trade, investment and capital flows. In the process, the world has become much more prosperous and well fed. But absolute poverty and food insecurity persist and have worsened in sub-Saharan Africa. The focus of globalization has not been on eliminating poverty and food security, leading to the conclusion that: "Current trends for achieving food security contradict hopeful assertions that hunger and malnutrition can be eradicated in our lifetime and are not consistent with political commitments by the international community substantially to reduce food and nutrition insecurity by 2015."[49] In the 1990s, the net decrease in the number of the hungry poor was barely 19 million while a decrease of over 100 million was achieved in the 1980s. The remaining 800 million plus of undernourished people constitute the "hard core of world poverty." While globalization offers opportunities for economic growth essential for the reduction of poverty and hunger, the world's poor have not been able to seize these opportunities. Strategic attention by national governments and the international community remains central for meeting political commitments to globally agreed goals, including the MDGs.

A human rights approach

The series of international conferences held throughout the 1990s was designed in part to create a force of international political will to take action to confront the global issues addressed, including that of poverty and hunger. At each conference, world leaders asserted that they were prepared, and that the political will existed, to take action and that the resources and know-how were available. Yet, lack of progress has led to the suggestion that a human rights approach should be adopted.

The case put forward in favor of this approach is that policy objectives come and go with changing governments, and the numerous declarations of intent to end world hunger and poverty are not legally binding, while legal obligations would remain in place beyond the volatility of politics.[50] Getting all countries to adopt this approach, particularly powerful nations like the United States that have shown aversion in the past, and translating legal commitments into operational strategies and action, would still present formidable challenges. Several UN bodies have adopted a statement of common understanding regarding a rights-based approach to their cooperation and development programs. FAO has adopted a set of voluntary guidelines to support the progressive realization of the right to adequate food in the context of national food security.[51] It remains to be seen, however, whether the human rights approach will prove to be more successful than the other commitments made over the past 60 years.

The way ahead

The world has witnessed dramatic changes in the last two decades that have had profound effects on all global institutions, including those concerned with food and agriculture.[52] The former East–West political divide has been replaced by more complex multilateral relationships among nations and the emergence of new regional powers. The architecture of the United Nations system that was created after the Second World War to respond to the global challenges of the time is now being critically examined and reforms are being proposed. At the same time, significant changes are taking place in international cooperation. Powerful multinationals have emerged with more resources than many states: their foreign direct investment reached $1.2 trillion in 2006.[53] Private foundations are providing vast resources at a time when many multilateral institutions are facing financial difficulties, with calls to do more with less through greater streamlining and efficiency. Those institutions concerned with food and agriculture have suffered disproportionately as the share of ODA devoted to agricultural and rural development was reduced by 50 percent during the 1990s.

The overall global food situation has shifted dramatically in recent years. Production is now growing more slowly and is inadequate to meet the demands of increasing population and income growth. The new and increasing demand for livestock products, higher-value crops, and biofuels is leading to sharp and dramatic increases in basic food prices, and threatening a world food crisis that could have a dire consequence for the hungry poor who spend most of their meager income on food. Existing production techniques and cropping patterns are coming under increasing stress as a result of climate change, urbanization, and increasing globalization. The call has gone out for a new "doubly green revolution," which would be even more productive than the first Green Revolution, and even more "green" in terms of conserving natural resources and the environment. Over the next three decades, the aim would be to repeat the successes of the first Green Revolution on a global scale, in many diverse localities, which would at the same time be equitable, sustainable, and environmentally friendly.[54]

A positive recent development has been a renewed awareness of the importance of agriculture as a "vital development tool" for achieving the MDG of halving the proportion of people suffering from extreme poverty and hunger by 2015.[55] Three out of every four poor people in developing countries live in rural areas, and most of them depend directly or indirectly on agriculture for their livelihoods. With rising land and water scarcity and the added pressures of a globalizing world, the future of agriculture is intrinsically tied to the better management of natural resources. Rapidly expanding domestic and global markets, innovations in markets, finance and collective action, and improvements in biotechnology and information technology, offer opportunities to enhance the role of agriculture in promoting development. But this will require national and international action to improve the governance of agriculture and to create a level playing field in such vital areas as: international trade, the provision of global public goods, helping developing countries address climate change, the major health problems of humans, plants and animals, and the equitable sharing and involvement of developing countries in the process and benefits of globalization. In sum, this calls for greater mobilization of individual and collective action not only to improve the lives and livelihoods of the rural poor, but to save our civilization on this one planet with finite resources.[56] In many ways, the global food and agricultural institutions described in this book will be in the front line of facing the emerging issues and in the concerted action that will be required to address them.

2 Origins

The origins of the four United Nations organizations concerned with food and agriculture can be traced back to State of the Union address that President Franklin D. Roosevelt gave to the joint session of the U.S. Congress on 6 January 1941. In that address, he made his famous declaration of hope, while the Second World War was being waged, for "a world founded upon four essential human freedoms," freedom of speech and worship, and from want and fear, "everywhere in the world."[1] This declaration was to form the vision for the Atlantic Charter that was signed between Roosevelt and British prime minister Winston Churchill in August 1941, with its reference to "the establishment of a wider and permanent system of general security," the Declaration of the United Nations, signed by 26 governments in January 1942, which pledged them to accept the principles of the Atlantic Charter as "a common program of purposes," and eventually the United Nations conference at San Francisco, California in June 1945 at which the UN was created and its charter signed.[2] This chapter describes the special circumstances and ways in which each of the four United Nations institutions (FAO, World Bank, WFP, and IFAD) were created, in the chronological order in which it happened, and the events leading up to the establishment of the CGIAR.

FAO

Even before the war was over and the United Nations established, President Roosevelt convened a United Nations Conference on Food and Agriculture at Hot Springs, Virginia, in the United States, in May/June 1943, which led to the creation of FAO.[3] The conference was strongly influenced by the "new science" of nutrition and its importance for health and well-being, already recognized by the League of Nations before the Second World War. FAO's founding conference was organized "to consider the goal of freedom from want in relation to food and agriculture."[4] It was recognized that "freedom from want means a secure, an adequate, and a suitable supply of food for every man." Its ultimate objective was defined as ensuring "an abundant supply of the right kinds of food for all mankind," hence the importance of dietary standards as a guide for agricultural and economic policies concerned with improving the diet and health of the world's population. The conference emphasized the "fundamental interdependence of the consumer and the producer." All inhabitants of the earth were consumers. At the time, more than two-thirds of adults were also food producers.

The bold declaration adopted at the conference stated:

> This conference, meeting in the midst of the greatest war ever waged, in full confidence of victory, has considered the world problems of food and agriculture and declares its belief that the goal of freedom from want of food, suitable and adequate for the health and strength of all people can be achieved.

The declaration identified the first task after winning the war to be the deliverance of millions of people from tyranny and hunger. Thereafter, a concerted effort was needed to "win and maintain freedom from fear and freedom from want. The one cannot be achieved without the other." But, the declaration stated: "There has never been enough food for the health of all people." Food production had to be "greatly expanded," for which "we have the knowledge of the means by which this can be done." It required "imagination and firm will" on the part of governments and people to make use of that knowledge.

The declaration recognized that:

> The first cause of malnutrition and hunger is poverty. It is useless to produce more food unless men and nations provide the markets to absorb it. There must be an expansion of the whole economy to provide the purchasing power sufficient to maintain an adequate diet for all. With full employment in all countries, enlarged industrial production, the absence of exploitation, an increasing flow of trade within and between countries, an orderly management of domestic and international investment and currencies, and sustained internal and international economic equilibrium, the food which is produced can be made available to all people.
>
> The primary responsibility for ensuring that people had the food needed for life and health lay with each nation. But each nation

could fully achieve that goal only if all worked together. The declaration ended:

> The first steps towards freedom from want of food must not await the final solution of all other problems. Each advance made in one field will strengthen and quicken advance in all others. Work already begun must be continued. Once the war has been won decisive steps can be taken. We must make ready now.

It became clear at an early stage of the conference that there was general agreement that a permanent multilateral organization in the field of food and agriculture should be established. It was also agreed that the organization should act as a center of information and advice on both agricultural and nutritional questions, and that it should maintain a service of international statistics. The conference agreed on the establishment of an Interim Commission in Washington, D.C. to draw up a detailed plan for the permanent organization for the approval of governments and authorities represented at the conference.

After two and a half years of preparatory work by the Interim Commission, FAO was established by representatives of 44 countries at the first FAO conference in Quebec City, Canada in October 1945.[5] An executive committee of 15 members was also elected. Washington, D.C. was designated as the temporary location of FAO but it was agreed that the permanent location should be at the United Nations on the understanding that this would also be the location of ECOSOC. Eventually, ECOSOC was placed in Geneva, Switzerland and FAO was located in Rome, Italy, where it inherited the library of the International Institute of Agriculture.

Sir John Boyd Orr of the United Kingdom was elected as its first director-general. He was already well known and respected for his pioneering work in nutrition. He had spent much time trying to improve the nutrition of poor people in the depressed areas of the United Kingdom. He had also taken part in meetings at the League of Nations in Geneva, Switzerland, including attending a committee charged with drawing up the standard diet needed for health. He had travelled extensively, visiting research institutions in many parts of the world. As a student of biology, a doctor of medicine, a practicing farmer, and a researcher, Orr was convinced that food should be considered as something much more than a tradable commodity. To him, the international community had a profound moral obligation to provide food for the hungry poor, just as it had provided them with medical care.

World Bank

Like FAO, the first part of what eventually became the World Bank Group, the International Bank for Reconstruction and Development (IBRD), was established before the United Nations was created. Concerned to establish a new international economic order once the Second World War was over, which would prevent the international economy from sinking back into the morass of the 1930s, a United Nations Monetary and Financial Conference was held at Bretton Woods, New Hampshire, in the United States, in July 1944, attended by representatives of 44 nations, to put the capstone on some three years of preliminary work and negotiations.[6] The letter of invitation to attend the meeting sent out by the U.S. secretary of state said that the objective of the meeting was "for the purpose of formulating definite proposals for an International Monetary Fund, and possibly [sic] a Bank for Reconstruction and Development." Clearly, the main focus was on the establishment of the fund. The bank was in some respects an afterthought. The articles of agreement for the IBRD, approved at Bretton Woods, were signed by 28 governments in Washington, D.C. in 1945, and the bank formally began operation on 25 June 1946.

The objectives of the IBRD and its administration and management were largely determined by the United States as other countries were not in a position to make substantial contributions to its functioning. The articles of agreement drawn up for the bank built in "fateful features." It would be project-focused, mainly creating physical assets that would be income-generating and self-liquidating. Loans were steered toward "productive" and "specific projects," restricting non-project lending to "exceptional circumstances." They called for "equitable consideration to projects for development and reconstruction" but the immediate purpose of the bank was seen by the main shareholders as helping in the reconstruction of the war-torn countries of Europe. These provisions provided a convenient shield against political pressure and an attractive selling point for marketing bonds to cautious post-war investors. Lending would depend on a country's creditworthiness and would involve much advisory and technical advice and conditionality.

The IBRD was not like an ordinary bank: it had to borrow money in order to lend. Most of the bank's money would come from the private money market with government guarantees. Hence, it would not be a burden on the taxpayer but the borrower would need to win a high credit rating on the New York financial exchange. Only 20 percent of its initial $10 billion capitalization was to be paid in and only 2 percent of that amount was payable in gold or dollars, the remaining 18 percent in the currencies of members. Since the United States was the only member country with a convertible currency, the bank's useable resources when it opened in 1946 with 38 members were the U.S. 20 percent subscription and the 2 percent subscriptions of each of the other members. The bank was to make loans only to governments, or to public and private entities, on the basis of a government guarantee of repayment. Four-fifths of the subscribed capital was to be used as a guarantee fund against losses. Its principle function was intended to be the guarantee of private markets. It was not to lend or guarantee loans to any borrower capable of borrowing on reasonable terms from other sources.

Critically, it was agreed that voting would be based on financial contribution, unlike the vote per country basis adopted in most of the rest of the UN system, thereby ensuring control by the main contributors. Initially, the largest shareholders were the United States, the United Kingdom, the Soviet Union, China, and France. Since the Soviet Union failed to ratify the articles of agreement, India moved into fifth place. The bank was to operate under the authority of a board of governors, consisting of one governor and one alternative for each member country. Daily operations were delegated to executive directors of which there were initially 12, one for each of the five largest shareholders and seven for the rest. And a joint annual meeting of the bank and IMF should take place to discuss common issues and provide a forum for international cooperation.

The first meeting of the governors of the bank and IMF was held at Savannah, Georgia in the United States in June 1946, at which discussions on organizational and management issues took place. The United States stressed that both the bank and the IMF were not business institutions in the ordinary sense and were not profit-making. They were not just two more financial institutions and their activities involved matters of high economic policy. A number of key considerations arose from this position. The United States' view prevailed that both institutions should be subject to close control by national governments. The executive directors were to be appointed by governments, were to act as directors, not advisors, should be located at the bank and IMF, and be only concerned with the institutions' activities.

It was agreed that the president of the bank should be an American citizen while the managing director of the IMF should be a European. In the bank's case, the choice of president has been in the gift of the U.S. president, with no ratification required by the U.S. Congress. The bank's president was to be the chief officer responsible for the organization, appointment and dismissal of officers and staff subject to the general control of the executive directors. Recruitment of staff was to be based on competence and not geographical quota as in most of the UN bodies. Since the bank and IMF could afford to employ more staff at higher average salaries, more consultants, produce more publications, and provide employees with better comforts, including first-class travel (which has subsequently been stopped) this engendered an elitist outlook free from UN controls. The location of the bank and IMF proved to be a contentious issue. Some favoured New York, where these institutions would be close to the United Nations and the New York financial market, and clear of political influence. The United States insisted on Washington, D.C. for both the bank and IMF as it was putting up most of the subscriptions for the operations of both institutions and to ensure close cooperation between the two institutions.

The bank began operations in the period immediately after the Second World War, when a number of international institutions were created with attachments to the United Nations. The Charter of the United Nations[7] reflected the concept of the United Nations as "the authoritative centrepiece of the international system" and the senior and active leader of a cooperative system.[8] It was envisaged that the UN specialized agencies would be concentrated with the United Nations in one place under the "principle of centralization" and architectural plans were drawn up in 1947 for that purpose. But this was not realized and the specialized agencies were set up in different locations. Both the IBRD and the IMF were established as independent specialized agencies of the UN with links to the UN system. According to the UN charter, the specialized agencies "shall be brought into relationship with the United Nations" (article 57) and the UN "shall also make recommendations for the co-ordination of [their] policies and activities" (article 58). For these purposes, ECOSOC could "define the terms on which the [specialized] agency concerned shall be brought into relationship with the United Nations ... subject to approval by the [UN] General Assembly" and "may co-ordinate the activities of the specialized agencies" (article 63). Fearing undesirable political control and influence and negative effects on its credit rating on the New York financial market, the bank distanced itself from the UN and other agencies in the UN system, making coordination difficult. But there are now many examples of cooperation between the bank and other organizations of the UN system, including, for example, between the bank's Agricultural and Rural Development Department and FAO's Investment Center.

The addition of the International Development Association (IDA) as the soft lending affiliate of the bank in 1960 radically changed the institution. It was described as one of those phenomena that underscore the role of happenstance in history. When the United States failed to make the proposal for a Special United Nations Fund for Economic Development (SUNFED) disappear, it co-opted the concept into the bank, where it had greater control over the use of funds through the voting structure.[9] This radically increased the bank's clients and resources. IDA funds, contributed by member countries and replenished every three years, are made available to the poorest developing countries in the form of low-interest credits and grants for an array of non-self-liquidating projects, including poverty alleviation and the social sector. It also enabled the transition from project to program lending. The seamless web between the two parts of the bank, IBRD and IDA, ensured by their shared management, staff and organizational structure, had a profound effect on the bank as a whole.

WFP

Few global institutions have been born in the personal and unusual way in which WFP was created. The birth of WFP was due to the inspiration of one man, George McGovern. At the time, he was the first director of the newly created Office of Food for Peace in the Executive Office of the president of the United States, John F. Kennedy, and special assistant to him. This is how, and why, it happened.[10]

During and after the Second World War, government incentives and advanced technology led to the accumulation of large food surpluses, particularly in the United States. This, in turn, led to the rapid expansion of the controversial United States food aid program. From its inception in 1945, FAO persistently advocated the constructive use of surplus agricultural commodities in food aid programs for development and emergency relief in developing countries. Equally important was the avoidance of potentially destructive effects through the dumping of unwanted surpluses in developing countries, thereby impeding agricultural development and trade. The chance to take action came when, in the context of FAO's Freedom from Hunger Campaign (1960–70), the UN General Assembly adopted a resolution in October 1960 on the "Provision of Food Surpluses to Food-Deficit People through the United Nations System" (Resolution 1496 (XV)). FAO was invited, in consultation with others, to establish "without delay" procedures by which, with the assistance of the United Nations system, "the largest practicable quantities of surplus food may be made available on mutually agreeable terms as a transitional measure against hunger," and requested to submit a report for approval.

The FAO director-general, B. R. Sen, appointed a group of five "high-level, independent experts" to assist him in responding to the request.[11] The whole emphasis of the group's report was to deal with the surplus problem not by curtailing production but by expanding demand. In a spirit of optimism that matched the time, the group considered that the resources to implement a far-reaching program were already available. In its opinion, a transfer of two-thirds to three-quarters of 1 percent of the gross national product (GNP) of the developed countries over a period of five years, and probably less for another decade, would provide sufficient means for helping people in developing countries to help themselves. (Under the European Recovery Program, popularly known as the Marshall Plan after its originator, George C. Marshall, secretary of state in President Truman's administration, the United States provided $13.5 billion of aid between 1948 and 1952, representing about 3 percent of its GNP, almost a third of which consisted of food, feed and fertilizers). Food aid from the food surpluses that existed was seen as an important part of the resources needed for economic development of developing countries. Far from being a waste, it could be a blessing, if matched by other resources, and used as an essential part of a coherent aid program, as it had been in the Marshall Plan, and would "turn the stone of surpluses into bread for development."

A central part of the group's case was that surplus food products could form an important part of capital in its original sense of a "subsistence fund." Food aid could be used to feed additionally employed workers during the period of construction before the fruits of their labor and investments could supply their needs, and rampant inflation would be avoided. Food surpluses used for economic development would enable hungry people to produce either their own food or other products to buy food. Freedom from hunger could ultimately be achieved only through freedom from poverty.

The group estimated that about $12.5 billion of agricultural commodities would become available over a five-year period as surplus to normal commercial markets either bilaterally or through the United Nations system. It recommended that two-thirds of these resources should be used in economic development programs, including the establishment of national food reserves in developing countries and an international emergency food reserve, and one-third for social development, including land reform, education and relief and welfare programs. While the major part of food aid would continue to be supplied bilaterally, the group recommended that it should be supplied within a consultative multilateral framework that would ensure that bilateral and multilateral aid would be provided within coherent and consistent country assistance programs that would combine financial, technical, and food aid.

The group's report was well received, particularly by officials in key positions in the United States, the main provider of food aid, and incorporated into the FAO director-general's submission to the UN General Assembly.[12] But before submitting it, he requested a meeting of an Intergovernmental Advisory Committee in Rome in April 1961 to obtain its views. President Kennedy asked George McGovern to represent the United States at the meeting, with the assistance of Raymond Ioanes of the U.S. Department of Agriculture and Sidney Jacques from the U.S. Department of State. Shortly after taking office in January 1961, President Kennedy had asked McGovern to undertake an evaluation of the past operations of the U.S. food aid program and propose ways of improving it. In his report, submitted to the president on 28 March 1961, which Ioanes had helped to prepare, McGovern wrote, among other things:

> We should support an expanded role for FAO—a role where it will have responsibility for developing and executing a multi-lateral food distribution program. There should not be fear that a multilateral approach will conflict with the US Food for Peace Program. On the contrary, world food needs are so great that there is need for both approaches.[13]

At the meeting in Rome, recalling the evaluation he had recently submitted to President Kennedy, McGovern suggested to the other members of the U.S. delegation that a concrete proposal be made in order to move the process forward. This came as a complete surprise. There had been no discussion, hence no agreement, on any proposal in Washington, D.C. prior to the departure of the U.S. delegation for Rome. Moreover, the meeting had been called only to provide advice and comments, not to present government positions. McGovern's colleagues felt that there was insufficient time to get any proposal approved in Washington, D.C. However, McGovern persisted. He requested the other members of the delegation to draft a proposal while he undertook to get clearance from the White House.

This unconventional procedure was even more unusual in that permission to proceed was sought over a weekend. McGovern contacted his deputy in the Office of Food for Peace, James Symington, by telephone and requested him to speak to Theodore Sorensen, special counsel to President Kennedy, about the draft proposal. Sorensen, a friend of McGovern who had the ear of the president, later spoke by telephone with McGovern, and "within 24 hours" permission was obtained to go ahead. This showed the close relationship, and high regard, McGovern enjoyed with President Kennedy.

The multilateral food aid program that McGovern proposed was circumscribed in a number of ways.[14] It was to be a three-year experimental program with a decision on its continuation dependent of an evaluation of experience. It was to be limited to $100 million in commodities and cash. The United States would be prepared to offer $40 million in commodities and possibly a supplementary cash contribution when, in 1961, the value of farm products shipped under the United States food aid program alone was $1.3 billion and U.S. food surplus stocks had reached 112 million tons. The activities of the experimental program were to be restricted to meeting emergencies and to pilot development interventions, such as school lunch programs and labor-intensive projects, in order to test approaches and develop diversified experience. The multilateral food aid experiment was meant to be a supplement to, and not a competitor of, the bilateral food aid programs. It was precluded from providing large-scale program food aid for balance of payment and budget support purposes, and support for political and commercial objectives that the bilateral programs provided. The multilateral nature of the proposal was stressed. The word "multilateral" occurred four times in McGovern's brief and concise statement. It was to be "a truly multilateral program with the widest possible contributions by member countries." This served notice that the United States was not prepared to address the food problems of developing countries alone. International burden-sharing was needed to tackle their dimensions, politically and financially. This would help both to meet the costs involved and to give an opportunity to all donors to contribute according to their comparative advantage in terms of food commodities and the kinds of food needed, money for transportation and administration, and services, such as shipping.

McGovern's proposal, and the concise, yet detailed, way in which it was presented, caught the delegates from other countries by surprise. They called for an adjournment to consider how to respond. Eventually, the proposal was accepted, and in the new spirit of international solidarity and burden-sharing in development cooperation that the Kennedy administration had ushered in,[15] the United Nations/ FAO World Food Programme was established in parallel resolutions were passed by the FAO Conference and the UN General Assembly on

24 November and 19 December 1961 respectively. At the end of the experimental period (1963–65), proposals were made to transform WFP into a "World Food Fund," a "World Food Bank" or an "Emergency Supply scheme," which came to nothing. Sufficient experience had been gained, however, and parallel resolutions were passed by the UN General Assembly and the FAO Conference in December 1965 for its continuation "for as long as multilateral food aid is found necessary."

IFAD

IFAD arose out of the world food crisis of the early 1970s and the World Food Conference of 1974. An overriding concern was to increase food and agricultural production in the developing countries, for which a substantial increase in investment was necessary. A major source of additional funding was seen to be the OPEC countries, which had considerably increased the price of oil. The resolution of that conference, which was endorsed by the UN General Assembly, recommended that IFAD "should be established immediately to finance agricultural development projects primarily for food production in the developing countries"[16] Contributions to the fund were to be made on a voluntary basis. The fund should be administered by a "Governing Body consisting of representatives of contributing developed countries, contributing developing countries, and potential recipient countries, taking into consideration the need to ensure equitable distribution of representation among these three categories and regional balance among the potential recipient representations." Disbursements from the fund were to be carried out through existing international or regional institutions in accordance with regulations and criteria to be established by IFAD's governing board. The fund was to become operative as soon as the UN secretary-general determined that "it holds promise of generating substantial additional resources for assisting developing countries and that its operations have a reasonable prospect of continuity."

The agreement establishing IFAD was signed in June 1976. IFAD began operations with the first meetings of its governing council in December 1977, and its first two loans were approved in April 1978. The hiatus between the establishment of the fund and the commencement of its operations was caused by disagreement over the level of contributions from the major donor countries of OECD and OPEC. From the beginning, the concept of "rough parity" between their respective contributions was fundamental and the basis for the equal voting power of these two blocs of donors. Initial funding reached just over $1 billion, with 58 percent and 42 percent from OECD and OPEC countries respectively. There does not appear to have been any agreement on what "rough parity" really meant, and some OECD countries, notably the United States, contended that it meant "equality." This issue was not resolved.

IFAD was, in principle, established like the other international financial institutions (IFIs), and as with the World Bank and the regional development banks, was charged with lending for development projects. However, it differed from them in several important respects.[17] IFAD was given a specific, single mandate, in one sector, to finance agricultural development project, primarily with the view to increasing food production in the developing countries. Other IFIs have broader responsibilities and lend to a wide variety of projects in many sectors. While the bulk of the funds available to other IFIs come from developed countries, in IFAD's case, a substantial part of its resources was to come from OPEC countries, representing an important development in North–South relationships.

In other IFIs, voting power is largely determined by formulas that measure the strength and size of each member country's economy or by the size of their contributions to the institution concerned. This method places control in the hands of the developed countries, and particularly the largest contributors. In contrast, in the UN General Assembly and most of the UN specialized agencies, each member country, irrespective of the size of its population or economy, is given one vote, which places the developing countries in a distinct majority. In IFAD's case, the method of voting represented a middle ground. Voting power was divided equally among the three categories of members, OECD, OPEC, and developing countries. For OECD and OPEC countries, voting was primarily determined by the size of each member's initial, and any additional, contributions to the fund. For developing country members, votes were allocated equally among them. This voting system was designed to allow each group an opportunity to achieve a majority, permit greater interaction between North and South, and give developing countries a larger role in influencing the management of IFAD's development aid.

Another significant difference was that while IFIs are normally directly involved in the entire cycle of projects for which they make loans, from identification, design, preparation and appraisal to implementation and evaluation. In IFAD's case, its founding resolution foresaw the disbursement of its funds to support projects identified and implemented by existing international and regional institutions. A compromise was reached, however, which gave IFAD direct involvement in the first half of the project cycle, up to and including project preparation, with other institutions responsible for the remaining half of the cycle. This compromise was reached between most of the OECD countries, who were opposed to the creation of yet another IFI, with the proliferation of staff and costs involved, and who preferred to give the additional funds to established IFIs, and the developing countries who wanted a new IFI that was more borrower-oriented.

CGIAR

The roots of the CGIAR lie in the pioneering agro-scientific work that led to the Green Revolution (GR). The GR was a remarkable achievement.[18] The use by farmers of new, research-based high-yielding seeds and technology transformed agriculture and thwarted the very real threat of famine in the developing world. The achievement was to deliver annual increases in food production that more than kept pace with population growth. Many factors contributed to the success of the GR but of central importance was the application of modern science and technology to the task of getting crops to yield more through what were referred to as "core programs" in international agricultural research centers and "outreach programs" through trials and tests in other countries.

The origins of the GR and the CGIAR lay in a joint venture between the Office of Special Studies, established by the Ministry of Agriculture in Mexico, and the Rockefeller Foundation in 1943. The Office, headed by a small team of scientists, which included Norman Borlaug, who was awarded the Nobel Peace Prize in 1970 for his pioneering efforts, worked at an experimental station on Mexico's rain-fed central plateau. Its remit was to improve the yields of the basic food crops, maize (corn), wheat and beans, the mainstay of the Mexican diet. Dramatic success was achieved. By 1960, over a third of Mexico's maize land was planted to new high-yielding varieties and total production increased from 2 to 6 million tons. At the same time, virtually all of Mexico's wheat lands were put under high-yielding varieties and average yields quadrupled.

Following this success, attention turned to Asia, where rice was the staple food in many countries. In 1960, the International Rice Research Institute (IRRI) was established in the Philippines as a joint venture between the government and the Ford and Rockefeller Foundations. By 1970, half of the Philippines' rice lands were planted to new varieties and the country achieved self-sufficiency in rice production in

1968 for the first time in decades. From the beginning, an objective was to produce high-yielding crop varieties that could grow in a wide range of conditions throughout the developing world. As early as the 1950s, successful trials of the new Mexican maize and wheat varieties were conducted in Asia and Latin America. To oversee the international efforts required, an outreach improvement program was established in 1971 under the umbrella of the International Center for the Improvement of Maize and Wheat (CIMMYT) in Mexico, and for rice from IRRI. Two other international agricultural centers were established for tropical agriculture in Colombia and Nigeria in 1967.

By this time, it became clear that the resources needed to sustain the international agricultural research core and outreach programs were far larger than could be provided by the two foundations, Ford and Rockefeller, alone. The foundations, together with the heads of FAO, UNDP and the World Bank, sought to persuade donors that agricultural development, and, therefore, agricultural research, deserved high priority on the international development agenda. A series of meetings was held between 1969 and 1971 at Bellagio, Italy, which finally resulted in the establishment of the CGIAR. At its inaugural meeting in January 1971, a "Statement of Objectives, Composition and Organizational Structure" was adopted that committed the CGIAR to examine the needs of developing countries for specialized efforts in agriculture, harmonize international, regional and national efforts to finance and undertake agricultural research, provide finance for high-priority agricultural research activities, and undertake a continuing review of priorities. A unique "strategic alliance" was born of members, partners and international agricultural centers to mobilize science for the development of agriculture throughout the developing world.

In these different ways the five global institutions were established. We can now turn to the different ways in which they operated.

3 Mandates, governance, and finance

This chapter describes the mandate, governance structure, staffing and financing arrangement of each of the global food and agricultural institutions in turn, beginning with the four United Nations bodies, FAO, World Bank, IFAD and WFP, and ending with the CGIAR. Each of these institutions has their own arrangement for managing their operations. Some have remained relatively unchanged since their foundation while others have witnessed several alterations and refinements.

FAO

FAO's mandate and constitution were established at the first FAO conference in Quebec City, Canada in October 1945. FAO was to:

- Raise levels of nutrition and standards of living of people.
- Secure improvements in the efficiency of production and distribution of all food and agricultural products.
- Better the condition of rural populations.
- Contribute toward an expanding world economy and ensure humanity's freedom from hunger.[1]

The functions of FAO were also set out fully, clearly and explicitly. The institution was to "collect, analyze, interpret and disseminate" information relating to nutrition, food and agriculture. It was to "promote and, where appropriate, recommend national and international action" concerning:

(a)   scientific, technological, social and economic research relating to nutrition, food and agriculture;

(b) improvement of education and administration relating to nutrition, food and agriculture, and the spread of public knowledge of nutritional and agricultural science and practice;
(c) conservation of natural resources and the adoption of improved methods of agricultural production;
(d) improvement of the processing, marketing, and distribution of food and agricultural products;
(e) adoption of policies for the provision of adequate agricultural credit, national and international; and
(f) adoption of international policies with respect to agricultural commodity agreements.

It was also to:

(a) furnish such technical assistance as governments may request;
(b) organize, in cooperation with the governments concerned, such missions as may be needed to assist them to fulfill the obligations arising from their acceptance of the recommendations of the Hot Springs conference and FAO's constitution; and
(c) generally to take all necessary and appropriate action to implement the purposes of FAO.

To execute this comprehensive mandate, the institution is governed by the FAO Conference of member states, currently numbering 192 countries. Each member has one vote and decisions are taken either by consensus, simple majority voting, or by two-thirds majority voting for changes to FAO's constitution. The FAO Conference meets every two years to review the work carried out by FAO and approve a "Program of Work and Budget" for the next biennium. It also elects a director-general of FAO for a six-year term of office. From its inception in 1945, directors-general have been elected in order from the United Kingdom, the United States (on two occasions), India, the Netherlands, Lebanon, and Senegal. The current and previous executive heads have been elected three times, to service a total of 18 years each.

The FAO Conference elects an FAO council of 49 members drawn from seven regional groupings (Africa, Asia, Europe, Latin America and the Caribbean, Middle East, North America, and the Southwest Pacific). The council acts as an interim governing body between FAO Conference sessions, with an independent chairperson appointed by the FAO Conference. Decisions are taken by consensus or simple majority voting. The council is assisted by a number of technical and special committees that are open to all member countries and registered observer organizations. These include technical committees dealing with: agriculture (covering crops, livestock, land and water, and related natural resources and policy issues); commodity problems and trade (with intergovernmental groups on the major food and agricultural commodities); fisheries; forestry; and commissions dealing with plant genetic resources, fertilizers, and food standards. There are also special committees relating to program, finance and constitutional and legal matters. Panels of experts have also been formed on Ethics in Food and Agriculture, Animal Production and Health, Forest Genetic Resources, and Plant Production and Protection.

The FAO secretariat at its headquarters in Rome, Italy operates through a number of departments dealing with: Human, Financial and Physical Resources, Knowledge and Communications; Agriculture and Consumer Protection; Economic and Social Development; Fisheries and Aquaculture; Forestry; Natural Resources Management and the Environment; and Technical Cooperation. On taking up office in 1994, director-general Jacques Diouf undertook a partial restructuring of the organization. He followed this up with a major reorganization of FAO in 2005, the most significant since its founding. While the previous director-general, Eduoard Saouma, had established FAO country offices, serving some 106 developing countries, in 1976, this was taken further by the current director-general, Jacques Diouf. With the objective of bringing FAO as close to its members as effectively possible, and creating a management style with delegation of authority and an environment that encouraged staff creativity and initiative, an extensive decentralized network was created of: regional offices for Africa, Asia and the Pacific, Latin America and the Caribbean, the Near East and Europe; sub-regional offices for Central Asia, Central and Eastern Europe, North, Central, East, West and Southern Africa, the Caribbean, and the Pacific Islands; liaison offices in Geneva, Switzerland, Washington, D.C., Brussels, Belgium, and Yokohama, Japan; and 78 offices throughout the developing word. At the same time, with the decline in FAO's resources (see below), the total staff of FAO has fallen by over 40 percent from 6,487 in 1990 to 3,597 in 2008. The most significant falls have taken place in the number and distribution of professional staff at FAO headquarters, particularly in the Department of Technical Cooperation, where staff numbers have fallen by 30 percent.

FAO activities are financed in part through assessed contributions of its members, set by the FAO Conference for each biennium, for its regular program, and partly from extra-budgetary funds from governments and private sources earmarked for specific programs and

70 Mandates, governance, and finance

activities identified by them. The United States and Japan make the largest assessed contributions to FAO. FAO is facing financial difficulties.[2] Total resources in real terms (net of extra-budgetary funds for emergencies) declined by 31 percent between 1994 and 2005 to $841.7 million for the biennium 2004–5. Net appropriations from assessed contributions declined by 22 percent to $522.7 million for the biennium 2006–7. Extra-budgetary resources (net of emergencies) declined by 50 percent. The FAO Conference approved a budget of $867.6 million for FAO's regular program for 2008–9, an increase of 13 per cent above the budget for the current biennium, although less in real terms in view of the depreciation in the value of the U.S. dollar Figure 3.1).

In the biennium 2004–5, three-fifths of extra-budgetary funds were for development activities and the remaining amount for emergencies. Donors are attracted to funding particular countries and regions according to their aid policies, priorities and preferences. Africa, Central America, and some Asian countries receive the bulk of extra-budgetary funding. The main providers of extra-budgetary funds in 2005 were the EU, Italy, the Netherlands, Japan, Germany, and Spain. Most of FAO's field program is extra-budgetary funded. Only

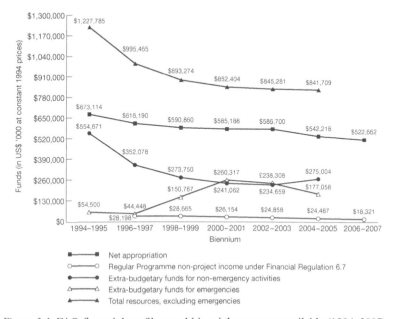

Figure 3.1 FAO financial profile: total biennial resources available (1994–2007)
Source: Independent External Evaluation of FAO (2007).

about 12 percent of funding for all projects in developing countries approved between 2001 and 2006 came from the regular budget. An increasing proportion of work at FAO headquarters is also financed from extra-budgetary sources. Extra-budgetary funds for development projects are mainly channeled through earmarked trust funds. These are essentially either unilateral trust funds, where a number of developing countries (for example, Brazil, Mexico, Nigeria, and Venezuela) provide their own funds for activities executed by FAO in their countries, or involve donor governments in a "Government Cooperative Programme." FAO charges up to 13 percent for servicing trust funds and their activities.

There are also other trust funds established by FAO, such as the "FAO Trust Fund for Food Security and Food Safety," established as a follow-up to the World Food Summit of 1996. Increasingly, FAO seeks to have "strategic partnership agreements" with donors designed to put into operation programs designed at FAO headquarters, with only a small percentage of extra-budgetary funding. For emergencies, a "Special Fund for Emergency and Rehabilitation Activities" was established in May 2003 to enable FAO to take initial rapid action and complementary action to ensure continuity of follow-up of emergency activities with a target funding established in November 2004 of $20 million.

World Bank

The mission of the IBRD and the IDA is:

> To fight poverty with passion and professionalism for lasting results. To help people help themselves and their environment by providing resources, sharing knowledge, building capacity, and forging partnerships in the public and private sectors.[3]

The articles of agreement of the IBRD called for equal consideration to be given to assisting projects for reconstruction and development. The major shareholder gave preference to reconstruction and the first major loan was given to France for that purpose. But the creation of the U.S. Marshall Plan in 1947, with its large program of assistance for the recovery of war-torn Europe, removed the need for the bank's priority in this area. Reconstruction remains an important focus of the bank's work, however, given the natural and man-made disasters and reconstruction needs of developing countries

The bank's portfolio of assistance was broadened, particularly after the inclusion of IDA in 1960, from large-scale infrastructure projects to include social sector project lending, poverty alleviation, debt relief, and good governance programs. This, in turn, sharpened the focus on poverty reduction as the overarching goal of the bank's entire work.

The bank has been likened to a cooperative, where its 185 member countries are shareholders, represented by a board of governors, who are its ultimate policy-makers. Generally, the governors are member countries' ministers of finance or development. They meet once a year at the joint meeting of the governors of the bank and the IMF. Between annual meetings, the governors delegate specific duties to a board of executive directors of 24 members who work full-time at the bank. The five largest shareholders, France, Germany, Japan, the United Kingdom, and the United States, each appoint one executive director. The other 180 member countries are grouped into constituencies that elect the remaining 19 executive directors. The board of executive directors is responsible for making policy decisions affecting the bank's operations and for approving all loans. The executive board meets twice a week in regular sessions and also as often as bank business requires. Each executive director also serves on one or more of the bank's standing committees on audit, budget, development effectiveness, personal, governance, and administrative matters. The executive board normally makes decisions by consensus. However, the relative voting power of individual executive directors is based on the shares that are held by the countries they represent. Currently the shares are: 16.39 percent for the United States, 7.87 percent for Japan, 4.49 percent for Germany, 4.30 percent for France, and 4.30 percent for the United Kingdom, with 62.61 percent for all other shareholders.

The bank's day-to-day operations are carried out under the leadership of the bank's president, managing directors, senior staff and vice-presidents (VPs). The president chairs meetings of the executive board and is responsible for the overall management of the bank. The vice-presidencies are the main organizational unit of the bank. Each VP reports mainly to a managing director, to the chief financial officer, or directly to the president. Each VP is responsible for a specific region of the world, a thematic network, or a central function. The network VPs cut across the regional VPs in the form of a matrix, which ensures an appropriate mix of experience and expertise. There is an Independent Evaluation Group to enhance development effectiveness through excellence and independence in evaluation.

Originally, bank operations were highly centralized in Washington, D.C. and carried out through short-term missions to developing countries. In recent years, through a policy of decentralization, reflecting the bank's commitment to operate in close partnership with its clients, of the 10,700 professional and support staff employed at the end of 2007, 3,800 were located in country offices throughout the developing world. The Agricultural and Rural Development Department (ARD) had 235 professional staff, of whom 92 were located in developing countries. Once a largely homogeneous team of engineers and financial analysts, the bank's staff now consists of a multidisciplinary and diverse group that includes economists, public policy experts, sector specialists, and social scientists.

As the world's largest development financing institution, the bank finances its development programs in two ways. In the case of the IBRD, it taps into the world's capital markets by offering highly rated IBRD bonds, notes and other debt securities. In the case of the IDA, contributions are received from donor countries on a replenishment basis. Additionally, specific activities can be funded by donors through trust funds managed by the bank. IBRD provides more than half of the bank's annual lending. Less than 5 percent of IBRD funds are paid in by countries when they join the bank. Member governments purchase shares based on their relative economic strength but pay in only a small portion of the value of these shares. The unpaid balance is "on call" as guaranteed capital to pay bondholders. IBRD's rules require that the sum of all loans outstanding and disbursed should not exceed the combined total of capital and reserves. Because it is a cooperative institution, IBRD does not seek to maximize profit but to earn enough income to ensure its financial strength and to sustain its development activities.

The bank's treasury is at the heart of IBRD's borrowing and lending operations and has developed considerable expertise since the bank was established. The treasury currently borrows around $10 to $15 billion annually in about 11 currencies. It has offered IBRD bonds and notes in over 40 different currencies and has opened up new markets for international investors through its issuance in emerging market currencies. It is an extensive user of interest rates and currency swaps with about $30 billion in annual volume and a swap book total around $150 billion. In its asset management business, the treasury now manages between $60 and $65 billion.

IDA is the world's largest source of interest-free loans and grant assistance to the poorest countries. It accounts for nearly 40 percent of total bank lending. IDA resources are replenished every three years by donor countries, which include developing countries that were once IDA borrowers as well as industrialized countries. While other development assistance institutions and agency are having financial difficulties, the 15th triennial replenishment of IDA in 2007 brought a record contribution from donors of $41.6 billion, 30 percent above the previous replenishment, reflecting donor confidence in an institution over which they have full control. As with IBRD, to date there has never been a default on an IDA credit.

Since it began operations in 1946, cumulative lending from the IBRD reached $420.2 billion by mid-2006. Lending for FY 2006 was $14.1 billion for 112 new operations in 33 countries. In the case of IDA, which was established in 1960, cumulative lending by mid-2006 had reach $170 billion. Commitments for FY 2006 were $9.5 billion for 167 new operations in 59 countries. For FY 2006, the combined lending from the IBRD and IDA of $23.6 billion by region was: Latin America and the Caribbean 25 percent, Africa 20 percent, Europe and Central Asia 17 percent, East Asia and the Pacific 14 percent, and the Middle East and North Africa 7 percent. By sector it was: 25 percent for law, justice and public administration, 14 percent for transportation, 13 percent for energy and mining, 10 percent for finance, 9 percent for health and other social activities, 8 percent for education, 7 per cent each for: agriculture, fishing, and forestry; industry and trade; and water, sanitation, and flood protection; and 1 percent for information and communication.

Developing countries are placed in different categories to determine their eligibility for IBRD and IDA lending. Two basic types of loans and credits are made: investment loans and development policy loans. IBRD serves countries that are defined by the bank as middle-income and creditworthy poorer countries. It provides these countries with access to capital on favorable terms, with longer maturity, and in a more sustainable manner than the financial market provides. Typically, an initial fee of 1 percent of the loan amount was charged, with a lending fee depending on the type of project, a charge of 0.75 percent on undisbursed balances, and a maturity period of 15–20 years, with a 3–8 year grace period. For all loans signed on or after 16 May 2007, however, the initial fee is 0.25 percent, and as of February 2008, the maximum maturity period of IBRD loans is 30 years. Specifically, IBRD loans: support long-term human and social development needs that private creditors do not finance; preserve borrowers' financial strength by providing support during crisis periods, when poor people are most adversely affected; promote policy and institutional reforms; create a favorable investment climate for private capital; and provide financial support in areas that are critical for poor people.

Eligibility for IDA assistance depends on a country's relative poverty, defined as its gross national income (GNI) per capita below an established threshold that is updated annually. The threshold for FY 2007 was $1,025. Some countries above that threshold may be eligible for IDA assistance because they lack the creditworthiness needed to receive IBRD assistance. Some countries below the established threshold may also be creditworthy for IBRD assistance. For IDA loans, commitment fees range from zero to 0.5 percent on undisbursed balances, which are set annually (0.2 percent for FY 2007), a maturity period of 20–40 years, with a 10-year grace period, an interest rate of 4 percent for hard-term credits approved in FY 2007, and a service charge of 0.75 percent. This concessional lending helps build the human capital, policies, institutions and physical infrastructure that is needed to achieve faster, environmentally sustainable growth. IDA's goal is defined as reducing disparities across and within countries, especially in terms of access to primary education, basic health, and water supply and sanitation, and to bring more people into the economic mainstream by raising their productivity and incomes. IDA also provides grants designed to facilitate development projects by encouraging innovation, cooperation between organizations, and stakeholder participation. In recent years, IDA grants have been used to: reduce the debt burden of heavily indebted poor countries (HIPCs), improve sanitation and water supplies, support vaccination and immunization programs, combat HIV/AIDS, support civil society organizations, and create initiatives to cut the emission of greenhouse gases.

The bank has recognized that many development efforts have failed because donors rather than governments they were trying to assist drove the agenda. Under its current development policy, the bank helps governments take the lead in preparing and implementing development strategies in the belief that programs that a country owns, and that have widespread stakeholder support, have a greater chance of success. All bank assistance is made within the context of a rigorous project cycle based on a poverty reduction strategy approach. Each assisted country devises a National Poverty Reduction Strategy (PRS), which creates a framework for donors to coordinate their assistance programs and align them with national priorities and targets for reducing poverty over a three-to-five-year period. In addition, the bank and the development community initiated a new approach to development assistance in the form of a Comprehensive Development Framework (CDF).[4] The CDF builds on lessons concerning development aid effectiveness and focuses on coordination among development partners in each PRS. The bank's Strategic Framework Paper (SFP) identifies two main pillars in the bank's assistance in fighting poverty: building a climate for investment, jobs, and sustainable growth; and empowering men and women to participate in development. One of the most visible changes in the bank in recent years has been in the increasing focus on poverty combined with a growing emphasis on meeting the MDGs.

The bank's blueprint for its work with a country is based on a Country Assistance Strategy (CAS) that is derived from the priorities in the country's PRS. The CAS is produced in cooperation with the government concerned and interested stakeholders. Each project assisted by the bank goes through a coordinated cycle of identification, preparation, appraisal, approval, implementation, supervision, and completion, and evaluation carried out by the bank's Independent Evaluation Group. A project may be dropped at any point in the project cycle from preparation to approval. An independent Quality Assurance Group monitors the quality of the bank's activities during implementation to facilitate better management. Another independent body, the Inspection Panel, provides a forum for citizens who believe they have been or could be harmed by a bank-supported project. Throughout this process, the bank provides technical assistance and training, and through its publications draws lessons from the experience gained.

WFP

The original purpose of WFP was to provide emergency assistance and explore the possibilities of using food aid to promote economic and social development through school lunch programs and labor-intensive projects. During WFP's initial three-year experimental period (1963–65), it was found that WFP could not respond quickly to emergency situations. Food commodities pledged to WFP were not held in storage but kept by donor countries around the world. Its cash resources were too limited to purchase food on the scale required and had to be used to purchase transport and logistics facilities. It took several months to deliver food from donor to recipient country. More time was often required to synchronize the arrival of consignments of different food commodities from a number of donors. Therefore, for its first 30 years, the bulk of WFP's assistance was provided for a wide range of development projects.

Escalation in man-made disasters in the 1990s following the end of the Cold War dramatically transformed WFP's portfolio of assistance. Up to that time, some two-thirds of WFP's assistance was provided for development projects and one-third for emergencies. In a short space of time, the reverse was to be the case. The International Emergency Food Reserve (IEFR) established by the UN General Assembly in 1975 to enable WFP to respond quickly to emergency food needs was strengthened in 1991 by the addition of an Immediate Response Account with an annual target of $30 million in cash to enable rapid purchases of food close to where emergencies occurred. A new working arrangement was also made between WFP and the UNHCR by which WFP assumed a major role in providing life-saving food to refugees and displaced persons.

When WFP drew up a new mission statement in 1994, 30 years after its establishment, it reiterated that its mandate would continue to be to: use food aid to support economic and social development; meet refugee and other emergency food needs, and associated logistics support; and promote world food security in accordance with the recommendations of the United Nations and FAO. Its core policies and strategies were defined as: saving lives in emergency situations; improving the nutrition and quality of life of the most vulnerable people at critical times in their lives; and building assets and promoting the self-reliance of poor people, particularly through labor-intensive works programs.[5] WFP would concentrate its efforts and resources on the neediest people in the poorest countries.

The organization was described as being "well placed" to play a major role in the *continuum* between emergency relief and development. WFP activities would be integrated at the country level so that they could respond to urgent needs while retaining core development objectives on the basis of the national plans, policies and programs of developing countries. WFP would continue to provide its transport and logistics expertise and assistance to others to ensure rapid and efficient humanitarian aid. Collaboration with other UN organizations, bilateral agencies and NGOs would be pursued. And WFP would play its part in bringing the issue of hunger to the center of the international agenda and in advocating policies, strategies, and operations that directly benefited the poor and hungry.

A unique feature of WFP's original constitution was that the new experimental program was to be carried out jointly between two "parent bodies," the United Nations in New York, and FAO in Rome. The rationale given for this unprecedented arrangement was that the United Nations functioned "in the general field of economic and social development," while FAO had special responsibilities "for securing improvement in nutrition and in the efficiency of food production and distribution." WFP activities were perceived to be included in the mandates of both parent organizations. It was also expected that the new program would provide substantial additional resources to support the work of both organizations. Therefore, neither would yield to the other and, as a compromise, WFP was made a joint undertaking.

WFP's governing body has been changed significantly on a number of occasions since the institution was established. Initially, it was set up as the Intergovernmental Committee (IGC) composed of 20 member states, increased to 24 in 1963, of which half were elected by ECOSOC and half by the FAO council, taking into consideration the need for balanced representation between developed and developing countries, and geographical coverage of all world regions. The IGC was to provide guidance on WFP's policies, administration and operations and approve assistance for development projects and emergency operations. Provision was made for two regular sessions a year and for holding special sessions as necessary. Decisions on important questions required a two-thirds majority of the votes cast.

The IGC was reconstituted in 1975 as the Committee on Food Aid Policies and Programmes (CFA). The UN General Assembly approved a resolution passed by the 1974 World Food Conference on "An improved policy for food aid," which called on the CFA to "formulate proposals for the more effective co-ordination of multilateral, bilateral and non-governmental food aid programmes and for co-coordinating emergency food aid."[6] In 1992, following far-reaching changes in WFP's constitution, which gave the CFA full powers of oversight of WFP activities and greater autonomy to the organization, the number of the governing body members was increased to 42 with 27 from developing countries and 15 from the "more economically developed nations."

In 1993, the UN General Assembly passed a resolution which resulted in the further transformation of WFP's governing body.[7] The governing bodies of the UN funds and programs (UNDP, UNFPA, UNICEF and WFP) were changed into executive boards of identical size and composition, and with similar functions and responsibilities. Each executive board was to consist of 36 members composed of eight members from African states, seven from Asia, four from Eastern Europe, five from Latin America and the Caribbean, and twelve from Western Europe and other states. The resolution further established common functions and working methods for the boards, under the authority of ECOSOC, although the joint undertaking of WFP as a UN/FAO organ was retained.

The functions of the boards were to: implement the policies formulated by the UN General Assembly and the coordination and guidance received from ECOSOC; receive information from, and give guidance to, the executive head of each organization; ensure that the activities and operational strategies pursued were consistent with the overall policy guidance given by the UN General Assembly and ECOSOC;

monitor the performance of each organization; approve programs of assistance; decide on administrative and financial plans and budgets; recommend new initiatives to ECOSOC and the UN General Assembly; and submit annual reports to ECOSOC, with a common structure, in order to ensure effective interaction between the UN General Assembly, ECOSOC and the individual executive boards.

WFP's executive director heads its secretariat and is appointed by the UN secretary-general and the FAO director-general after consultation with WFP's governing body. To date, in order of appointment, executive directors have been from the Netherlands, India, El Salvador, the United States, Canada, Brazil, Uruguay, and Australia. The last three executive directors have been from the United States, two of whom are women. Following the major changes in WFP's constitution, which came into effect at the beginning of 1992, the executive director is responsible for the operation and administration of WFP's resources, approval of emergency assistance up to a level delegated by the governing body, and staff appointments up to and including the most senior level. Executive directors are appointed for five years with the possibility of one further five-year term.

The structure of the WFP secretariat has undergone significant changes in recent years to reflect the major shift in its program of assistance from being a major UN development program to the world's largest humanitarian organization operating on the frontlines of hunger in almost 80 countries. The hub of WFP's activities is its Operations Department, which is responsible emergency operations and development projects. It is organized on a regional basis, with regional bureaus and country offices in Asia, North, West, East and Southern Africa, and Latin America and the Caribbean. The department also has divisions for Program Management and Transport and Food Procurement, and an Assessment Analysis and Preparedness Service.

There is a Fund Raising and Communications Department with links to the donor community and to the private sector, and an Administrative Department for staff and financial matters. WFP's Policy and External Affairs Department has expanded in recent years. It contains services and units that support WFP's special interest in nutrition, school feeding, combating HIV/AIDS, gender, mother and child care services, social protection and livelihoods, and the transition from emergencies to rehabilitations and development. The department also supervises WFP offices in Addis Ababa, Ethiopia for relations with the African Union, New York for connections with the United Nations and UN organizations and government agencies in North

America, and in Geneva, Switzerland for links with UN and international agencies there.

To execute its growing responsibilities, the number of WFP staff has increased significantly in recent years, particularly in the developing countries. Professional staff located in the field increased from 607 at the end of 2002 to 802 at the end of 2006, while at headquarters the number increased over the same period from 268 to 443. Total WFP professional staff increased from 915 (of whom 360 were women) to 1,295 (511 women). Total WFP staff, including general service employees, increased from 1,383 to 2,561 over this period. With locally recruited staff, more than 90 percent of WFP's global workforce of some 10,000 employees works outside WFP headquarters, often in difficult circumstances. The dedication and motivation of this workforce is WFP's greatest asset. WFP's executive board approved a Programme Support and Administrative Budget for 2008–9 of $345 million in October 2007, a reduction of 21 percent in real terms from the previous budget. This has resulted in an overall reduction of around 290 posts with the largest cuts being made at WFP headquarters, liaison offices and regional bureaux. The aim is to manage these reductions in way that do not harm WFP operations for bringing food to the hungry and most vulnerable beneficiaries (see Chapter 5).

All contributions to WFP's resources are made on a voluntary basis in the form of appropriate food and feed commodities, services such as ocean transport, and cash. The original aim was to provide at least one-third of total contributions in cash and services, in the aggregate, to cover the cost of transporting the food commodities provided to recipient countries. All WFP assistance is provided to governments in developing countries on the basis of requests submitted by them. Contributions to WFP's resources may be accepted from intergovernmental bodies, other public sources, and NGOs but, until recently, almost all resources have been provided by member states of the United Nations and FAO. Faced with declining resources, a concerted effort has been made since the late 1990s to identify new non-traditional funding sources. For the first time, large food commodity contributions were obtained from the private sector. A "Friends of WFP–USA" was launched to encourage private and corporate contributions in the United States. And contributions have been received increasingly from NGOs, farmer groups and private individuals.

The nature and composition of WFP resources, and the chosen methods of their deployment, call for complex food aid management arrangements. Over the years, WFP has gained a considerable reputation for being able to move large amounts of food commodities, often

Mandates, governance, and finance 81

in difficult circumstances, throughout the developing world. Although the bulk of foods made available to WFP consist of different types of cereals, a wide variety of foods and feedstuffs have been provided, including dairy products, fats and oils, canned meat, fish and fruit, pulses, mixed and blended foods, sugar, and beverages. As preference has been given to providing food rations directly to beneficiaries that are calculated on the basis of their nutritional requirements, the delivery of a number of food items from different donor countries has to be synchronized to arrive in recipient countries at the same time. Each consignment had to be appropriately labeled and provided in containers the size and form of which facilitates distribution to beneficiaries.

A relatively small number of donor countries have provided most of WFP resources. The United States has been the major donor from WFP's inception. But over 100 countries, including many developing countries, have made contributions at one time or another (Table 3.1).

The Achilles heel of WFP's funding has been shortage of cash resources. As a food aid organization, WFP made a unique entry into the United Nations system. The impressive growth of its resources was in large part due to the fact that food aid was additional to financial aid, and there was relatively little competition from other organizations for the kinds of resources that it was designed to deploy. WFP has performed its functions efficiently with the lowest administrative overhead of any UN agencies (around 7 percent of disbursements), but increasing demand for more cash resources has put WFP in direct competition with other UN and non-UN organizations that operate entirely with financial contributions. Several factors contributed to

Table 3.1 WFP annual contributions 1998–2007 (U.S.$ millions)

Year	No. of contributions	Total	United States	European Union*
1998	49	1704.4	873.0	516.3
1999	52	1512.5	721.2	463.7
2000	59	1694.2	795.9	443.2
2001	53	1906.6	1201.2	449.3
2002	60	1821.6	939.3	562.8
2003	67	2555.1	1458.9	662.9
2004	70	2242.0	1065.0	695.5
2005	80	2724.9	1174.2	876.2
2006	96	2703.7	2423.1	747.6
2007	88	2712.5	1182.2	763.4

Notes: * European Union member states and commission.
Source: World Food Programme.

WFP's increasing cash shortage. A major factor was that some donors, particularly the larger contributors, have not provided one-third of their contributions in cash or services. Another is that increasing involvement in emergency operations called for more cash contributions. WFP undertook to cover the internal transport, storage, and handling costs in the poorest developing countries for the food aid it provided. Those costs increased considerably, particularly as it was in those countries that many of the large-scale and complex emergencies occurred.

Yet another reason for the rising need for cash contributions were the modalities required to get food quickly to where it was most needed. WFP was restricted to selling its food commodities in developing countries to generate cash resources in only a small number of exceptional cases. (By 1986, after 24 years of operation, sales had been permitted in only 16 percent of all WFP-assisted projects, involving 15 percent of the total quantity of food aid committed by that date.) Three other modalities were used.: "triangular transactions," whereby a donor bought food commodities in a developing country to be used as food aid in other developing country; commodity exchanges, in which a food commodity, say wheat, supplied as food aid to a developing country was exchanged for another commodity, say maize, which was used as food aid; and commodity purchases in a developing country to be used as food aid in that country. This last modality is particularly effective in providing a speedy, initial response in emergency situations, and is being increasingly favored by donors, but it requires careful management in order not to create counterproductive effects.

IFAD

The original purpose of IFAD, set out in the resolution of the 1974 World Food Conference, was "to finance agricultural development projects primarily for food production in the developing countries." Its mandate, defined in the agreement establishing IFAD of June 1976, which made the institution a UN specialized agency, was both broadened and narrowed.[8] Its mandate was defined as to finance project and programs specifically designed to improve agricultural production, but it was added that this should be done particularly in the poorest food-deficit countries and in ways that would raise the income, productivity and nutrition of the rural poor. From inception, therefore, IFAD has sought to finance agricultural and rural development that specifically benefits the rural poor, with a distinctly small-farmer focus.

Its overarching mission became to "enable poor rural people to overcome poverty" through country-specific solutions. This involved a number of instruments, including increasing access to land and other natural resources, financial services, markets, and technology, and largely reflected changing ideas about the causes of poverty and how development assistance should be delivered to eradicate it in sustainable ways.

IFAD's seminal study on *The State of World Rural Poverty* in 1992 strongly supported its broadened but focused mission.[9] It drew from the fund's unique field experience and sought to forge a closer connection between the issues of poverty and sustainable growth. The perspective that emerged from IFAD's study was not that growth achieved by the better-off would pull the poor out of poverty but that "mobilization and enhancement of the resources and activities of the poor themselves can uphold their dignity and free them from the shackles of misery, while at the same time making a vital contribution to overall sustainable growth." The study established that poverty was largely a rural problem. Out of a world population at the time of some 4 billion, more than 2.5 billion lived in rural areas, of whom some 1 billion lived below the poverty line. The study also advanced knowledge as to who the poor were, where they were located, and what were their livelihoods. It observed that the mass of the rural poor were self-employed. It was through improvement in the means of production directly accessible to them that their prosperity depended. These assets and services included land, water, technology, commercial services, and credit, provided in an economic policy framework conducive to their optimal exploitation. The poor had not benefited from investments in the agricultural sector because of policy and institutional failures. By its mandate, IFAD had been forced to deal with these problems, which required, among other things, better targeting of resources, reorienting institutions, decentralization, participation in decision-making by the poor themselves, and demand-driven research and extension for the rural poor.

Another seminal report was published by IFAD in 2001.[10] It showed that progress in poverty reduction had slowed during the 1990s and was one-third of what was needed to meet the MDGs (see Box 1.1). It underlined that poverty is multidimensional, so its reduction must be multi-targeted, straddle a number of disciplines and encompass economic, social, political, and institutional factors. Four aspects were identified as being critically important for understanding the challenges facing rural poverty reduction: institutions, markets, technology policy, and asset arrangements that needed to reflect the critical role of food staples in the livelihoods of the rural poor. Rural poverty reduction increasingly required better allocation and distribution of water. Growth alone would not be sufficient to meet the MDGs. And particular groups, especially women, and methods, especially participation and decentralization, merited special attention. The report emphasized that poverty reduction was not something governments, development institutions, or NGOs could do for the poor. The poor themselves had to seize responsibility, as agents of change, for their own development.

IFAD's *Strategic Framework 2007–2010* sets out its current goal and objectives. The goal is "to empower poor rural women and men in developing countries to achieve higher incomes and improve food security." It objectives are to "ensure that poor rural people have better access to, and the skills and organization they need, to take advantage of six essential factors":

- natural resources, especially secure access to land and water and improved natural resource management and conservation practices;
- improved agricultural technologies and effective production services;
- a broad range of financial services;
- transparent and competitive markets for agricultural inputs and products;
- opportunities for rural off-farm employment and enterprise development; and
- local and national policy and programming processes.

Six "principles of engagement" have been establishment to implement IFAD's strategic framework. IFAD focuses on its strength in agriculture and rural development, while working with partners to meet the other needs of poor rural communities. The poorest and most marginalized and vulnerable rural people with the capacity to benefit from IFAD-supported programs and projects are targeted, with special consideration given to gender difference, and a particular focus on women, and recognition of the special needs of indigenous people and ethnic minorities. Poor rural women and men are empowered to take advantage of economic opportunities and achieve higher incomes and better food security for themselves by building their individual capacities and helping them develop and strengthen their own organizations and communities. IFAD encourages innovation, tests new approaches, and works with governments and other partners to learn from experience, and replicate and scale up successes. It also works systematically to make development partnerships more effective. And it designs and manages programs and projects for quality, impact and sustainability by ensuring ownership and leadership by governments and poor rural people themselves.

Membership of IFAD is open to any state that is a member of the United Nations, any of its specialized agencies, or of the International Atomic Energy Agency. Its 165 members are classified into three lists: list A (primarily OECD countries), list B (primarily OPEC countries) and list C (the rest of the world), which are further subdivided into three regional groupings: Africa; Europe, Asia and the Pacific; and Latin America and the Caribbean). Its governing council is IFAD's highest decision-making body. Each member state is represented in the council by a governor, alternate governor, and any designated advisers. Observers may also attend sessions of the council whose status has been approved by the IFAD executive board. All powers of the fund are vested in the council, which meets annually to take decisions on such matters as approval of new rules, appointment of IFAD's president, approval of the administrative budget, and adoption of broad policies, criteria, and regulations. Council sessions are chaired by the chairman of the Governing Council Bureau, which is composed of a chairperson and two vice-chairpersons, representing the three lists of member states described above, who serve a two-year term.

An executive board, IFAD's second main governing body, consists of 18 elected members and 18 alternate members (eight from list A countries, four from list B countries, and six from list C countries), who serve for a three-year term. The board meets three times a year. As with the council, the total number of votes is calculated on both membership and contributions to IFAD's resources. The board decides on IFAD's program of work, approves projects, programs, and grants, and, subject to final approval by the council, adopts and recommends action on matters relating to policy, the annual administrative budget, applications for membership, and staffing. The board also overseas the work of IFAD's Office of Evaluation, which reports directly to it. Sessions of the board are chaired by IFAD's president.

A new and complex system for calculating members' votes was approved in 1997. Under the new system, the total votes of all members are divided into two groups, original votes and new replenishment votes. Each of these is subdivided into two further groups, membership votes and contribution votes. It was agreed that of the original 1,800 votes, 790 are membership votes divided equally among all members. After subtracting the membership votes from the original

1,800, the remaining 1,010 contribution votes are distributed among member states in accordance with their paid share of cumulative resources in 1997. For subsequent replenishments, 100 new votes are created for the equivalent of $158 million of contributions to the replenishment's regular resources. These votes are also divided into membership and contribution votes. New membership votes are divided equally among member states. Contribution votes are allocated according to a member's share of total paid contributions within each replenishment. Membership votes are redistributed each time a new member state joins IFAD. The objective is to give all members a say in decision-making and to encourage increased and speedy payment of contributions to the fund's resources.

IFAD is headed by its president, who is responsible for the day-to-day administration of the fund. The term of office of the president is for four years, renewable only once. Four presidents have been appointed since IFAD was established, three from OPEC countries (Saudi Arabia, Algeria, and Kuwait), and the current one from Sweden. The internal structure of IFAD's secretariat is made up of the Office of President and Vice-President and three departments for External Affairs, Finance and Administration, and Program Management. The latter is the hub of IFAD's operations. It consists of five Regional Divisions (for West and Central Africa, East and Southern Africa, Asia and the Pacific, Latin America and the Caribbean, and the Near East, North Africa, Central and Eastern Europe and the newly independent states), and a Technical Advisory Division with technical expertise in agronomy, livestock, rural infrastructure, rural finance, natural resource management, the environment, gender, public health and nutrition, household food security, and sustainable livelihoods.

IFAD is also home to a number of strategic partnerships in the form of a Global Environment Facility Unit, a Global Mechanism for the Convention to Combat Desertification, the International Land Coalition, and the Belgium Survival Fund. The number of IFAD's professional staff has increased from 191 at the end of 2003 to 242 by mid-2007, of whom 110 are female, and 30 percent are from developing countries. The total number of IFAD staff, including general service employees, increased from 414 to 485 over the same period. In the framework of IFAD's pilot field presence initiative, staff have been out-posted in 15 countries on a pilot basis where innovative projects have been approved to facilitate continuous dialogue with government, beneficiaries and partners on progress made and problems encountered.

Contributions to IFAD have not lived up to the initial promise, generated at the 1974 World Food Conference, of providing substantial additional resources for food and agricultural development in the developing world, as Table 3.2 shows. The conference resolution recommending the establishment of IFAD was initiated and sponsored by almost all the OPEC countries. Additions to IFAD's core resources are made through a replenishment process, with targets approved by its governing council. As a result, compared with other international financing institutions, IFAD is a small organization with an annual lending program below that of the World Bank's IBRD and IDA, and the regional development banks.

IFAD is nevertheless a prominent player in the development of agricultural and rural development in a number of developing countries. Two prominent features of its assistance program have been innovation and partnership, with a focus to leverage impact well above its financial size, partly by co-financing and partly by facilitating the scaling-up of investment. Assistance is provided in the form of loans and grants. Loans are provided to developing member countries on highly concessional, intermediate and ordinary terms. Grants have been a key element in alleviating poverty since IFAD's inception. Over the past 30 years, IFAD has committed about $625 million in grants to support research-for-development programs that have had an impact on small-scale agriculture throughout the developing world. IFAD has also joined the international aid effort to address the debt problems of highly indebted developing countries by providing assistance to them on grant terms rather than through loans (Table 3.3).

Table 3.2 IFAD resources: pledged initial contributions and replenishments

Replenishment	Period	Amount (U.S.$'000)
Initial contributions	1978–80	1,025,829
First	1981–83	1,090,165
Second	1985–87	485,907
Third	1989–96	567,589
Fourth	1997–99	451,351
Fifth	2001–3	451,271
Sixth	2004–6	509,147
Seventh	2007–9	642,531
Total	1978–2009	5,229,788

Source: IFAD, Secretary's Office, April 2008.

CGIAR

The original focus of international agricultural research that led to the foundation of the CGIAR was to increase substantially the production of the staple foods maize, rice, and wheat, through the development and dissemination of high-yielding varieties. Inspired by these early successes, a special partnership was formed within the global agricultural research community in 1971 to address the chronic food supply deficits in many developing countries through production-oriented research.

The strategic and economic reasoning in support of the CGIAR mission to expand and coordinate international efforts in transferring and adapting scientific knowledge to the conditions of developing countries runs along these lines.[11] Implicit in this original mission was a primary focus on the production of international public goods (IPGs) that are non-exclusive in access and non-rival in use, and have widespread applicability beyond national boundaries. The comparative advantage of the CGIAR derives partly from the fact that private firms operating through markets have limited interest in public goods since they do not have the capacity to capture much of the benefit through

Table 3.3 IFAD operational activities (1976–2007), U.S.$ millions

Operational activities	2003	2004	2005	2006	2007	1978–2007
Loan approvals						
Number	25	24	32	31	40	788
Amount	403.6	408.7	499.3	515.0	563.0	9,979.6
Grant approvals						
Number	70	87	66	109	73	2061
Amount	20.3	33.3	36.6	41.8	34.4	625.1
Total	424.0	442.0	515.0	556.8	597.4	10,604.7
Co-financing	124.9	167.2	118.7	108.3	427.4	7,482.2
Multilateral	124.5	69.8	72.1	67.3	401.2	5,935.2
Bilateral	0.0	8.6	38.0	31.8	23.2	1,233.2
NGO	0.0	0.0	1.6	0.6	1.0	26.8
Other	0.3	88.8	6.9	8.6	2.0	287.1
Domestic contributions	184.1	296.6	414.8	282.7	278.7	9,321.6
Total program and project cost	712.5	875.6	1,018.1	910.8	1,272.8	26,836.7

Source: IFAD Annual Report 2007.

proprietary claims. Socially desirable levels of investment in such goods can only be elicited from the public sector. CGIAR investment in developing IPGs complements investments by both the private sector and governments who would invest in national public goods, irrespective of potential spillovers. Although it contributes less than 5 percent to the total global agricultural research budget devoted to the developing countries, the CGIAR has, therefore, played a fundamental role in helping spur agricultural growth and poverty reduction in developing countries.

CGIAR's mission has evolved and expanded over time to reflect changes in development thinking and emphases in the international community (Figure 3.2). The CGIAR commodity improvement mandate quickly expanded from maize, wheat, and rice to included other key food crops, such as legumes (beans, cowpeas, pigeon pea, and chickpeas), roots and tubers (cassava, yams, potato, and sweet potato), and other cereals (sorghum and millet) that were widely consumed as basic foods throughout the developing world, and to encompass better management of livestock and pastures.

By the beginning of the 1980s, through a network of 13 international agricultural research centers, the CGIAR was actively involved in varietal improvement and crop management research for most crops and cropping systems of major importance in the developing world. Recognizing the critical role that good agricultural policies and strong national institutions played in fostering agricultural development, two new centers, IFPRI and ISNAR, were incorporated into the CGIAR.

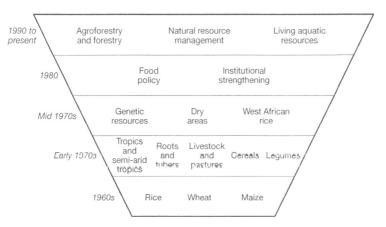

Figure 3.2 CGIAR's evolving research agenda
Source: CGIAR secretariat.

And as recognition of protection and conservation of the natural environment as vital factors for sustainable agricultural development emerged in the 1990s, five additional centers were added to the CGIAR network for genetic resource conservation, forestry, agroforestry, water, and aquatic resource management. By this time, the CGIAR mission had been expanded well beyond raising food production to "achieve sustainable food security and poverty reduction in developing countries through scientific research and research-related activities in the fields of agriculture, forestry, fisheries, policy and the environment."[12]

In its 37-year history, the CGIAR's mission has broadened considerably from a strongly supply-side to a considerably more demand- (often donor) side orientation. It has added to its agenda for delivering concrete research products, such as improved crop varieties, to one of "developing approaches, articulating problems and delivering common agendas and solutions to partners. In doing so, its multifaceted role as a moderator, initiator, facilitator, stimulator and a bridge to broader stakeholder groups has become increasingly important."[13] The challenge is to replicate the successes in helping to raise the productivity of basic food crops in the broader development agenda it has now adopted.

The CGIAR was initially established as an informal organization with the single purpose of increasing basic food production through the application of the latest agricultural research. It was considered that no written charter or definition of roles and responsibilities were necessary. Instead, six main principles guided the CGIAR's operations: donor sovereignty, research center autonomy and authority, consensus in decision-making, independent technical advice, informal status, and a non-political and non-ideological perspective. Decisions on establishing priorities and goals, on approving budgets, and opening new research centers were reached by consensus. Membership was open to any government or private agency that supported the CGIAR mission and was prepared to provide financial support. During its history, no donor has left the CGIAR after becoming a member.

At inception, the organization of the CGIAR consisted of three components: the Consultative Group (CG), consisting of the entire membership; the autonomous international agricultural research centers; and an independent Technical Advisory Committee (TAC). The CG grew to become an informal association of 64 independent public and private sector members (25 developing countries, 22 industrialized countries, 13 regional and international organizations, and four private foundations) with the World Bank, FAO, UNDP, and later IFAD as co-sponsors.[14] It was agreed that the CG's chairman should be a vice-

Mandates, governance, and finance 91

president of the World Bank, nominated by the bank's president in consultation with the other co-sponsors. Members provided financing, policy guidance, and advice to the CGIAR centers. The centers were established as autonomous institutions, each with its own charter, international board of trustees, director, and staff. Initially, representatives from the centers met with all CG members at a "Centers Week" in Washington, D.C., where they had the opportunity to attract general donor interest in their projects, a practice which has subsequently ceased. The director and secretariat of the CG were made administratively a department of the World Bank, which appoints the staff and meets their costs.

At its first meeting in 1971, the CG created the TAC as a source of high-quality, independent, scientific and technical advice. The TAC's role was to evaluate all research projects undertaken by the CGIAR centers, ensure the relevance, and enhance the quality of the science available to the centers, assess the impact of the centers' work, and help mobilize global scientific expertise. In 2003, the TAC was transformed into a Science Council (SC) to reflect the increasing need to focus on scientific matters. Distinguished scientists and research managers from developing and developed countries have served on the TAC and SC. It has its own secretariat, based administratively at FAO headquarters in Rome. The work of the SC is undertaken by standing panels of experts on: monitoring and evaluation; priorities and strategies; impact assessment; and mobilizing science.

Major changes took place in the mandate, direction, membership, and funding of the CGIAR during the 1990s due to a confluence of several factors both inside and outside the institution. No longer was an informal, undefined association of members adequate for the advance of the institution. At its annual general meeting in 2004, the CGIAR adopted *The Charter of the CGIAR System*, with revisions in 2006 and 2007, defining in detail its constituent parts, their roles and responsibilities, and its mission and objectives.[15] The three pillars of the CG system were defined as:

- the Consultative Group, the primary decision-making body consisting of CGIAR members, which meets once a year at its annual general meeting, usually in a member country, with a chair nominated by the president of the World Bank and endorsed by the CGIAR, and its executive council with 20 members and a director selected by the CGIAR chair after an international search process by a search committee consisting of the CGIAR co-sponsors;

Mandates, governance, and finance

- the Science Council of six members and a chair all identified through an international search by an independent selection committee established for the purpose by the CGIAR, which helps to maintain the high quality of science in the CG system; and
- the independent international agricultural research centers supported by the CGIAR, and centers committee.

These entities are supported by the CGIAR System Office, which has a pivotal role in the integration and administration of the entire CG system.

The activities of the CGIAR centers are financed primarily through annual grants from CGIAR members. Members are urged to provide unrestricted contributions to the center, which allows flexibility regarding the allocation of funds based on CGIAR priorities. Resources are transferred in one of three ways:

- directly to each of the CGIAR centers;
- through mechanisms established in the World Bank and administered through the CGIAR secretariat, including the CGIAR Multi-Donor Trust Fund, with the funds disbursed on the instructions of the member concerned; or
- to centers of members' choice through a third party such as an international institution other than the World Bank.

Member support for CGIAR research activities expanded significantly during the first 15 years of its operation. From an initial funding base of $19.5 million in 1972, support broadened and deepened. By 1987, the then 35 members were investing over $240 million each year in the existing 13 CGIAR centers. Today, the aggregate annual contributions from the 64 members are just under $440 million. A small group of donors have provided the major share of contributions to the CGIAR but this is changing. While the top 10 donors accounted for 78 percent of total CGIAR resources in 1994, a decade later they accounted for 64 percent, suggesting a broadening of support. The developing countries, who stand to gain most from the CGIAR's efforts, currently contribute only 4 percent to the total budget, indicating that there is a long way to go before the CGIAR becomes an organization predominantly financed and managed by the developing countries themselves.

During the early years of the CGIAR, a relatively large proportion of funds was contributed by donors in an unrestricted way and not earmarked for any particular project or type of activity. This has changed over time. Restricted (targeted) funding has increased to over half of contributed resources, threatening the integrity and functioning of the CGIAR as one system for coordinating research and funding. As the allocation of CGIAR resources is dominated by center autonomy and authority and donor sovereignty, this has resulted in distortions in funding among the 15 centers and the increasing number of mission objectives. As a result, a major change over the last 30 years has been the shift in focus away from the CGIAR centers focused on increasing food production, and toward those concerned with protecting the environment, saving biodiversity, and improving policies (Table 3.4). A relatively recent additional development has been increasing support for large multi-institutional research programs, as in 16 Systemwide (inter-center) Programs and four Global Challenge Programs that address specific problems of regions or global significance using the expertise of center programs and expanded partnerships, which has added further to the complexity of the entire CGIAR system.

Having examined the ways in which these institutions function, details will be given in the next chapters of the kinds of policies, programs, and projects that each of them have pursued.

Table 3.4 CGIAR funding by type of center, 1972–2005

	1972–75	1976–79	1980–83	1984–87	1988–91	1992–95	1996–99	2000–2003	2004–5
Commodity-focused centers									
Total ($m)	15.6	42.23	63.5	79.2	105.1	95.5	108.6	119.16	128.89
% CGIAR	47.85	49.24	45.26	43.68	45.46	37.58	33.76	32.61	29.89
Eco-regional/commodity-oriented centers									
Total ($m)	16.2	40.56	68.2	88.2	103	100.2	115	125.59	142.47
% CGIAR	49.69	47.26	48.61	48.65	44.55	39.43	35.75	34.37	33.04
Natural resource management centers									
Total ($m)						31	50.6	64.19	88.73
% CGIAR						12.20	15.73	17.57	20.58
Policy/institutional strengthening centers									
Total ($m)	0.8	3.0	8.6	13.9	23.1	27.4	47.5	56.42	71.05
% CGIAR	2.45	3.49	6.13	7.66	9.99	10.79	14.76	15.44	16.48

Source: Prabhu Pingali and Tim Kelley, *The Role of International Agricultural Research in Contributing to Global Food Security and Poverty Alleviation: the case of the CGIAR* (Amsterdam, the Netherlands: North Holland, 2007).

4 Policies, programs, and projects

This chapter gives details of the policies, programs, and projects of each institution. Space does not permit a full description of all their work. Instead, an attempt is made to provide a broad sweep of the activities undertaken, with a concentration of what are regarded as their key activities.

FAO

This particularly applies to FAO, the primary multilateral global food and agricultural institution. Over the past 60 years since its establishment, there have been few aspects of food and agricultural development that it has not covered in response to its extensive and detailed mandate (see Chapter 3).

Early years

The experience of FAO's initial years was to cast the future scope and direction of the organization. When FAO's first director-general, Sir John Boyd Orr, proposed that a World Food Board be established under FAO's administration to ensure world food security, by linking nutrition, health, and agriculture with trade and industry, the major industrialized countries objected. They were not prepared to accept any centralized multilateral world food security arrangement which might weaken their national initiatives and powers of control. The climate of opinion was against multilateral action in operational fields as distinct from advisory or information-providing roles, leading to Boyd Orr's famous statement: "people ask for bread and we give them pamphlets."

During its first 15 years, FAO was the pre-eminent world agricultural organization, and enjoyed a rapid growth in resources and

96 *Policies, programs, and projects*

influence. FAO embarked upon a studies and reports program covering all aspects of the state of food and agriculture after the Second World War. A series of seminal and authoritative publications were produced, which drew the contours of the problems facing world food and nutrition security.[1] FAO was also consciously aware, as the only organization of its kind, of the prime importance of working with governments, especially in developing countries, to increase global food production. For this purpose, FAO's regular resources were annually augmented with extra-budgetary contributions from the UN Expanded Program of Technical Assistance (EPTA) and the UN Special Fund, and from UNDP when it was created in 1965 by an amalgamation of those two UN bodies. By 1951, FAO was able to execute 100 projects in 35 developing countries involving over 2,000 scientific and technical experts from 32 countries.[2] By 1959, over 1,700 experts had served in FAO projects in the field, 1,600 fellowships had been awarded, and 100 training centers organized. In 1956–57, about $16 million, or about 95 percent of FAO's total extra-budgetary resources, came from EPTA. It was a considerable blow to FAO, therefore, when UNDP decided in 1976 to move into thematic programming and national execution of UNDP projects. As a result, UNDP support for FAO's projects went from 74 percent of FAO's total extra-budgetary resources in 1970 to 5 percent in 2000.

Other historical incidents were to change the focus of FAO's work and reduce its authority. In 1971, FAO reluctantly became a co-sponsor with the World Bank and UNDP of the CGIAR, thereby ceding, to a large extent, its role in agricultural research. In 1974, the World Food Conference, called to address the world food crisis of the early 1970s, adopted a series of resolutions, which made inroads into what was formerly FAO territory. The fact that the conference was held in Rome, Italy where FAO's headquarters is located, but in a different part of the city, and under UN, not FAO, auspices, was interpreted as lack of confidence in the organization. In reality, FAO was the first to issue a warning of the impending world food crisis in the early 1970s, and played a major role in preparations for the conference and in its conduct. FAO's work was reflected in a number of the conference resolutions. However, the conference did recommend the setting up of an International Fund for Agricultural Development (IFAD) to attract resources for agricultural development separate from those provided to FAO. It also recommended the creation of a World Food Council (WFC), as a UN ministerial body, to coordinate and follow up "policies concerning food production, nutrition, food security, food trade and food aids as well as other matters, by all the agencies of the United

Nations system," including FAO, and the setting up in FAO of a Committee on World Food Security to submit periodic and special reports to the WFC on the state of world food security.[3]

Following the conference, the election of the next FAO director-general, Edouard Saouma, in 1976, marked a major juncture in FAO's history. A Maronite Christian from the Lebanon, Saouma had a distinctly different personality, and sharply different views, from his predecessor. An agricultural engineer, he had been director-general of Lebanon's National Agricultural Research Institute and minister of agriculture. He joined FAO in 1962, 14 years before becoming director-general, first as FAO regional representative for Southwest Asia in New Delhi, India (1962–65), and then for 10 years as director of FAO's Land and Water Development Division (1965–75). He was to be elected director-general on three consecutive occasions and to serve as FAO's director-general for 18 years.

Saouma witnessed what he, and others in FAO, regarded as the humiliation of his organization at the 1974 World Food Conference. He described how "a careful reading of the [FAO] Constitution gave me inspiration."[4] His view was that the text "clearly expresses the primacy of the Member Nations." FAO "before anything else" was a place where they could meet, enter into dialogue, and agree on joint action, "with the assistance of the body of specialists they have established to help them." The constitution also called for FAO to be aware of the needs of each country, for which "FAO should be by their side, in their homeland, and not only exercising vigilance from far away in Rome."

An extraordinary session of the FAO council was called for by Saouma in July 1976 to amend his predecessor's budget for the biennium 1976–77, and to begin to repair the damage that he considered his predecessor has done. He reduced the number of proposed new posts by 330, dispensed with 155 proposed meetings, and reduced the number of FAO publications and documents. These amendments resulted in savings of over $20 million out of a total budget of $167 million. Saouma allocated these newly released resources in three main areas. First, he strengthened FAO's Investment Centre, which worked with the World Bank, regional banks and other financial sources to prepare agricultural investment projects. Second, he set up a Technical Cooperation Programme to respond quickly to the requests of countries in need. Third, he established 78 FAO country offices, with FAO representatives serving 106 developing countries, beginning a process of decentralization that was continued and deepened by his successor.

World food security was identified by Saouma as one of FAO's major objectives. At the fortieth anniversary of FAO in 1985, he

98 *Policies, programs, and projects*

proclaimed "we must strive to attain food security for the whole earth." He organized a World Conference on Agrarian Reform and Rural Development in July 1979 and an International Conference on Nutrition, jointly with WHO, in 1992, both at FAO headquarters, to establish FAO as the lead agency for the coordination of action in the UN system in these fields. He was concerned to retain FAO's interest and involvement in activities to achieve world food security through a mixture of pragmatic and political action. This put him on a collision course with the major developed countries that paid the bulk of FAO's assessed contributions, which led to financial crises as they reduced or delayed their payments.

Saouma's successor, Jacques Diouf from Senegal, FAO's first director-general from Africa, also focused on world food security as a major objective of FAO. His first action was to propose the holding of a World Food Summit, which was held at FAO headquarters in 1996. This was followed by another World Summit in 2002, which adopted an *International Alliance Against Hunger* and resulted in annual reports on *The State of Food Insecurity in the World*, beginning in 1999.[5]

FAO Strategic Framework 2000–2015

Against this background, the FAO Conference approved *The Strategic Framework for FAO 2000–2015,* which locates the totality of the institution's efforts within the 15-year framework of the MDGs established at the UN Millennium Summit in 2000. Three interrelated global goals are identified:

- Access of all people at all times to sufficient nutritionally adequate and safe food, ensuring that the number of chronically undernourished people is reduced by half by no later than 2015.
- The continued contribution of sustainable and rural development, including fisheries and forestry, to economic and social progress and the well-being of all.
- The conservation, improvement and sustainable utilization of natural resources, including land, water, forest, fisheries, and genetic resources for food and agriculture.

FAO's mission was defined as "to help build a food-secure world for present and future generations." To achieve this goal, FAO will assist its members in: reducing food insecurity and rural poverty; ensuring an enabling policy and regulatory framework for food and agriculture, fisheries and forestry; securing sustainable increases in the supply and availability of food; conserving and enhancing the natural resource base; and generating knowledge of food and agriculture, fisheries, and forestry.

FAO's vision is to remain fully responsive to the ideals and requirements of its members and to provide leadership and partnership in helping to build a food-secure world. It aims to be: a center of excellence and an authoritative purveyor of knowledge and advice in food and agriculture; a pre-eminent repository and provider of multidisciplinary capacities and service in the areas of its competence; and an active partner of organizations both within and outside the UN system; a well managed, efficient and cost-effective institution; a mobilizer of international will and resources to assist its members; a responsible manager of resources entrusted to it; and an effective communicator and advocate for its own goals and those of its members.

Agricultural and nutritional problems

Within this strategy, and with the focus on a "food-secure world," FAO's Committee on Agriculture conducts reviews of agricultural and nutritional problems every two years in order to propose concerted action by FAO member nations. The committee last met in April 2007 and identified five major concerns. The first related to the interaction of agriculture and the environment. In the committee's opinion, environmental sustainability in agriculture "is no longer an option but an imperative." The crucial challenges were: conservation of biodiversity, with climate change expected to cause modifications to biodiversity at all levels, including ecosystems, species, and genes; modifications in agricultural practices, as it was revealed that current practices, such as deforestation, cattle feedlots and fertilizer use, currently accounted for about 25 percent of greenhouse gas emissions;[6] and the shift to bioenergy, which raised concerns for food security as land and other productive resources were taken out of food production.

The second issue was reconciling increasing livestock production with the need to protect the environment to meet the growth in demand caused by the rise in population and incomes. The committee found that farm animal biodiversity, sustainable management and genetic improvement of local breeds were essential if countries were to meet their future food needs and respond to the changing production environment. FAO coordinates the development of a Global Strategy for the Management of Farm Genetic Resources and produced the first *State of the World's Animal Genetic Resources for Food and*

Agriculture in September 2007 as a basis for intergovernmental policy-making in animal genetic resources.

The third major issue was coping with water scarcity. Given the state of global water scarcity, agriculture would be under close scrutiny to account for the water it uses, calling for sound management of agricultural water use. Fourth, profound changes in agri-food systems, and the "agribusiness boom," had significant implications for economic growth, poverty alleviation, and food security. On the positive side, expanding markets offered farmers new value-added opportunities, compared to primary production, and exporters and agro-processing companies were providing inputs and services to the farming community. But the benefits were not automatic and would not necessarily be shared by all. Small-scale farmers were particularly at risk. Governments therefore needed to create enabling conditions for agribusiness investment that also enhanced the livelihoods of poor rural and urban communities. The final major issue concerned the need to give special focus to the problems of agricultural development in Africa and to boost agricultural production in the region by encouraging a shift to what was called "conservation agriculture."

Fisheries and forestry

From FAO's inception, its departments of Fisheries and Forestry have played pioneering and leading roles in mapping, assessing and conserving the resources of these two sectors, and keeping those involved informed through their annual and other publications.[7] Both sectors have become increasingly important in terms of ensuring world food security on a sustainable basis in the face of climate change and global warming.

Up to the 1980s, FAO's Fisheries Department concentrated on developing fisheries and aquaculture to ensure growth in production to meet increasing consumption. International fish trade increased dramatically over the two decades from $6.1 billion in 1980 to $56 billion in 2001. Developing countries' net receipts from fish exports increased from $3.4 billion to $17.4 billion over the same period, greater than the net receipts of all other agricultural commodity exports combined. As many resources became fully or over-exploited, the focus has turned to fisheries and aquaculture management to ensure sustainability. Aquaculture continues to grow more rapidly than all other food-producing sectors. FAO projects that while production from marine and inland fisheries will stabilize or fall over the next 30 years, aquaculture production will almost double. FAO's Committee on Fisheries is the only global intergovernmental forum where major international fisheries and aquaculture issues are examined and recommendations made to all concerned. It has sub-committees on fish trade and the rapidly growing aquaculture sector. It seeks to promote cooperation among the regional fisheries management organizations that have emerged to ensure conservation and sound management, for which FAO provided technical and administrative support. In response to worldwide public concern about the state of world fishing resources and related ecosystems, FAO has promoted the extended application of the *Code of Conduct for Responsible Fisheries* and the strengthening of national capacity to combat illegal, unreported, and unregulated fishing.

FAO's Forestry Department's annual publication on the *State of the World's Forests 2007* offers a global perspective on the forest sector worldwide, including its environmental, economic and social dimensions.[8] Release of the results of the *Global Forest Resources Assessment 2005* provided new and more comprehensive information than ever before for evaluating the state of the world's forests. It showed that the world had just under 4 billion hectares of forest, covering about 30 percent of the world's land area. Forests are unevenly distributed around the world, with 43 countries having a forest area greater than 50 percent of their total area, and 64 countries with less than 10 percent. Five countries (Brazil, Canada, China, the Russian Federation, and the United States) have over half the world's total forest area.

Over the 15 years 1990–2005, the world has lost 3 percent of its total forest area at the rate of 7.3 million hectares a year (20,000 hectares a day). The highest losses have occurred in Africa and Latin America. The carbon stocks in the forest biomass have decreased by about 5.5 percent globally over the 15-year period, with greatest losses in the tropical regions, while the carbon stocks in Europe and North America have increased. A good sign is that many countries have designated their forest areas for conservation by almost 11 percent to 96 million hectares. An adverse trend is the decline in the primary forests in most tropical countries owing to population growth, agricultural expansion, poverty, and commercial logging.

FAO's Forestry Department undertakes on average about 10 new projects each year to strengthen national forest institutions through FAO's Technical Cooperation Programme, but demand from countries is considerably higher than FAO's ability to respond. A National Forest Programme Facility supports the efforts of over 40 countries to increase the participation of all stakeholders in the forestry decision-making process, but demand for additional assistance far exceeds its capabilities. FAO chairs the *Collaborative Partnership on Forests*, an

102 *Policies, programs, and projects*

informal, voluntary, arrangement among 14 international organizations and secretariats with substantial forest programs, which was set up in 2001 to promote the sustainable management of all types of forests and the livelihoods of forest-dependent people. FAO's Forestry Department helps developing countries and countries in transition to modernize and improve their forestry practices. It champions a broad vision of sustainable forest management through policy advice, forest assessments, and technical support to governments when fostering partnerships with civil society and industry in the implementation of national forest programs.

Special programs

FAO has undertaken a number of special programs in helping to build a world without hunger

Special programs for food security

A Food Security Assistance Scheme (FSAS) was established in 1976 to assist developing countries achieve food security. The FSAS attempted to deal not only with short-term food supply problems but also with improvements in food production on a continuous basis. It exemplified a merge of efforts under FAO's regular program of work with projects funded from extra-budgetary resources entrusted to FAO by donors. It also identified projects that might be funded from other multilateral and bilateral aid programs. The FSAS mobilized over $50 million in its first eight years of operations. Initially concentrating on food reserves, storage and emergency needs, the scheme was gradually broadened to deal with other elements of a food security system, including marketing, information systems, and economic and social incentives for increased food production.

To reinforce the impact of the SFAS, a Special Action Programme for the Prevention of Food Losses after Harvest was launched in 1977. Its aim was to help small farmers reduce the considerable post-harvest food losses, which were estimated at more than 20 percent in many developing countries, thereby contributing directly to increased food availability. The program was financed by voluntary contributions from FAO member countries, initially benefiting from an input of $10 million from the FAO budget surplus for the years 1976–77.

A Food Security Action Programme was adopted in 1979 to provide more aid to low-income, food-deficit countries to enable them to cope with their food import needs and to compensate for insufficient food production, lack of storage facilities, and the construction of national food reserves. The objective was to reduce dependence on food imports and food aid, foster trade among them, and establish regional and sub-regional food reserves. Yet another element was the need for balance of payments support in the event of exceptional variations in their food import bills caused by poor harvests and food price rises. FAO and the WFC were able to convince the IMF to set up a special food import facility for this purpose

In 1994, the director-general, Jacques Diouf, called for a review of FAO's priorities, programs, and strategies. This review concluded that improving food security should be reaffirmed as FAO's top priority. A Special Programme for Food Security (SPFS) was launched with the ultimate objective of helping developing countries develop national SPFSs large enough to make a significant difference in the fight against hunger.[9] These programs would have two phases. The first phase would involve pilot projects that would demonstrate the possibilities of rapidly increasing the yields of staple foods and improving household and national food security. The second phase would involve the formulation of bankable projects that would mobilize the investment required to remove constraints hindering widespread adoption of viable technologies.

The SPFS was started in 1995 with pilot demonstration projects in 15 countries and a restricted budget of $3.5 million from FAO's regular resources. Ten years later, by the end of 2005, 105 countries had implemented pilot SPFS activities, more than $775 million had been mobilized, of which over $300 million came from the involved countries themselves, and national programs of food security were getting underway in 52 countries. The SPFS projects were reviewed based on standard FAO evaluation procedures. During the first decade, most SPFS projects were too small to have a measurable impact on national food security. Positive impacts were achieved, however, in terms of: increasing yields, effectiveness of the extension methods employed, rapid adoption of new technologies, increases in farm household welfare, improved livelihoods at the community level, and raising awareness and institution-building.

Looking ahead, from a total coverage of around 1.5 million people at the end of the first decade, the number of direct beneficiaries was projected to increase to around 30 million people by 2010, and with indirect beneficiaries, to 80 million by 2012. During the early years of the SPFS, financial contributions from FAO were frequently used to jumpstart the process. SPFS projects were normally executed by FAO in collaboration with national project teams. However, South–South cooperation (SSC) has been a fundamental and integral part of the SPFS implementation strategy from inception. By mid-2006, 37 SSC agreements had been signed in which the cooperating countries have committed to provide up to 2,600 specialists. This cooperation will play a critical role in the implementation of the national programs for food security. FAO has entered into an agreement with China to deploy an additional 3,000 experts and technicians to national and regional programs for food security. Similar agreements are being made with other advanced developing countries. The SPFS is now FAO's flagship initiative for reaching the goal of halving the number of hungry in the world by 2015 set by the 1996 World Food Summit.

Emergency and rehabilitation operations

FAO involvement in emergency and rehabilitation activities has increased significantly as disasters have increased worldwide, from fewer than 100 in 1975 to more than 400 in 2005, with the sharpest rise from the 1990s. The scale and complexity of emergency operations have also increased. The frequency of emergencies is likely to increase in the future as a result of political tensions in many food-insecure countries, HIV/AIDS, and large-scale natural disasters associated with climate change. FAO assistance in this area rose in real terms from $45 million in 1994–95 to $175 million in 2004–5, and absorbed 40–50 percent of extra-budgetary resources. FAO is well placed to respond to emergencies. Many take place in rural areas and often involve widespread destruction to agriculture, fisheries, and forests. To determine its most appropriate response, FAO has distinguished different types of emergency (slow or rapid developing, natural or man-made, and complex) and identified six phases in its sequence of response: prevention, preparedness, early warning, impact and immediate needs assessment, relief and rehabilitation activities, and reconstruction and sustainable recovery measures.[10]

FAO provides its expertise in the full range of agricultural sector activities to many partners, including NGOs and civil society organizations, for which it has developed guidelines for emergency and rehabilitation operations in agriculture, fisheries, and forestry. FAO is a member of the International Strategy for Disaster Reduction System (ISDR) and helps member countries develop policies and practices for agriculture, fishing, and forestry. FAO performs two major roles: detection, monitoring and coordination; and immediate disaster recovery.

Three measures have strengthened FAO's detection, monitoring, and coordination roles. Experience has repeatedly shown that accurate, timely and commonly available information of an impending disaster, coupled with a sound and speedy response, are key factors in mitigating the effects of emergencies. FAO's pioneering work resulted in the establishment of a Global Information and Early Warning System (GIEWS) in 1968 to detect where emergency situations were likely to develop. At the 1996 World Food Summit, this work was complemented when it was decided to develop Food Insecurity and Vulnerability Information and Mapping Systems (FIVIMS). These systems identify groups and households particularly vulnerable to food insecurity and the reasons for the food insecurity. FAO was requested to provide the technical secretariat for FIVIMS on behalf of an inter-agency working group of 25 members from bilateral, multilateral, and regional organizations, and international NGOs. FAO established in 1994 the Emergency Prevention System for Transboundary Animal and Plant Pests and Diseases (EMPRES), which provides advance warning and early detection of outbreaks, rapid reaction, application of the results of research on new surveys and control tools, and promotion of pest and disease control techniques that respect the environment.

In its role in immediate disaster recovery, FAO works with WFP through joint missions to assess the impact of disasters on the food supply situation of afflicted countries and provided seeds and tools for agricultural recovery programs. In 2006, FAO was engaged in 350 emergency projects in 60 countries and regions, over half of which were in Africa. These projects were almost entirely funded from short-term extra-budgetary contributions from member countries. They involved over 60 professional officers and consultants who also helped train staff in their roles and responsibilities in emergency operations. FAO also benefited from resources generated by the UN secretary-general's Consolidated Appeals for emergency funds. A Special Fund for Emergency and Rehabilitation Activities (SFERA) has been introduced to provide FAO with a quick reaction capability, but this is limited as most funds are linked by donors to specific emergencies.

Plant health and genetic resources

FAO has played a pioneering and leadership role in the development of global instruments for plant protection, pesticides, food safety, and plant genetic resources, reflecting a shift of focus over the years from a direct involvement in crop production to a global governance role. At the same time, there has been a move to a systems, as opposed to a single crop, approach including: urban and peri-urban agriculture; integrated crop-pasture-livestock systems; production and biodiversity in crop and grassland systems; good agricultural practices and organic agriculture;

conservation agriculture, alternative crops, and plant nutrition, with technical support to various global and regional networks.

The pioneering International Plant Protection Convention (IPPC), an international treaty relating to plant health, was adopted by the FAO Conference in 1951 and amended in 1979 and 1997. It had been signed by 166 governments by October 2007. The convention has been deposited with the FAO director-general since its adoption. It seeks to secure action to prevent the spread and introduction of pest plants and products and to promote appropriate measures for their control. The IPPC is governed by the Commission on Phytosanitary Measures, which adopts international standards for phytosanitary measures. The IPPC aims to harmonize phytosanitary measures throughout the world, emphasizing cooperation and exchange of information, and the provision of technical assistance to developing countries. The IPPC has an important role in international trade by encouraging countries to ensure, through phytosantiary certification, that exports do not introduce new pests to their trading partners. FAO provides the IPPC secretariat, which coordinates the activities of the convention.

FAO pioneered the introduction of integrated pest management (IPM) in the early 1960s. Spectacular results were reported in the 1980s on rice in Indonesia, which were extended to Southeast Asia, and to crops other than rice. This led to the development of the Farmers' Field School approach. A global integrated pest management facility was established by FAO, UNDP, and the World Bank in 1997 to support cooperation in IPM. The emphasis was on putting the farmer in charge as the crop manager. IPM reduced farmers' costs, increased yields, improved health and food safety in farming communities, and protected the environment.

FAO's early history of working to ensure safe and judicious use of pesticides led to the International Code of Conduct on the Distribution and Use of Pesticides. FAO's long history in working with WHO to ensure food safety through the preparation and issuance of food standards was formalized in 1961 by the setting up of a joint Codex Alimentarius Commission to protect consumers and promote international trade in agricultural commodities by: formulating standards on food safety, pesticides, veterinary drug residues, and contaminants; setting labelling requirements and standards for analysis and sampling; recommending uniform codes of hygienic handling requirements; and promoting mutual recognition of systems for food inspection and certification. In 1999, the commission established an ad hoc Intergovernmental Task Force on Foods Derived from Biotechnology to consider the health and nutrition implications of such foods. FAO issued a statement on biotechnology in March 2000 in which it stated that while biotechnology provided powerful tools for the sustainable development of agriculture and the food industry, it supported a science-based evaluation system that objectively determined the benefits and risks of genetically modified organisms on a case-by-case basis. FAO has set up a Trust Fund for Food Security and Food Safety.

From inception, FAO has sought to preserve biological diversity in plant and animal life. The Convention on Biodiversity of 1995, the first legally binding framework for the conservation and sustainable use of biodiversity, recognizes the knowledge, innovation and practices of indigenous and local communities and specifically encourages the equitable sharing of benefits arising from their utilization. FAO has championed the rights of farmers and through the International Undertaking on Plant Genetic Resources for Food and Agriculture of 1983 (amended in 1989), and other measures, has sought to strengthen intergovernmental control over crop germplasm, held in trust under the auspices of the United Nations, and to prohibit intellectual property claims on this material.

Investment Centre

FAO's main support for investment in agriculture comes through its Investment Centre (IC). The center provides assistance to member country governments in the preparation of agricultural investment projects for funding by international financial institutions (IFIs). The IC was originally established as the World Bank/FAO Cooperative Programme in 1964. The bank approached FAO to assist in accelerating the preparation of agricultural projects for its funding when it established the reduction of poverty as its main goal and large additional resources became available through the creation of IDA. Subsequently, the regional development banks and IFAD have sought IC technical assistance in the preparation of agricultural projects for their funding. IC services are partly funded from FAO's regular program and partly through payment of fees from the IFIs. The World Bank, the main user of IC services, pays a guaranteed annual fee for an agreed number of weeks of service, which covers about three-quarters of IC costs. The other IFIs pay at agreed rates, covering two-thirds of IC costs.

The IC provides a range of services aimed at increasing the flow of investment into agricultural and rural development and enhancing investment performance. Its main task is to assist FAO member countries in the formulation and preparation of agricultural projects they submitted for external assistance. In doing so, it works on behalf of member governments and in partnership with IFIs. The ensuing stages of project appraisal, implementation, and evaluation are the responsibilities of the assisted governments and IFIs. On project completion, the IC frequently assists with the preparation of a final report. In carrying out its tasks, the IC's overall aim is to strengthen the capabilities of member governments to carry out the work involved.

The IC is part of FAO's Technical Cooperation Department. As one of FAO's largest divisions, and with a multidisciplinary staff, it resembles a mini-FAO, although it maintains close collaboration with other FAO departments and divisions which are able to provide specialized technical expertise and support. By 2004, at the 40th anniversary of its establishment, the IC had helped to formulate more than 1,200 development projects in 138 countries, involving an investment of over $74 billion, of which $43 billion was external financing (Table 4.1).[11]

With the decline in ODA to agriculture, a significant increase in bilateral and private sector lending, and the increased capabilities of developing countries, there has been a decline in the demand for IC services. The number of IC professional staff has fallen from 85 in 1996 to 57 in 2006. An issue of conflict of interest has been raised in that IC is often seen as an extension of the IFI concerned rather than representing the interests of FAO member governments. An additional problem is that as IC no longer provides the majority of staff involved in project preparation, it cannot assure that FAO's views and approaches to agricultural development are respected, and that those of the IFIs, with which FAO does not always agree, may prevail.

Table 4.1 FAO Investment Centre prepared projects approved, 1964–2004

Financing institution	Starting date	Approved projects (no.)	Total investment (U.S.$bn)	External investment (U.S.$bn)
World Bank	1964	779	61.6	34.6
IFAD	1977	213	5.9	3.8
AFDB	1968	148	3.4	2.3
ADB	1968	50	2.6	1.7
IDB	1974	21	0.4	0.3
EBRD	1994	14	0.7	0.3
Total	–	1225	74.6	43.1

IFAD = International Fund for Agricultural Development
AFDB = African Development Bank
ADB = Asian Development Bank
IDB = Inter-American Development Bank
EBRD = European Bank for Reconstruction and Development
Source: FAO Investment Centre data.

Technical Cooperation Programme

The Technical Cooperation Programme (TCP) is the only fund at FAO's disposal to respond quickly to requests from member governments for urgent, small-scale technical assistance for development or to meet emergencies. Its creation in 1976 by Director-General Saouma was controversial. Opponents accused Soauma of creating a "slush fund" for his own personal use to curry favor in developing countries for political purposes, including his own re-election. The TCP may also be used to enable FAO to work as a partner with other sources of external support, and to commit funds in the UN system and with donor coordination bodies. The TCP provided about 10 percent of FAO resources for technical cooperation in the biennium 2004–5. The TCP budget for the 2006–7 biennium is $98.8 million. Requests for TCP assistance are normally submitted or endorsed by member governments, or by regional or interregional organizations, or by national NGOs or other national institutions or associations, if endorsed by the government concerned. Requests may be prepared with the assistance of an FAO country, sub-regional or regional representative, or by an FAO mission. Requests are approved if they meet the criteria laid down by FAO's government bodies for TCP development and emergency assistance.

From its creation in 1976 to the end of 2005, the TCP has funded almost 8,800 projects with a total value of more than $1.1 billion. The main categories of expenditure have been: 48 percent for advisory services; 28 percent for emergencies; 13 percent for training; and 8 percent for development assistance. Africa has benefited most from TCP assistance, with 32 percent of total allocations going to that region, followed by Asia, with 31 percent, Latin America and the Caribbean, 21 percent, the Near East, 10 percent, Eastern Europe, 9 percent, the Southwest Pacific, 4 percent, and interregional projects 4 percent.

TCP assistance has been relatively small per project and per country (Table 4.2). The average size of TCP assistance per project was $228,000 for the period 2001–6. For country programs, more than half the countries receiving TCP assistance received less than $1 million over the same period; about a quarter received over $3 million, largely for meeting emergencies.

An independent evaluation of the TCP found that the spread of allocations among regions broadly reflected relative need in relation to food security, poverty, and dependence on agriculture, but the reason for distribution among individual countries was not clear or transparent. Flexibility and rapid response to requests were frequently constrained by lengthy delays in approval. TCP funds were also used as a

110 *Policies, programs, and projects*

Table 4.2 Geographical distribution of FAO Technical Cooperation Programme, 2004–5

Region	Total net delivery (U.S.$'000)	Percentage (%)	Average net delivery per:	
			Project (U.S.$)	Country (U.S.$)
Africa	44,452	40	101	945.8
Asia	22,529	16	129	126.5
Caribbean	4,931	6	74	308.2
Central Asia	3,265	3	105	466.4
Europe	6,308	6	91	286.7
Inter-regional	4,118	2	242	n.a.
Latin America	15,389	14	103	905.2
Near East	11,075	10	96	738.3
Pacific	3,237	4	75	231.2
Total	115,304	100	104	n.a.

Source: *Independent External Evaluation of FAO* (2007), 94.

buffer for late payment of assessed contributions by FAO members as it is the only funding available in FAO's regular program that is not fully committed. It was clearly unsatisfactory that what is regarded as a priority area of FAO's work should be used as a reserve fund, thus giving it less priority than other FAO programs.

FAO country representatives now spend as much time disseminating policy advice on how to implement national food security programs as on providing technical assistance for increasing food production. A "right to food" approach has been adopted since FAO's governing body adopted a set of voluntary guidelines to support the progressive realization of the right to adequate food in the context of national food security.[12] FAO's Strategic Framework 2000–15 stipulates that the organization is expected to take fully into account "progress made to further a rights-based approach to food security." A Right to Food Unit has been established in FAO's Economic and Social Department to monitor progress and provide information and training material.

A knowledge organization

FAO's special and unique contribution to the international community is as developer and disseminator of knowledge, information, and data concerning the whole spectrum of issues and concerns relating to food and agriculture. When FAO moved from Washington, D.C. to Rome in 1951, it inherited the library of the International Institute of

Agriculture. FAO's virtual library now consists of: the David Lubin Memorial Library on-line, one of the world's finest collections of food, agriculture and international development information, containing FAO's institutional memory and over 60 years of accumulated knowledge and experience among its 1 million volumes; the FAO corporate document repository, an electronic library of FAO publications and documents started in 1998 with over 6,000 items; FAO library catalogues, a multilingual on-line catalogue of documents; and the FAO sales catalogue.

FAO has developed a series of statistical databases covering all aspects of food and agriculture, the most prominent of which are listed below. AQUASTAT is a global information system on agriculture and water, which provides users with comprehensive data on the state of agriculture and water management across the world, with emphasis on developing countries and countries in transition. FAOSTAT is an on-line multilingual database, currently containing over 1 million time-series records for over 210 countries and territories on agriculture, nutrition, fisheries, forestry, food aid, land use, and population. AGROSTAT and FAOSTAT–Food Quality provide information and data from the Codex Alimentarius Commission on food quality standards and related subject, such as pesticide residues and veterinary drug residues in food. FAOSTAT–Agriculture provides statistics on crops, livestock, irrigation, land use, fertilizer and pesticide consumption, and agricultural machinery.

FAOSTAT–Nutrition provides data on food commodities and supply, food balance sheets, food aid, and population. FAOSTAT–Fisheries provides statistics on fish production and fish products, complemented by FISHERS, a database that provides users with access to fishery statistics of various sorts. FAOSTAT–Forestry provides statistics on the imports and exports of wood and wood products, complemented by FORIS, a database containing statistics on forestry and forest issues on a country-to-country basis. GLIPHA, the *Global Livestock Production and Health Atlas*, provides an overview of information relating to animal production and health through the combination of maps, tables, and charts. The PAAT Information System combines information from FAO, WHO, IAEA and the AU Inter-African Bureau for Animal Resources to promote integrated trypanosomiasis control through coordinated international action with the ultimate goal of improving food security and sustainable agricultural and rural development. The Programme Against African Trypanosomiasis (PAAT) is a forum to guide and assist 37 affected countries. TERRATAT provides land resource potential and

112 Policies, programs, and projects

constraints at country and regional levels. The Joint FAO/IAEA Division has a database on nuclear techniques in food and agriculture.

The computer and Internet revolutions have provided many new opportunities and ways of creating and distributing knowledge, and have reduced the costs involved. FAO's fundamental and unique roles with respect to knowledge management for food and agriculture, and its ability to fulfill its mandate as a global broker of essential information and data, should be fully supported by the donor community, and will require effective and strategic partnerships with many other organizations.

World Bank: agricultural and rural development

For an institution intent on "fighting poverty with passion and professionalism for lasting results"; that recognizes that poverty exists mostly in rural areas, where agriculture is the main livelihood; and that receives growing contributions to its resources while those of other institutions have declined; the enigma has been a fall, not rise, in its assistance to the agricultural sector over the past 20 years (Figure 4.1).

Early years

The bank's historians have followed the path of the bank's agricultural assistance over the past four decades.[13] As they put it, for an institution that in the 1970s would become agriculture's most active and generous official international promoter, the bank got off to a slow start. In the early days, before IDA, Eugene Black, the bank's president

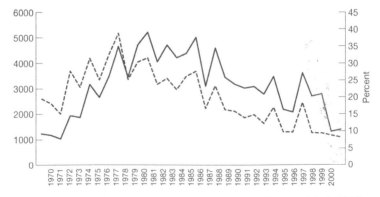

Figure 4.1 World Bank (IBRD+IDA) assistance to agriculture (1970–2001)
Source: World Bank, Reaching the Rural Poor (2003).

Policies, programs, and projects 113

(1949–62), was preoccupied with establishing the bank's creditworthiness in the New York financial markets. The kinds of projects that best served this purpose were those promising directly to generate returns that would service the bank's loans. Many agricultural projects were not self-liquidating in this sense, and most required local cost support, which the bank's articles prevented. The bank saw itself more as a capital transfer specialist and less as a comprehensive development promoter obligated to pursue all major aspects of development.

There were other reasons for the bank's reluctance to give priority to supporting agriculture. The leading development economists of the day favored industrialization as the main route for quick and sustained development. There was also what was described as a "cultural gap" between the lawyers, investments bankers and policy economists who populated the young bank and those concerned with developing agriculture. The highly centralized operations of the bank out of Washington, D.C., were conducted through short-term missions to developing countries, where bank staff met primarily with government officials in the departments of finance and planning with little interest in agricultural matters. To some extent, the bank was let off the hook by the development of other aid institutions. As we saw above, FAO was launched a year before IBRD and quickly entered into a variety of agricultural developing initiatives with additional resources provided by other UN bodies. During the 1950s, agricultural and rural development was also high on the agendas of new bilateral aid agencies, NGOs and foundations like Ford and Rockefeller.

President Woods' initiatives (1963–68)

All this was to change with the advent of IDA and the emergence of two new bank presidents, George Woods (1963–68) and Robert McNamara (1968–81). When Eugene Black eventually welcomed IDA into the World Bank Group in 1960, he recognized that the new soft credits it provided should flow mainly to the neediest countries heavily dependent on agriculture. In a major policy paper to the bank's executive board in January 1964, however, Woods noted that agriculture, which employed two-thirds of the working population of the developing world, had received on 8 percent of the loans provided by the bank from its opening in 1946 to mid-1963. About a quarter of IDA credits had been channeled to agriculture but the sector's portfolio was still small. Woods mandated a quick doubling of the bank's program of agricultural assistance and announced in 1964 the bank's

114 *Policies, programs, and projects*

intention to expand its lending to agriculture (and education) in cooperation with the appropriate UN specialized agencies.

An agreement was made with FAO for its staff to help increase the preparation of agricultural projects for bank lending. At the same time, the bank increased the number of specialists in its own agricultural department. Woods recommended that agricultural promotion be concentrated on specific high-return efforts and that governments be encouraged by bank lending to engage coherently in all the various elements of rounded agrarian-reform packages. Early concentration was on water development, irrigation, and flood control projects. Funding was also provided to finance roads and other necessary installations, and the provision of technical, financial and organizational services, which indirectly gave incentives for land reform programs that the bank lacked authority to fund directly. Woods challenged several of the bank's orthodoxies, such as funding local costs and certain recurrent costs, and that the projects it supported must be financially self-liquidating.

The McNamara presidency (1968–81)

The arrival of Robert McNamara as the bank's president in 1968 was to result in taking bank lending to agriculture to a new and sustained level. Bank lending for agricultural and rural development in the 1970s grew in real terms at an annual rate of 13.5 percent from less than $1.5 billion in 1970 to almost $5.3 billion in 1980. A number of external factors stimulated McNamara's pro-poor agenda with a focus on small-scale peasant agriculture. By the mid-1960s, the development promotion community was seized with the importance of increasing agricultural production, especially in the aftermath of two consecutive droughts in the populous countries of South Asia. This triggered support for high-yielding varieties of staple food crops, which eventually led to the Green Revolution and a spectacular growth in food production. At the same time, economic and anthropological studies had shown that farmers could be expected to respond to better economic incentives but had been given little chance, trapped in repressive markets with controlled prices.

McNamara played a leadership role in the conferences that led up to the creation of the CGIAR in 1971 and in persuading FAO and UNDP to become co-sponsors along with the bank. He got the bank's executive committee to agree to make a major contribution to the new institution. He also got them to approve an arrangement whereby the bank's president would nominate the CGIAR chairperson, after informal consultation with CGIAR members, who from 1974 has been the bank's vice-president overseeing its work on agriculture. In addition, it approved his proposal to house the CGIAR secretariat in the bank as part of the bank's administration, and for its entire staff to be employed by the bank. McNamara enthusiastically embraced both agricultural growth and rural equity. He saw no need to sacrifice the expansion of output in order to strengthen the poor or to accept a quality discount for large volume lending. And he was not wedded to either a single or multiple-track programming for rural projects.

During the McNamara presidency, the bank focused on employment-creation as a major avenue to poverty reduction. In his address to the 1972 annual general meeting of the bank and the IMF, McNamara said: "Unemployment ... must be attacked head on [through] the building of market roads; construction of low-cost simple housing; reforestation programs; expansion of irrigation and drainage facilities; highway maintenance; and similar low-skill, labor-intensive projects." He favored labor-intensive work schemes to increase employment and create the infrastructure necessary for agricultural and rural development. And he adopted the concept of "redistribution from growth," a modified version of a concept first developed by Hans Singer during the ILO pilot employment mission to Kenya in 1972,[14] as the signature concept of the bank's approach to poverty alleviation as a means of distributing the benefits of development to the poor.

While the share of total bank agricultural lending to Asia was consistently highest, at between 40 and 44 percent, Africa's share increased to 15 percent but was overtaken by the share going to Latin America and the Caribbean (24 percent) in the decade of the 1980s. In terms of the types of agricultural projects supported, irrigation and drainage schemes dominated the portfolio, reaching over half of the bank's agricultural lending in the decade of the 1960s but decreasing sharply thereafter following increasing international criticism. During the McNamara presidency, multipurpose area development projects and agricultural credit schemes were particularly favored, reaching over 21 percent and 15 percent of total bank agricultural lending respectively.

Declining attention

With the departure of McNamara, bank lending for agriculture dropped, in real terms, from $5.4 billion in the early 1980s to an average of $3.96 billion for the four fiscal years 1990–93; its share of total bank lending fell from 30 percent to 20 percent. By the end of the millennium, the share was to fall further to around 8 percent. A number of reasons have been put forward for this decline.[15] These have included: falling agricultural commodity prices that made agriculture less profitable in developing countries; increased competition within ODA, especially from social sectors; emergency responses to numerous crises; opposition from farmers in some donor countries to support agriculture in their major export markets; and opposition from environmental groups who saw agriculture as a major contributor to natural resource destruction and environmental pollution.

In the agricultural sector itself, big agricultural projects have fallen out of favor. The bank was heavily criticized for the damage large dam and irrigation projects have done to poor people and the environment. A double issue of the *Ecologist* was published in 1985 in order "to expose to world leaders the role played by [the] Bank ... increasing the present escalation of human misery, malnutrition and famine in the Third World." This led the bank to reappraise its work in this area and to the creation of a World Commission on Dams that established international guidelines. What has been referred to as the "agroskepticism" of many donors may relate to their experience with past unsuccessful agricultural interventions, such as large-scale integrated rural development projects and the training-and-visit system, which were both promoted heavily by the bank.

New-style agricultural projects are smaller and require less funding. Quality problems have occurred with agricultural projects, in part due to low world prices and consequently low economic returns, although this is now changing with the sharp upturn in the prices of food and agricultural commodities on world markets. Agriculture has not been the priority of ministers of finance. And increasing priority has been given to sub-Saharan Africa, where the problems of agricultural development and rehabilitation are particularly problematic and take more time to solve.

A major factor was the shift to structural adjustment lending in the 1980s. During this decade, many developing countries faced a world economic recession of unprecedented magnitude since the 1930s. Often encouraged and supported by the IMF and the World Bank, they sought to adjust their economies to the realities of their internal and the international conditions. Unless far-reaching structural and sectoral adjustments were made, drastic demand-restricting measures would have to be imposed in order to avoid total economic collapse, with serious political consequences. The measures imposed with IMF and World Bank advice and support were to have disproportionate social costs on the poor, leading to the call by UNICEF and others for "adjustment with a human face" to protect the vulnerable and promote economic growth with equity.[16]

Adjustment programs also had a negative effect on the agricultural sector and on food security in developing countries.[17] An evaluation of the 10-year experience of the bank with adjustment program lending at the end of the 1980s concluded that: "Adjustment lending ... is both a potentially high pay-off and high-risk instrument. There is, therefore, the need to continue to adapting and improving the policies and procedures of structural lending to increase its effectiveness."[18] Negative effects of adjustment on the poor were often certain and immediate, while their assumed long-term positive effects remained uncertain. They also tended to be more contractionist, exacerbating inequality of income, rather than expansionist, which would involve the poor in the development process and contribute to equitable and sustainable development.

Another factor was seen to be a professional and technical staff constraint in the bank itself.[19] The bank's shift toward adjustment lending in the 1980s, in combination with its reorganization and the new emphasis on internal budget austerity, penalized potential agricultural development projects, which were frequently costly and time-consuming to prepare and implement even when returns were high. These shifts were also seen to reduce and marginalize the bank's technical staff engaged in agricultural and rural development, and its age structure meant that a retirement crisis could occur in 1990–93. Outside consultants would not enable the bank to respond to the challenges of the 1990s if it continued to shed its in-house agro-technical capabilities. This would be especially disturbing for Africa, where new types of projects were needed, and where past failures were seen to be partly due to inadequate technical, institutional, and agro-economic preparation.

The ultimate concern was that persistent declines in the share of agricultural development projects in total bank lending, and even more in real values, would eventually constitute quantity signals both to bank staff and borrowers, that agricultural and rural development was not a sector on which to spend scarce time and energy for quality improvements. At the same time, bank leadership was distracted elsewhere. The growing preoccupation with the debt crisis, mostly in Latin America, and with economic reconstruction in Eastern Europe, threatened to dilute the bank's role as a development institution focused on poverty reduction. And no other large lender was able or willing to pick up this mission.

As the work of IFAD and IFPRI has shown, the bank failed to take into account the many causes of rural poverty that lie outside the command of its market economics, and may even be exacerbated by it.

The add-on of concern with such issues as governance and corruption is a move in the right direction but is insufficient to come to terms with the many non-economic causes of poverty. As a review of the bank's Independent Evaluation Group in 2008 stated, over time the importance of agriculture in the bank's rural strategy has declined.[20] Both arising from and contributing to this, technical skills to support agricultural development have also declined. The review noted that technical experts in agricultural and rural development in sub-Saharan Africa declined from 40 in 1997 to 17 in 2006, where they are needed most. Results have fallen short of expectations because, among other things, of weak political support and insufficient appreciation of reality on the ground. In addition, the bank's data system and support was found to be insufficient to adequately inform the bank's efforts to develop agriculture in Africa across a broad front.

From vision to action (1996)

In mid-1995, with the appointment of a new president, James D. Wolfensohn (1995–2005), the World Bank renewed its commitment to supporting agricultural and rural development. The bank's action plan, *From Vision to Action in the Rural Sector* (1996), recognized that it was not difficult to make the case for greater bank involvement in improving the rural economy.[21] The bank's mandate was to help developing countries reduce poverty. Sustainable rural growth and development could make a powerful contribution in three critical areas: global and national food security; increasing rural incomes and reducing poverty; and sustainable management of natural resources. Three "equally important" challenges lay ahead: world food needs could double over the next 30 years; rural poverty must be reduced; and environmental degradation must be reduced. Action was required not only to increase agricultural production but equitable and sustainable rural growth and development.

If these aims were so important, why were they receiving so little emphasis? There had been a significant decline in demand for, and commitment to, rural development in the developing countries, in the bank itself, and in the international community. Actions to resuscitate demand were needed in all three dimensions. Countries had reduced their commitment to rural development for several reasons. Agriculture was often viewed as a declining sector, and not important for development. Falling real food prices had led to complacency toward the agricultural sector. The rural poor had little political voice and the political power of urban elites had led to an urban bias in policies, institutions, and expenditure patterns in developing countries. Greater understanding of these political economy issues was badly needed. At the World Bank, the focus on agricultural and rural development had declined "primarily because the process of strategy formulation has been weak, and because many past bank-assisted project and programs have performed poorly," apart from IFC's agribusiness portfolio, which showed what could be done with well-planned and executive action. The international community had also become complacent, partly because of long-term declining international food prices and partly because of poor coordination among the very many institutions and organizations involved.

The action plan proposed three ways of tackling these problems. At the country level the development of Country Assistance Strategies was proposed in order to foster renewed commitment to rural growth. In the bank, the focus was on strengthening collaboration among the different entities that constituted the World Bank Group, strengthening staff capacities and capabilities, and enhancing cooperation with the other main actors involved in agricultural and rural development. The third element was the development of regional action plans based on the reality that countries and regions varied greatly with regard to the conditions and needs of their rural economies and that there was no simple approach to rural development that would work for all countries. The action plan proposed a whole new way of doing business with five key recommendations: a broad rural focus in place of the narrow sectoral focus of the past; partnership with countries and the broader international community to integrate rural concerns in overall country development strategies; involvement of all parts of the World Bank Group; addressing long-ignored issues, such as land reform, gender, and food consumption policy issues; and addressing old issues in new ways.

Reaching the rural poor (2003)

In 2003, the bank recognized that its rural development strategy, which was launched in 1997, "had a decisive influence on global thinking—but disappointing results on the ground." In 2001, lending for agricultural projects was the lowest in the bank's history, less than 8 percent of total bank lending, whereas in the early 1980s it accounted for more than 30 percent (Figure 4.1). A renewed strategy for rural development, *Reaching the Rural Poor. A Renewed Strategy for Rural Development* (2003) was therefore proposed, consisting of five pillars: an enabling environment for broad-based growth; an enhanced agricultural productivity and competitiveness; non-farm economic growth; improved social well-being, managing risk and reducing vulnerability; and enhanced sustainability of natural resources.[22] Four "thrusts" were identified for implementing these objectives. First, integrating the needs of the rural poor in national policy dialogues in the preparation of poverty reduction strategy papers and country assistance strategies for each assisted country. Second, scaling up investments and innovations, which had been below expectations. Third, improving the quality and impact of bank operations, with rural projects now performing on a par with or better than bank projects as a whole. Fourth, implementing global corporate priorities and enhancing partnerships. Trust funds mobilized and managed by the bank's Agricultural and Rural Development Department have been increased and a Global Donor Platform for Rural Development has been established for harmonizing donor rural activities in target countries.

As a result, the declining trend in lending to agriculture and to rural development in general has been halted, and in some sub-sectors reversed. (Table 4.3)

Agricultural growth for the poor (2005)

In 2005 the World Bank published a major report, *Agricultural Growth for the Poor. An Agenda for Development (2005)*, linking agricultural growth with the reduction of poverty.[23] In its foreword, the director and sector manager of the bank's Agricultural and Rural Development Department pointed to the importance of agricultural development for meeting the MDGs of poverty and hunger reduction, gender equality, and environmental sustainability. The report acknowledged that: "The potential and the urgency for securing agriculture's prominence in the development agenda have never been greater" but that "international support to agriculture has declined sharply since the late 1980s." Referring to the bank's new rural development strategy that had been approved in 2003, the report identified priorities for public support to agriculture that harnessed change to benefit the poor. These included: fostering the provision of global public goods and services; accelerating policy reform; developing institutions to support the private sector; fostering decentralization and empowerment of the poor; and investing in core public goods and stimulating market development.

Five key areas were listed by which the international community was encouraged to take concerted action to get agriculture back onto the development agenda. First, involving agricultural stakeholders more closely in policy and investment decisions. Second, tailoring investment

Table 4.3 World Bank (IBRD/IDA) commitments to agriculture,* 2000–7 (U.S.$ millions)

	FY 00	FY 01	FY 02	FY 03	FY 04	FY 05	FY 06	FY07
By region								
Sub-Saharan Africa	123	286	308	318	287	295	685	394
East Asia and Pacific	132	110	151	119	358	253	373	269
Europe and Central Asia	324	416	644	342	175	153	160	63
Latin America and Caribbean	104	72	100	61	387	238	299	105
Middle East and North Africa	121	51	5	199	33	229	15	212
South Asia	67	116	328	251	255	955	400	765
Total	872	1,051	1,536	1,289	1,495	2,122	1,932	1,807
By sector								
Agric. ext. and research	48	112	70	48	117	247	423	156
Crops	17	34	487	96	80	64	50	140
Irrigation and drainage	261	197	335	220	769	1,069	403	912
Animal production	84	8	25	23	61	32	145	37
Forestry	75	111	128	166	29	63	131	148
Gen. agr./fish/for sec.	353	333	202	660	330	458	601	324
Agric. market and trade	27	89	221	72	85	95	139	55
Agro-industry	8	166	68	4	24	94	42	35
Total	872	1,051	1,536	1,289	1,495	2,122	1,932	1,807

* Includes fishing, forestry, agro-industry, markets and trade
Source: World Bank.

needs more closely to financial instruments. Third, reducing processing costs for agricultural projects. Fourth, identifying innovative channels to support direct investments in agriculture. And, finally, enhancing the quality of bank lending, and sharing what had been learned with other donors and sources of funding. The report concluded that "the agricultural sector can command greater attention by clearly communicating the impact of agricultural investments on economic growth and the welfare of the poor." The scene was therefore set for a major review of the role and importance of agriculture in economic development, which was taken up in the bank's *World Development Report* (WDR) for 2008, the first time in 25 years that a WDR had been devoted to this subject.[24] The expectations are that a significant increase in the bank's lending to agricultural and rural development will now take place.

WFP

WFP's executive committee approved a *Strategic Plan 2004–2007* in 2003, which set the goal and objectives for WFP over that period.[25] The core program goal was "to contribute to meeting the MDGs through food-assisted interventions targeted on poor and hungry people." In order to achieve that goal, WFP operations would be targeted on five strategic priorities: (1) saving lives in crisis situations; (2) protecting livelihoods in crisis situations and enhancing resilience to shocks; (3) supporting the improved nutrition and health status of children, mothers and other vulnerable people; (4) supporting access to education and reducing gender disparities in access to education and skills training; and (5) helping governments establish and manage national food assistance programs.

From development to emergencies

In little more than a decade, WFP was transformed from being a major UN development program into the world's largest humanitarian organization (Table 4.4).[26] The transition was not easy, partly because of the speedy and scale by which events occurred that forced the change in direction.

By the end of its first 30 years of operations, WFP had invested over $13 billion, involving more than 40 million tons of food, in 1,600 development projects to combat hunger and promote economic and social development throughout the developing world. In the process,

Table 4.4 WFP: from development to emergencies (U.S.$ millions)

Year	Total commitments	Development projects	Emergency operations	PRO/ PRRO*	Total relief
1980	670.5	479.0	191.5	n.a.	191.5
1984	1,158.7	**925.0	233.7	n.a.	233.7
1990	947.2	480.0	131.6	335.6	467.2
1995	1,357.1	248.0	665.2	443.9	1,109.1
2000	1,158.3	185.0	576.9	343.4	920.3
2006	2,665.0	268.2	729.0	1,233.3	1,962.3

1980–95 = commitments
2000–6 = total expenditure
PRO = Protracted Relief Operations
PRRO = Protracted Relief and Recovery Operations
* WFP commitments to this category began in 1989.
** Historically highest annual commitment to development projects
Source: World Food Programme.

WFP had become the largest source of grant development assistance to the poor in developing countries. Three notable distinctions stood out. WFP had become the largest source of assistance within the UN system to development projects involving and benefiting women in developing countries, the largest provider of grant assistance for environmental protection and improvement activities in developing countries, and the largest purchaser of food and services in developing countries among UN bodies, and a major supporter of South–South trade. A broad category of agricultural and rural development projects received about two-thirds of development aid, mainly through labor-intensive work programs, while projects for human resource development, mainly through nutrition improvement programs for mothers and children, and through school feeding programs, received one-third. During this time, there was a gradual shift to sub-Saharan Africa as the main recipient region for WFP development assistance.

Five milestones may be singled out in the inexorable rise in WFP's involvement in emergency operations. First, were the food crises in Africa in the 1970s and 1980s caused mainly by drought. They propelled WFP's involvement in emergency operations not only in terms of increasing the amount of emergency food aid it delivered but also through its role in the coordination of food aid from all sources in large-scale international relief operations. Second, was the approval given by its governing body for WFP to help meet the internal transport, storage, and handling costs in the least-developed countries of the food aid it provided. This placed a heavy additional burden on WFP's limited cash resources, particularly after the steep increase in world food and oil prices in the early 1970s. Limited sales of cereals donated to WFP were permitted in eligible countries to offset these internal costs, but this created difficulties as internal costs rose and larger volumes of grain were needed for sale.

A third factor was the increased responsibility given to WFP's reconstituted governing body, the Committee on Food Aid Policies and Programmes, for the more effective coordination of food aid from all sources, including emergency operations. Fourth, was the creation of an International Emergency Food Reserve (IEFR) by the UN General Assembly in 1975. The reserve was to be placed at the disposal of WFP to strengthen its capacity to deal with crisis situations throughout the developing world. While the IEFR increased resources available for emergencies, difficulties were created when donors did not live up to the modalities they agreed to for its operation. The reserve was originally intended to be a multilateral standby facility to provide WFP with an initial, quick-response capability to meet emergency situations whenever and wherever they occurred throughout the developing world. It was not like a bank account readily available for WFP to use, but a voluntary facility to provide emergency relief from food stocks and budgeted funds kept in donor countries. A high proportion of contributions were tied and designated to specific food commodities and emergencies *after* they had occurred. And cash contributions fell short of requirements. The IEFR was strengthened in 1991 with the addition of a cash reserve with an annual target of $30 million to enable rapid purchases of food to be made close to where emergencies occurred. And a subset of WFP development assistance was established in 1989 for assistance to protracted refugee and displaced person operations, lasting one year or more, which relieved pressure on WFP emergency resources but reduced those available for development.

More than any other factor, the escalation in man-made disasters, and the concomitant new working arrangements between WFP and the UN High Commissioner for Refugees (UNHCR), which came into force in January 1994, greatly increased WFP's involvement in emergency operations. The two organizations agreed to pool their resources and share their expertise and experience. While these joint working arrangements strengthened the response of the two organizations, they carried far-reaching implications for WFP. WFP undertook to respond to refugee and displaced persons emergency and relief needs on a priority basis. If WFP's resources did not expand proportionately, an increasing share would go to protracted relief operations (PROs) at the expense of its development assistance. This, in turn, would reduce the amount of borrowing from WFP-assisted development projects in times of emergency, and limit WFP support for disaster prevention, preparedness and mitigation activities.

One of the most tragic developments of the late 1980s and 1990s was the outbreak of disasters caused not by nature, but by man. The scale, complexity, and duration of these man-made disasters increased considerably in Africa, Asia, and later, in the former Yugoslavia and Soviet Union. In 1970, there were 2.5 million refugees throughout the world; in 1980, 11 million; and in 1993, over 18 million.[27] In addition, there were 24 million people displaced from their homes in their own countries. In 1997–98, some 50 million people were the victims of forced displacement, of whom 22 million were refugees and 28 million displaced persons. Each disaster was a saga of man's inhumanity to man, the fortitude of the civilian population, particularly women and children, in the face of appalling suffering, and the sacrifice of relief workers, national and international, a number of whom have lost their lives or been seriously injured.

No two disasters are the same but these large and complex emergencies shared common features. Most of the human conflicts now occur not between, but within, developing countries, resulting in death, displaced persons and refugees. Most of the victims are not soldiers, but women and children, the most vulnerable group. Conflicts have occurred in poor countries or newly created states following the collapse of the previous political order. Few have the resources, administration, or logistics to cope without considerable external assistance. Several disasters have been exacerbated by a lethal combination of war, civil disturbance, and drought. The international community has given generously to come to the aid of the afflicted. Steps have been taken to improve coordination within the UN system, and with the many agencies and NGOs, to provide food and other basic needs quickly and effectively to those in distress. Still, the linkages between humanitarian aid and peace-making and peace-keeping operations remain dangerously confused. There are as yet no clearly established rules, guidelines, and modalities so that the ways in which humanitarian assistance is provided can become part of the solution, and not part of the problem. This may be understandable given the nature and increasing number of emergencies in recent years. But progress should be quickened in implementing the many proposals that have been made.

Emergency operations have not only been large and complex but often more protracted in nature, adding to resource and other problems, and leaving less for meeting new and other types of emergencies. Protracted Relief and Recovery Operations (PRROs) have special characteristics, which set them apart from other emergencies. Solutions to four particular problems have had to be found. First, how to provide an assured and continuous supply of food that is not only adequate for good health but sufficiently varied to avoid monotony, and flexible enough to meet changing needs. Second, how to coordinate supplies of food with other non-food basic needs. Third, how to cater for the developmental as well as the survival needs of the victims in terms of the nutrition, health, education, and training, and, where possible, provide employment and income-earning opportunities. A fourth problem has added yet another dimension to WFP assistance in PRROs. Once the immediate needs of people affected by disasters are addressed, the focus shifts to helping rebuild their lives and livelihoods. For food-insecure people, the crisis continues after the cause(s) of the disaster subside(s). PRROs deal with the later stages of an emergency. The main objective is to help re-establish and stabilize livelihoods and household food security and continue to improve the nutritional status of vulnerable groups. This involves a "continuum" of action between

126 *Policies, programs, and projects*

relief and development, emphasized in a UN General Assembly resolution in 1991, in which relief assistance supports and protects development, and development mitigates the effects of disasters, implying that well executed relief and recovery operations can make a major contribution to future development.[28]

As the food-aid organization of the UN system, WFP has automatically assumed a major role in providing life-saving food to refugees and displaced persons as well as to the victims of natural disasters like floods, droughts, and earthquakes over the past 30-plus years. Some examples are given to show both the scale and diversity. In the 1970s, WFP provided food and helped to coordinate international relief efforts to 25 million people in seven Sahelian countries of West Africa afflicted by six successive years of drought. In the 1980s, even more assistance was required for an estimated 30 million people in 21 of the most seriously affected African countries that faced famine. WFP had early experience of what was to come in man-made disasters in the civil war in eastern Nigeria in 1968. Another profound experience was the international relief operation in the 1970s for Kampuchea (Cambodia), one of the largest, most protracted and complex ever undertaken, following the devastating civil war that affected the entire country. WFP went to the aid of the Afghan refugees living in Pakistan in the 1980s, one of the largest refugee populations ever recorded.

Even more difficult to handle were the large and complex humanitarian relief operations in Rwanda and Burundi, both landlocked countries in central Africa. A new, large and additional dimension was added to WFP emergency operations in 1992 following the break-up of the former political order in Yugoslavia and the Soviet Union and the formation of new republics. WFP was also called upon to monitor food distribution to 22 million people in Iraq in the aftermath of the Gulf War, the imposition of economic sanctions, and the implementation of the UN Security Council resolution that allowed the sale of Iraqi oil to pay for food and other essential imports. Most recently, WFP has played a prominent part in the large-scale relief operations following the devastating earthquake in Kashmir, the Indian Ocean tsunami, and the largest current humanitarian operation in Darfur in western Sudan (Table 4.5).

These emergency operations have common features. They have been difficult to resource fully and constantly. Obstructions to food delivery have threatened large-scale malnutrition and death. They have often taken on a regional dimension as they straddle the frontiers of several countries, further complicating their operation. Versatility and ingenuity have often had to be employed in finding solutions to major

Table 4.5 Beneficiaries of WFP assistance, 1998–2006 (in millions)

Categories	1998	1999	2000	2001	2002	2003	2004	2005	2006
People assisted, total	75	89	83	77	72	104	113	97	88
In emergency operations	50	59	43	43	44	61	38	35	16
In PRROs	6	11	18	14	14	27	25	38	47
In development projects	18	20	22	20	14	16	50**	24	24
Number of countries	80	83	83	82	82	81	80	82	78
Food delivered (million tons)	2.8	3.4	3.5	4.2	3.7	6.0*	5.1	4.2	4.0
Operational expenditure (U.S.$ billions)	1.2	1.4	1.5	1.7	1.6	3.3	2.9	2.9	2.7

Notes: PRRO = Protracted Relief and Recovery Operations
* Includes 1.4 million tons provided through the Iraq Oil-for-Food program
** Includes 26 million people in the Iraq bilateral operation
Source: WFP annual reports.

transport and logistics problems in very difficult circumstances in order to get food through to those in dire need. The costs of operations are often very high. Relief workers are exposed to considerable risk and, tragically, to loss of life. Overall administration has been difficult to control as often there has been little government or other capacity to plan and implement these large-scale and complex operations. Coordination among the many government and aid agencies involved has been necessary, but difficult to maintain, not only to provide the food required but also other essential needs such as water, fuel, shelter, basic medicines, security, and human rights.

Several factors facilitated WFP's transition from a largely development to a mainly emergency organization. Particularly important was the widespread deployment of its staff throughout the developing world, the establishment of close working relations with government officials and departments, and the build-up of strong partnerships with other UN and international organizations and NGOs. Critically important were the creation of transport and logistics expertise and experience to get food to poor, hungry, and afflicted people in a timely and cost-efficient manner, maintaining a fine balance between speed and cost of delivery. Ultimately, the more spent on delivery, the less is available for providing food. WFP has built up a considerable reputation in transport and logistics operations, and its expertise and services are now sought by many aid agencies both within and outside the UN system.

Another factor has been the creation of early warning and early action systems to detect a nascent emergency situation and to act with precision in its pre-emption or mitigation. A special emergency preparedness and response unit was set up at WFP headquarters for this purpose. Since its establishment, WFP has worked closely with FAO in the operation of the Global Information and Early Warning System (GIEWS) to provide the earliest indication of a disaster. Joint FAO/WFP missions are also sent to disaster areas to estimate the extent of destruction and the effect on the food supply situation so that arrangement can be made for the speedy provision of food aid. More recently, WFP has joined an inter-agency working group to design Food Insecurity and Vulnerabilty Information and Mapping Systems (FIVIMS) to identify groups and households particularly vulnerable to food insecurity. In addition, WFP has created its Vulnerability Analysis and Mapping (VAM) system. While FIVIMS provides guidance on norms and standards for use by national information and mapping systems, VAM supports the application of these approaches at the country level. The common objective is to identify who are food-insecure or vulnerable to food insecurity, why they are so, and where they are located. The revolution in information and communications technology has revolutionized the ways in which humanitarian work can be done. A situation room has been established at WFP headquarters to keep constant track of emerging disasters, and the response to them, and instant and continuous communications are maintained between WFP headquarters and field staff, and between all those involved in the disaster areas, through communication networks and mobile phones.

A further factor has been the wider and more versatile use of different modalities to get food aid to beneficiaries quickest and at the least cost. Greater use has been made of triangular transactions, but especially significant has been an increase in the purchase of food in developing countries for use as food aid. In 2006, over 2 million tons of food was purchased by WFP at a cost of $600 million, 77 percent (in value terms) in developing countries. The purchases were made in 84 countries, 70 of which were in the developing world. The largest purchases were made in Africa (780,000 tons) and Asia (653,000 tons).

Special development programs

While the greater part of WFP assistance has gone to emergency operations, support has still been provided for specific development programs.

School feeding programs

Feeding children in primary schools was identified as one of WFP's main activities from its inception.[29] By the end of 1995, 33 years after WFP began operations, over $2 billion of WFP aid had been committed to 200 primary school feeding programs throughout the developing world. While the number of primary school children reached was small compared to their total number, to say nothing of the number who do not attend school, the number of beneficiaries was more noticeable in some countries and regions. In Africa, for example, most of the primary school children in Botswana, Lesotho, Mauritius, and Swaziland were reached. In other countries, such as Algeria, Brazil, Colombia, and Sudan considerable numbers of school children benefited. Since the start of the new millennium, the number of children and countries benefiting from WFP school feeding programs has steadily increased (Table 4.6).

Three interrelated objectives of these programs were established: improving child nutrition and health; increasing the range of school enrollment to include the children of poor households, including girls, encouraging greater regularity of school attendance, and reducing drop-out rates; and, thereby, improving school performance. School feeding programs are strongly supported by the general public and by politicians in both developing and developed countries. And they are considered to be relatively easy to implement, and to create no displacement effects as they involved additional consumption, although experience has revealed a number of difficulties.

The extensive evaluation literature on primary school feeding programs has shown that the nutritional, health, and educational benefits they promise are difficult to achieve in the reality of many developing countries. In addition, the general obstacles to educational progress in developing countries, particularly in Africa, tend to reduce the gains that food aid could assist in achieving. Investment in teacher training

Table 4.6 WFP primary school feeding programs, 2000–2005

Year	Children (millions)	Number of countries
2000	12.3	54
2001	15.0	57
2002	15.6	64
2003	15.2	69
2004	16.6	72
2005	21.7	74

Source: WFP.

and school infrastructure is often inadequate. The effectiveness of school feeding depends crucially on the degree to which governments in developing countries are taking steps, within their capabilities, to improve the basic education system. School feeding programs address an age group that has passed the greatest risk of acute malnutrition, and it is difficult to repair the effects of inadequate food intake in the pre-school years in catch-up programs. Dependence on imported food could create inappropriate food habits, which could be counter-productive to attempts to reach self-sufficiency. In the absence of adequate personnel, teachers can be diverted from their educational roles to engage in food preparation and distribution. The neediest children, those who did not go to school, or attended infrequently, were rarely reached, particularly in rural areas that had the poorest educational facilities. Evaluators therefore concluded that school meals programs had a built-in bias against the rural poor, and for urban areas.

An additional factor, which was often overlooked, is the opportunity cost to poor households of sending children to school. This often presents a barrier to school attendance. Children of poor families make a significant contribution to total household subsistence and income. Rather than providing only a meal at school, it might be necessary to give additional assistance. This would augment the stock of human capital by improving nutrition and health, increase schooling, and provide income transfers to the poor and disadvantaged to enable them, perhaps for the first time, to make longer-term investments that would raise their productivity and increase their income-generating potential. Seen in this way, food aid would be demand-enhancing rather than merely supply-augmenting.

Supported by strong donor interest and contributions, WFP is now expanding its school feeding program, taking account of earlier WFP experience. The school meals provided are governed by local tastes and customs, nutritional needs, the availability of local foods, ease of operation, and available resources. School meals and take-home rations may be combined. Between 2000 and 2004, WFP studied more than 1 million students in over 4,000 schools in 32 countries in Africa. The results suggested that school feeding has strong impact on absolute enrollment in WFP-assisted schools. Average absolute enrollment increased by 28 percent for girls and 22 percent for boys during the first year of the program. The combination of take-home rations for girls with on-school feeding saw a sustained increase in girls' absolute enrollment of 30 percent from year to year.

In April 2000, UNESCO, UNICEF, WHO, and the World Bank agreed on a shared framework (FRESH) to strengthen school health, hygiene and nutrition programs. In partnership with FAO, UNICEF, and WHO, WFP is now providing food for education as part of an "essential package" of other health improvement and education courses. TNT, a global mail and logistics company, is WFP's largest global corporate partner and donor to school feeding programs. It sends volunteers to developing countries for three months to work directly with WFP-assisted school feeding programs. TNT contributes a minimum of $500,000 directly to each country that hosts TNT volunteers. The funds are used for food and much needed school infrastructure. Due to the success of the volunteer program, other large corporations have contacted WFP to discuss similar partnership arrangements. A target has been set to reach 50 million children by the end of 2008 through WFP's school feeding program.

HIV/AIDS

Given the role of nutrition in maintaining the health and livelihoods of people living with HIV and AIDS, in 2006 WFP provided food and nutrition support to over 2.3 million people in 51 countries through care, treatment, and mitigation interventions.[30] WFP recognizes that food is an essential part of the syndrome in the global fight against HIV and AIDS. Good nutrition can delay the onset of AIDS-related illness and improve the quality of life of those living with the disease. Food can help vulnerable children stay in school and help affected families stay together. Food, combined with drug treatment, can help people living with HIV or tuberculosis feel better and help them adhere to the treatment. When family members are sick with HIV, they work less. As incomes decline, less money is available to buy food or pay for health care. Without assistance, the likely and serious consequence is malnutrition for the sick wage earner and the rest of the family. When poor and hungry people are affected by HIV, food helps to mitigate the impact. For these reasons, WFP advocates that food should always be part of treatment and care programs. Medicines alone are not enough.

Orphans are more likely to suffer from chronic malnutrition than children with parents. WFP's food for education program can help give orphans and other vulnerable children the nutrition, skills, and confidence they need to lead healthy and productive lives. Education is an effective way of mitigating both the impact and spread of HIV/AIDS. WFP and its partners are using school feeding programs as a platform for HIV/AIDS awareness and prevention education. In addition, home-based programs that target the chronically ill can be used to

132 *Policies, programs, and projects*

identify and reach vulnerable children by helping them access education and training opportunities.

In an effort to mitigate the impact of HIV/AIDS in families and communities, WFP ensures that food is part of a larger package of assistance provided to afflicted households. Food in asset-creation and training programs also encourages longer-term livelihood security, providing children with a better chance of survival. The Junior Farmer Field and Life Schools initiative is an innovative program implemented with FAO in several countries. It provides vulnerable adolescents with agricultural skills and crucial information about health and nutrition. To help strengthen agriculture, WFP also supports conservation farming in countries like Zambia and community-based agricultural activities in Swaziland.

Nutrition policies and programs

Given the importance of nutrition in combating malnutrition and poverty, and in meeting the MDGs, WFP is taking steps to mainstream nutrition in all its operations. Nutritional considerations have been important to WFP since its inception. It was decided to provide its food assistance on the basis of nutritional objectives as additional food consumption to avoid any counter-productive effects on agricultural production in recipient countries and on international trade, in conformity with FAO's Principles of Surplus Disposal.[31] WFP rations were calculated to meet the particular nutritional needs of specific groups. The aim was to provide a food ration which, together with local foods, made up a complete and balanced diet. When beneficiaries were almost entirely dependent on WFP for their sustenance, a full family ration was provided. Where the quantity of local foods available was more substantial, the WFP ration was reduced *pari passu* within the overall nutritional target. Where workers were separated from their families and WFP food rations were only distributed to them, the calorie level aimed at was higher to take account of the level and conditions of work.

The special problems of providing adequate rations constantly and consistently to refugees and displaced persons in emergency situations was recognized at a conference on "Nutrition in Times of Disaster," organized by the SCN and the International Nutrition Planners Forum and held in Geneva, Switzerland in September 1988, at which it was recommended that for emergency food rations "a practical working figure for the minimum energy requirement should be 1,900 kilocalories/person/day for a sedentary population." A special statement was issued in 1993 by the UN Administrative Co-ordination Committee (ACC), the highest administrative body in the UN system, on the advice of the SCN, which recommended that "the protection and promotion of the nutritional well-being of afflicted populations be fundamental goals of agency policy and programmes concerning refugees and displaced persons."[32] Guidelines were subsequently agreed between WFP and UNHCR on food rations for refugees. When refugees were dependent entirely on external food aid, the total food available to them from all sources should provide an intake of no less than 1,900 kilocalories of energy per person a day, of which at least 8 percent should be in the form of protein and 10 percent in the form of fat. The calories of energy could be modified depending on the circumstances of the refugee population.

While generous, the international response to emergencies has been inconsistent, sometimes based more on political considerations than on real need. The avoidance of high malnutrition rates and mortality in certain emergencies, for example, contrasts starkly with the lack of success in others. The logistics involved in reaching afflicted people, and providing them with adequate food rations consistently, can be formidable and costly. But pioneering and innovative efforts have been made, such as using triangular transactions, food exchange arrangements, and especially local food purchases to expedite and maintain the provision of adequate and appropriate food rations.

Recognizing the importance of nutrition for combating malnutrition, disease and poverty and for achieving the MDGs, WFP has undertaken to mainstream nutrition in all its operations.[33] The 1974 World Food Conference passed a resolution on "Policies and programmes to improve nutrition" and called on the concerned bodies of the UN system, including WFP, to prepare projects for assisting governments in developing countries to improve nutrition.[34] From its inception in 1963, WFP provided assistance to nutrition improvement programs for mothers and pre-school children. By the end of 1995, WFP had committed assistance to 196 projects in this field, valued at $1.5 billion. The provision of supplementary food to mothers and children remains central to many of WFP's activities, but much has changed in recent decades in three important senses. First, food delivery is no longer the only objective, and programs are better tailored to the problems they seek to overcome. Second, increased attention has been given to maximizing the nutritional value of the food rations provided. And third, the scope of nutrition programming has extended to other interventions. Good problem analysis clarifies the role of food. Complementary resources and skills are needed for nutrition interventions. And the focus has moved to preventing malnutrition, not just treating it.

WFP has placed emphasis on enhancing the quality of the food it provides not only through balanced food rations but also by adding nutritional value through micronutrient fortification. WFP is collaborating with UNHCR and the University of London Institute for Child Health to develop a software tool to enable staff to better assess and compare alternative food ration compositions. A technical advisory group of experts under the auspices of the United Nations University is working on WFP's behalf to review potential new commodities in terms of quality, safety, nutritional value, and operational feasibility bearing in mind WFP's shipment, storage, and handling requirements. WFP is also expanding its role in food fortification measures. Other ways are being pursued to enhance the contribution of nutrition. In school feeding programs, for example, nutrition education is being introduced to increase awareness of its importance and micronutrient deficiencies are being reduced through school meals. De-worming is also being practiced on a growing scale to ensure that the food consumed by the child provides maximum nutritional benefit. In income-generating activities, WFP is encouraging the local production of fortified blended foods to help tackle micronutrient deficiencies.

Chronic malnutrition, the silent killer, often goes unnoticed, while good nutrition is largely invisible. A major problem is weak human and institutional capacity, often where it is most needed. Interventions are hampered by the limited outreach of delivery infrastructure, a lack of skills in disciplines beyond medical training, and limited availability of non-food resources. A greater shift toward community programming is one way to overcome institutional weaknesses, but it is not an easy option, requiring investment in time and effort. Among competing priorities, nutrition may still be sidelined. Communities often focus on pressing tangible needs, such as clean water, sanitation or roads. WFP seeks to overcome these problems through establishing partnerships with other UN bodies with similar concerns, institutions, and NGOs, helping to obtain non-food resources, and better documentation of nutritional impact.

WFP undertook to pursue two other approaches to enhance the nutritional impact of its assistance. Nutrition problems in emergencies would be systematically analyzed and the most appropriate responses would be defined based on up-to-date knowledge and best practice.[35] Special effort would be made to ensure that nutritionally adequate foods were provided in a timely manner. WFP staff would design and implement effective nutrition-related objectives and report on results. Collaboration with partners that offer complementary nutrition skill would be increased. Increased funding would be sought to enhance

WFP's cash resources to support nutrition objectives. And more attention would also be paid to the underlying causes of malnutrition, not only during emergencies but in longer-term development activities.

WFP would increase its efforts to meet micronutrient deficiencies among the beneficiaries of its assistance through the distribution of appropriately fortified foods.[36] Support would also be given for national and international fortification initiatives, particularly for people in emergencies and those living with HIV/AIDS. This would be done while respecting WFP's procurement specifications and quality control procedures. The effectiveness and impact of fortification would be documented. WFP would also expand its local initiatives to produce fortified blended foods and biscuits, and in the milling and fortification of cereals.

Gender policy

Research and experience have shown that women play pivotal roles in the health and social and economic development of their families, communities, and nations. This has often been done in the face of formidable constraints. Nowhere was this more evident than in maintaining the three pillars of food security: sustainable food production; economic access to available food; and nutrition security for all family members.[37]

Improvements in household welfare depend not only on the level of income, but on who earns and controls that income. In many developing countries, women, relative to men, tend to spend their income disproportionately on food for the family and improvements in their children's nutrition, health, education, and general growth and development. Ensuring household nutrition security through the combination of food and other factors, such as child care and access to clean water and sanitation, are almost the exclusive domain of women. This raised the question of how to take gender-sensitive factors into account in the design, implementation, and evaluation of WFP-assisted development projects. Although women's roles had been recognized, there remained a great deal of tokenism in supporting and strengthening their activities. Women continued to be "helped" often through projects exclusively for them, thereby marginalizing their impact.

The United Nations Decade for Women (1976–85) provided the impetus and opportunity that helped to make a difference. In common with other aid agencies both within and outside the UN system, WFP was stimulated, for the first time, to take stock of what it had done to improve the status of women, enhance their contribution to development, and identify what more might be done in future. WFP's first policy paper on the subject was presented to its governing body in 1975.[38] Two important facts emerged. First, the inclusion of women in the development process could not be taken for granted but had to be a deliberate and conscious concern. Second, because of the close affinity between women and food, food aid had a special potential for improving women's status, providing as it did a vehicle for bringing new ideas, particularly in rural areas, and offering possibilities to women for assuming new roles in addition to their traditional tasks. WFP declared its full commitment to meeting the aims of International Women's Year in 1975. The executive director declared that: "Common sense urges it; common humanity demands it. Not just for this year but for all the years to come."

A number of studies and reports were presented to WFP's governing body throughout the United Nations Decade for Women, making it one of the most documented of any single issue. Surveys showed the high proportion of women engaged in the labor force of WFP-supported food-for-work projects. When linked with a package of development services, functional literacy, training in income-generating activities, and access to savings and credit schemes, poor women had the chance, for the first time, of breaking the cycle of abject poverty and joining the mainstream of development. However, two sets of obstacles and imperatives emerged from WFP's 10-year experience during the UN Decade for Women. The first were institutional factors within WFP, which were shared by other aid organizations. These mainly related to conceptualizing the issues for the advancement of women during the various phases of the project cycle. The second consisted of factors conditioning the roles and status of women within the countries receiving WSFP assistance and linking national macro-economic policies to actual living conditions at the family and village level.

A WFP strategy to the year 2000 was approved in 1985 to assist governments in developing countries in the fuller integration of women in national development programs, particularly in the field of food security.[39] This included: improving support for women in food production; establishing priorities in food-for work programs; intensifying support for female education and training; supporting community-based skills training for employment, income generation, and nutritional improvement; strengthening collaboration with other aid agencies both within and outside the UN system; and improving the operational dimensions of WFP activities. Other issues were subsequently highlighted. One cross-cutting concern was the need for greater recognition and appreciation of the "continuum" in women's productive and reproductive roles. Both roles are performed in a continuum of labor time allocations, which have a finite limit. A major failure of both national policies and programs, and of international assistance, was that by addressing women's reproductive roles in the social sector, and their production roles in the economic sector, separately and dysfunctionally, they dichotomized in development programming what was not separated in reality. The resultant additional burdens placed on women tended to lower their productivity and diminish their capacity to fulfill their domestic responsibilities, including child care.

Another issue concerned whether development projects should be designed and supported exclusively for women. While it was recognized that there were certain conditions under which separate projects for women might be undertaken, experience showed that improving women's status was best obtained in projects targeted at the family as a whole. These findings underlined that successful policy formulation and projects required gender analysis, and should involve gender mainstreaming in all WFP activities.

By the beginning of the 1990s, WFP had emerged as the largest single source of grant assistance in the UN system for development projects that involved and benefited women in the rural areas of the developing world. Of the $3 billion of WFP assistance invested in operational development projects at that time, over half directly supported the advancement of poor rural women. This did not include the substantial emergency relief food provided to the victims of natural and man-made disasters, most of whom were women and children.

WFP's strong and persistent attempts to enhance the status of women and their role in development over a period of two decades were capped by a far-reaching commitment made on its behalf by its executive director at the Fourth World Conference on Women in Beijing, China in 1995. WFP would use its food aid to change behavior and improve the status of women. While beliefs and prejudices that did so much damage to women worldwide could not be quickly changed, "Each small change in behaviour will one day pay-off in a change in attitude." In countries with major gaps in literacy, education, and basic skills between the sexes, WFP would commit at least 60 percent of its resources to women and girls. In emergencies, WFP would see to it that women took the lead in managing the relief food provided in cooperation with NGOs and other UN agencies. More than 50 percent of WFP school feeding resources would be allocated to girls. WFP funding for women's literacy projects would be doubled. WFP would also expand the use of food aid in refugee camps to support training for women in basic education, work skills, family planning, health, and nutrition. WFP would target food aid better to overcome vitamin and mineral deficiencies among women, by fortifying or adjusting WFP food rations. WFP staff would be more attuned to women's issues and would be assessed for their performance on gender issues. And more women would be employed and promoted by WFP with the minimum aim of attaining the UN secretary-general's goal of 25 percent of high-level posts for women and full gender equality by 2000.

There had already been an impressive change since 1992 when, for the first time, a woman, Catherine Bertini, a United States national, was appointed as WFP's executive director. By 1995, the number of women in high-level appointments had been increased to 22 percent. By the end of 2006, nearly 40 percent of WFP professional staff were women. An action plan was drawn up to meet WFP commitments by 2001. Consultations were held with WFP's operating partners on how to carry out its policy to distribute a targeted 80 percent of relief food in emergencies directly to the senior female of a household. And a memorandum of understanding was signed with NGOs which included reference to the involvement of women at all levels of food aid planning, management, distribution, and monitoring.

This consultation process resulted in WFP's *Gender Policy 2003–2007*, approved by WFP's executive board in 2002, which established eight "enhanced commitments" to women to ensure food security:[40]

- Meet the specific nutritional requirements of expectant and nursing mothers and adolescent girls and raise their health and nutrition awareness.
- Expand activities that enable girls to attend school.
- Ensure that women benefit at least equally from the assets created through food for training and food for work.
- Contribute to women's control of food in relief food distribution of household rations.
- Ensure that women are equally involved in food distribution committees and other program-related local bodies.
- Ensure that gender is mainstreamed in programming activities.
- Contribute to an environment that acknowledges that the important role women play in ensuring household food security and that encourages both men and women to participate in closing the gender gap.
- Make progress toward gender equality in staffing, opportunities, and duties, and ensuring that human resources policies are gender sensitive and provide possibilities for staff members to combine their personal and professional priorities.

A survey was conducted in 48 countries in 2004–5 to see how WFP's *Gender Policy 2003–2007* was being implemented and to provide a baseline for future surveys. The survey showed some impressive gains but also a number of shortcomings. Micronutrient-fortified food was provided to all mothers at 89 percent of the project sites visited. At 90 percent of the project sites, at least half the assisted mothers attended awareness-raising sessions on nutrition, health and child care practices. But de-worming medications were provided at only 19 percent of project sites. At many sites adolescent girls were not targeted at all, and awareness-raising sessions on HIV/AIDS prevention were offered at only 61 percent of the sites. In school feeding projects, 48 percent of students provided with WFP food in 2004 were girls, close to the 50 percent target set. But the gender gap persisted, with boys exceeding girls by more than 15 percent in primary schools in one-third of the countries visited, and by 25 percent in secondary schools in a quarter of the countries visited.

In food-for-training projects, women made up 61 percent of the trainees, approaching the target set of 70 percent. However, data on adolescent girls were rarely available and at 88 percent of the project sites they were not involved. In food-for-work projects, 55 percent of the workers were women and adolescent girls. To enhance women's participation, flexible timing and working shifts were offered at 74 percent of the project sites. In 36 percent, there was no participatory consultation to define work activities. In emergencies, both men and women were well aware of food distribution modalities but consultations on the location of food distributions took place at only 48 percent of the relief sites. Beneficiary food distribution committees existed in 92 percent of the food-for-work projects, with women comprising at least half of the representative- and more than half of the executive-level members, at about 70 percent of the work sites. Leadership training for women participating in committees was not sufficiently provided in all activities: just 28 percent at relief sites, 31 percent at food-for-work sites, and 54 percent in the training programs. In only half the WFP country offices in the countries visited did contingency plans prepared since January 2005 explicitly reflect and address gender issues. Clearly, the survey showed that while progress had been made in implementing WFP's gender policies, much remains to be done.

Ending child hunger and undernutrition initiative

WFP and UNICEF joined forces in 2006 to spearhead a global initiative entitled Ending Child Hunger and Undernutrition, based on their long and profound practical experiences.[41] They were also stimulated to take this initiative by efforts to reform the UN system and the international consensus afforded by the UN Millennium Summit of 2000 and the adoption of the MDGs. This provided an opportunity for UN bodies supporting food- and nutrition-related programs to strengthen their capacities and serve as catalysts to address the global problem of child hunger and malnutrition.

The size and complexity of the problem, and the failure of past efforts to mount a broad and sustained attack on the problem, indicated that a strong global partnership was needed, focused on action, to achieve progress for children. There are roughly 400 million children under 18 years of age suffering from hunger and undernutrition. WHO and UNICEF estimate that 149 million children under five years are underweight, a key indicator of undernourishment. More than 5 million children under five years die each year from diseases from which they would have survived were they not undernourished. Experience over many years had shown that not only was access to more food required but the provision of a package of assistance was needed, which addressed not only health, education, and other related concerns, and the social, human rights, and political environment into which children were born and brought up, but also the grinding poverty of their economic condition.

The initiative has four intended outcomes:

- Increased awareness of hunger and undernutrition and an understanding of potential solutions.
- Strengthening national policies and programs affecting hunger and nutrition.
- Increased capacities for direct community action on child hunger and nutrition.
- Increased efficiency and accountability of global efforts to reduce child hunger and undernutrition, through monitoring and evaluating the initiative's interventions and impact on children.

Four groups would work to reduce child hunger and malnutrition over a 10-year period: individual members; a steering committee to provide oversight and direction; a high-level partners group consisting of key UN agencies, NGOs, and members of civil society and the private sector to provide strategic guidance at the global level; and a secretariat, based in Rome, with a senior UNICEF official as team leader, staff provided by WFP and UNICEF, and technical guidance from FAO, with a budget of $2.2 million a year. WFP and UNICEF will act as advocates and catalysts in pursuing the goals of the initiative.

The aim is to satisfy immediate needs while addressing systemic problems. The size of the global problem is daunting but is highly concentrated. Almost three-quarters of the world's underweight children live in 10 countries; 80 percent live in 16 countries. About 85 million families affected by child hunger live in countries where the prevalence of underweight among children under five years of age is greater than 10 percent. The experience of UNICEF and WFP has shown that the problem can be tackled operationally given adequate, sustained, and coordinated resources and programs. The focus would be on the most affected countries for the first two years with strategies and priorities formulated for later action. The initiative will distinguish between "child hunger" and "family hunger" and will promote various interventions targeting poor households to enable them to bring up healthy children.

The UN Standing Committee on Nutrition (SCN) estimates that the direct cost of inaction on child hunger and undernutrition is between $20 billion and $30 billion a year. The estimated annual cost of providing a set of interventions for 85 million families in countries with severe child underweight problems is put at $8 billion. This could not be absorbed immediately but an additional $1 billion raised internationally could be programmed immediately.

WFP and UNICEF executive boards authorized the WFP and UNICEF secretariats to continue to develop the initiative and approved their roles in the 2007–8 work plan and first year of the initiative, with a budget of $1.31 million from each organization. The UN High Commissioner for Refugees, Antonio Guterres, has been confirmed as the inaugural chair of the partners group.

IFAD

The signature concepts of IFAD's work program are "innovation" and "partnership." Since its early days, IFAD was a pioneer in supporting innovations, such as microcredit in the Grameen Bank in Bangladesh in 1979. With its focus on increasing agricultural production and improving the living conditions of the rural poor in developing countries, it engaged in the development of strong partnerships with a multitude of stakeholders, including governments, international and regional IFIs, NGOs, farmers' organizations, and local rural organizations. It targeted small farmers, landless people, nomadic herders, artisanal fishermen, and rural women. As IFAD broadened its interventions toward a more effective and an impact-driven fight against rural poverty, so did the types of activities carried out by its projects.

142 *Policies, programs, and projects*

IFAD's mandate now is about the identification, design, and implementation of sustainable projects and programs that enable the rural poor themselves to overcome poverty (Table 4.7).

IFAD's assistance is now firmly focused on Africa and Asia, where most of the rural poor live (Table 4.8).

Independent external evaluation: assessment of project performance

An independent external evaluation of IFAD was carried out in 2004 and 2005, the first since the fund began operations in 1978. At the time, it was one of the most ambitious exercises of its kind undertaken for a United Nations agency. It showed a number strengths and weaknesses in the performance of IFAD lending portfolio.[42] It should be remembered that IFAD had chosen the difficult road of trying to help poor rural people to help themselves out of poverty, often in the most disadvantaged locations. IFAD's assistance had also moved increasingly into innovative and higher-risk interventions. The results of the independent external evaluation are therefore not only instructive for IFAD as it plans its future program of work, but also for other food and agricultural institutions intent on reducing rural poverty.

The evaluation was wide-ranging. It aimed to: determine IFAD's contribution to rural poverty reduction; examine the relevance of its mission and objectives; assess its corporate learning and performance;

Table 4.7 IFAD assistance by type of project, 1978–2007

Project type	No. of Projects	% of total projects	IFAD assistance (U.S.$ millions)	% of total
Agriculture	241	31	3,053	30
Credit	110	14	1,568	16
Fisheries	23	3	153	2
Irrigation	52	7	792	8
Livestock	33	4	350	3
Marketing	11	1	170	2
Program loan	12	2	166	2
Research	46	6	522	5
Rural development	233	30	3,179	32
Settlement	4	1	70	1
To be decided*	1	0	10	0
Total	766	100	10,033	100

* Pending component analysis
Source: IFAD secretariat.

Table 4.8 IFAD assistance by region, 1978–2007

	1978–1986	1987–1996	1997–2006	2007	1978–2007
Western and Central Africa					
1	326.5	616.2	723.3	107.8	1,773.8
2	41	63	58	7	169
Eastern and Southern Africa					
1	340.7	565.6	777.3	149.2	1,832.8
2	31	53	51	9	144
Asia and the Pacific					
1	894.0	867.6	1,283.6	172.1	3,217.3
2	54	64	66	8	192
Latin America and the Caribbean					
1	321.4	480.3	697.7	49.7	1,549.1
2	37	46	42	5	130
Near East and North Africa					
1	386.6	480.8	704.7	88.1	1,660.1
2	35	38	52	6	131
Total					
1	2,269.2	3,010.4	4,186.6	566.8	10,033.0
2	198	264	269	35	766

1 = Total assistance (U.S.$ million)
2 = Number of programs and projects
Source: IFAD Annual Report, 2007.

and make recommendations on policy directions and steps to improve IFAD's performance. In each of these areas, the evaluation identified a range of strengths and weaknesses and made a series of recommendations. These subsequently led to, and shaped, IFAD's action plan for improving its development effectiveness.

The evaluation noted that while lending to agricultural projects had remained the major part of IFAD portfolio, other types of projects had received its support, including artisanal fisheries, rural finance, irrigation, livestock, marketing, research, settlement, rural infrastructure, and undifferentiated rural development. As IFAD's agenda and portfolio expanded, its assistance had become more thinly spread over an increasingly complex and diffuse range of activities. This lack of focus was reflected in IFAD's then-current Strategic Framework, which provided the intellectual and policy framework for its program of assistance, and which was considered to be "largely permissive, ruling almost everything in and very little out."

The evaluation found that the performance of IFAD-supported projects had shown a modest improvement after 2000, and had further improved in 2003. Two-thirds of the IFAD-financed projects evaluated were expected to achieve development objectives. Half of the projects reviewed were redesigned at mid-term, many of them substantially, suggesting the need for modifications in the design process. Targeting assistance at the poor, particularly those in remote and marginal areas, presented special problems, as most aid agencies have experienced. About half of IFAD projects did not represent a good use of resources invested. Economic analysis and planning were not always in line with the current nature of investment.

In rating performance, the evaluation found that the IFAD projects fitted country development priorities, and IFAD strategy and beneficiary needs, in 60 percent of the cases, and were rated "high." The extent to which project design targeted the right people with appropriate activities was rated "substantial," at 55 percent, as was effectiveness of the development intervention's major objectives, at 67 percent. Some of the project implementation difficulties rose from the performance of the borrower, the government of a developing country, and were largely beyond IFAD's control. In 40 percent of projects, the performance of the borrower was rated as "modest." The overall performance of IFAD and the cooperating institution was rated as "modest," at 45 percent.

The evaluation noted the difficulties of trying to undertake project supervision out of Rome, and the need for closer contact between partners, governments, and poor people in developing countries. This pointed to the value of a decentralization of IFAD staff, at least in key countries with innovative and complex projects, to facilitate a continuing dialogue between all the parties involved, which IFAD is now addressing.

The introduction of a Country Strategy Opportunities Paper in 1995 was intended to provide a medium-term framework for IFAD operations at the country level. The aim was to define IFAD's specific role and future direction, locate the strategy within IFAD's corporate and regional objectives, and identify the links between interventions at the country level. It also aimed to establish links with national policy processes and opportunities for engaging in a policy dialogue specifically focused on improving the welfare of the rural poor. However, the evaluation found that there had not been sufficient time for this approach to develop the synergies between projects, between aid instruments (loans and grants), and between projects and policy processes.

A crucial part of the evaluation concerned the impact of IFAD's assistance on rural poverty. Not surprisingly, it was found that project impact varied widely. A few high-impact projects contrasted with lower performance overall. In terms of impact on family or household income levels, 47 percent of the projects evaluated were rated as "substantial," 47 percent as "modest," and 6 percent as "high." Research, extension, and organizational interventions, often supported by credit or irrigation, to increase food production for consumption or sale, are historically core areas of IFAD assistance. The evaluation found that almost half the projects evaluated performed satisfactorily, while slightly over half were under-achieving. Roads, irrigation, and other water infrastructure were the largest stand-alone investments that IFAD made. Overall, the impact of IFAD investment in these areas was assessed as "modest." There were some notable examples of good performance in the rural financial services sector, even if credit interventions were generally less effective. Although health and education investments were not a major feature of IFAD-supported projects, they generally had a positive impact. Mixed results were achieved in projects that sought to conserve the environment and encourage the sustainable use of natural resources.

A major change in IFAD's portfolio of assistance has been the shift from a strong emphasis on agricultural production and productivity to a much broader agenda for poverty reduction and empowerment of the poor. IFAD's interventions were not only about transferring improved technologies and methods, but also focused on assisting the rural poor to establish their own, and frequently informal, institutions. The evaluation found that where IFAD-supported projects strengthened existing local institutions, the impact was positive, even if the institutions did not automatically represent the poorest groups or women. Creating new institutions posed more difficulties, and were rarely sustainable unless people had a good sense of mutual trust. The evaluation examined the key question of sustainability of benefits accruing from IFAD investments from two perspectives: whether the stream of benefits would continue when IFAD assistance came to an end; and whether the institutional changes induced by the project were likely to continue. It was found that in less than half the projects nearly or actually closed was sustainability achieved.

Innovation is seen as central to the achievement of IFAD's broadened mandate. The ability to scale-up successful and replicable innovations increases the value of IFAD's assistance and its impact on

146 *Policies, programs, and projects*

poverty. The evaluation found that the overall evidence showed that there was little to distinguish IFAD's work from that of other development agencies. Despite a few highly innovative projects and others that contained and promoted innovative elements, IFAD did not contribute to the creation, promotion, replication, and lesson-learning process in any systematic way. A paper on "Initiative for mainstreaming innovation" was presented to IFAD's executive board in December 2004. It took full note of the findings of the evaluation and acknowledged that changes in culture and learning are necessary elements for success.

The overall conclusions of the evaluation were that as a whole, IFAD's portfolio of assistance was broadly pro-poor but lacked strategic coherence. The impact of IFAD's projects was variable, as in most development organizations, but with a little under half of all projects falling below expected levels of poverty impact, there was a need for better performance. While acknowledging that comparisons with other international financial institutions were difficult, the evaluation found that on the basis of best data available, "IFAD lags its comparators on measures of projects at risk, time to project effectiveness, and quality of supervision."

IFAD'S action plan

IFAD's took the findings of the independent external evaluation seriously. Its response was to draw up an "Action Plan" to improve and increase its development effectiveness, efficiency, and relevance in helping its member countries reduce rural poverty. The plan, which was approved by its executive board in December 2005, defined more than 40 deliverables in the broad areas of strategic planning and guidance, project quality and impact, and knowledge management and innovation. The action plan's outputs have focused on: ensuring a clear definition of corporate strategic objectives; building new tools and processes to improve IFAD's development effectiveness; establishing a planning and management frame for improved organizational effectiveness; and developing a comprehensive approach to results measurements and reporting. The process has been guided by an Action Plan Management Team, consisting of IFAD senior managers, supported by a small Action Plan Secretariat. The Action Plan Management Team members themselves headed a series of working groups of staff members, who were responsible for preparing the specific outputs of the plan. By the end of 2007, two years after the independent external evaluation had been presented, 14 of the deliverables

Policies, programs, and projects 147

to be presented to IFAD's executive board had been approved, most of the other deliverables had been completed, and the outputs of the action plan were starting to transform the way IFAD goes about its business.

IFAD's new Strategic Framework 2007–2010 was approved by its executive board in December 2006. It specifically sought to respond to the finding of the independent external evaluation. It explained how IFAD could best discharge its mandate and use the instruments at its disposal to maximize its contributions to reducing rural poverty. It also defined IFAD's comparative advantage and, among other things, explained how IFAD was to be managed and organized in order to deliver on the defined development objectives. A results measurement framework was also established to monitor progress and reporting has started.

A series of reforms have been started to improve IFAD's development effectiveness. The starting point was a new results-based country strategic opportunities program (COSOP), which defines a coherent country programs within the national policy framework for reducing rural poverty. IFAD is also increasingly taking responsibility for supervising the projects it finances rather than outsourcing this function to a cooperating institution. By the end of 2007, over half of the project portfolio had been directly supervised. IFAD's field presence pilot program has been mainstreamed with improved headquarters backing. IFAD's executive board has also approved a series of policies and strategies including: a targeting policy; an innovation strategy; and a knowledge management strategy. Steps have been taken to ensure that these policies and strategies are taken into account at the project design and implementation stages.

A range of reforms have been implemented to strengthen IFAD's organizational effectiveness and efficiency, underpinned by its knowledge management systems. A Corporate Planning and Performance Management System has been established to focus IFAD's human and resources on the objectives defined in its Strategic Framework. IFAD is also improving its financial efficiency. Each year, it is reducing its budget on administration and its project development support to its member governments as a proportion of its program of work and increasing the proportion of expenditures on operational as opposed to non operational costs. Steps have also been taken to strengthen the management of its human resources. Recognizing that a key factor in any change process is an enabling organizational culture, IFAD has undertaken to create a culture that is results-driven and valued-based.

IFAD has developed a set of linked reporting tools to measure and report on its progress in achieving results. At its apex is an annual

Report on IFAD's Development Effectiveness (RIDE), which was prepared for the first time in 2007. This showed that IFAD was broadly on track to meet its 2009 action plan targets for effectiveness, efficiency and relevance. Performance for innovation and poverty impact had improved substantially, although particular attention would have to be given to sustainability. Performance of organizational effectiveness and efficiency was either on track or partially on track in terms of better country program management, better project design, and better implementation support, and partially on track in terms of improved resource mobilization and management, improved human resources management, and improved administrative efficiency. Improved performance in all these areas reflected both the successful introduction and initial mainstreaming across the organization of numerous initiatives, the explicit focus placed on achieving results, and the gradual establishment of a results culture within and across the organization.

Partnerships

IFAD's *Annual Report 2006* states: "Partnerships are fundamental to IFAD's work."[43] From inception, they have been a strong feature of IFAD's operations. An impressive network of relationships has been formed over the past 30 years. To scale-up and broaden investment in IFAD-initiated projects, partnerships have been established with 57 bilateral and multilateral donor organizations in co-financing ventures. Over 1,000 NGOs have been involved in IFAD-supported projects, more than 80 percent of them from developing countries. IFAD's relationship with the private sector has involved working with corporations at the project level, investigating means to access capital markets, and establishing partnerships in the ongoing dialogue on new technologies.

In response to the need for a coordinated international effort on development and knowledge-sharing, IFAD has established an extensive network with its research-for-development partners. IFAD grants have been provided to support international, regional, and sub-regional institutions and centers of excellence on thematic issues, technology development, and piloting of innovative pro-poor activities. Over the past 25 years, IFAD has committed about $120 million for CGIAR-led research programs as a co-sponsor with widespread impact on small-scale agriculture in developing countries. IFAD has also supported the Global Forum for Agricultural Research (GFAR) since its inception in 1996, and is on its steering committee In 2006, IFAD established a partnership with the Consultative Group to Assist the Poor (CGAP), a strategic technical group that supports donors in the area of rural finance, which undertakes research into innovative ways of bringing microfinance services to poor rural people. Electronic regional networks have been established with IFAD support. A knowledge-based, Internet-based network for rural development in Asia and the Pacific region, funded by IFAD, links 30 IFAD-supported rural development projects in the region. A similar network links 30 IFAD-funded projects in West and Central Africa. Another network links 40 IFAD-supported projects in Latin America and the Caribbean. A fourth network links 10 IFAD-supported projects in the Near East and North Africa region.

The Farmers' Forum is an emerging, bottom-up, process of consultation and dialogue between small farmers' and rural producers' organizations, IFAD, and governments, focused on rural development and poverty reduction. Fully aligned with IFAD's strategic objectives, the forum is rooted in partnerships and collaboration at the country and regional levels. The forum meets every two years for a global consultation, in conjunction with IFAD's governing council. Participants are invited to the governing council, where they take part in round-table discussions, with a concluding statement to the forum delivered by a farmers' leader.

IFAD would like to see its own policies and operations influenced by the perspectives of poor rural people and their organizations, and has stepped up its support for building up the capacity of their organizations. In 1998, IFAD approved its first flexible lending mechanism program in Mali under the direct management of the national farmers' and civil society organizations. This pioneering initiative has been followed by others in Senegal, Rwanda, Burkina Faso in Africa, in India, and in Brazil, Peru, Bolivia, and the Dominican Republic in Latin America. A particularly innovative "First Mile" pilot project, implemented in collaboration with the Agricultural Marketing Systems Development Programme of the government of Tanzania, is attempting to build agricultural marketing systems for the benefit of the rural poor through the use of modern communications technology, including mobile phones, the Internet and e-mail.

The importance that IFAD attaches to forming strong partnerships is epitomized by the fact that the directors and secretariats of four international collaborative arrangements are hosted at its headquarters.

Belgium Survival Fund (BSF)

The BSF was created by the Belgian parliament in 1983 in response to the drought and famine that took the lives of more than 1 million people in East Africa during the 1980s. The BSF provides grants to assist development projects in some of the poorest countries in Africa, helping extremely poor people to become healthier and more productive. Since 1984, IFAD and BSF have been engaged in a joint program to promote the common goal of enabling poor rural people overcome poverty through improved food and nutrition security. By the end of 2006, the BSF had provided $184 million, which has enabled IFAD to provide grants for 40 programs and projects in African countries, for the evaluation of those activities, and to cover administrative costs. The BSF is housed in IFAD's External Affairs Department.

International Land Coalition (ILC)

The ILC works to increase poor rural people's access to land and productive resources. It serves as a global forum for policy dialogue and convenes joint programs and activities among intergovernmental, governmental and civil society organizations. The ILC is independently governed by an Assembly of Members and a 14-member Coalition Council. IFAD hosts its director and secretariat and is one of its main funders. In 2006, the ILC participated in an external evaluation of its operations, which was carried out by IFAD. The evaluation stressed the continuing importance of the coalition's role in advocating a pro-poor land tenure agenda. It produced recommendations on how it can grow into its role as a global convener on land issues. In Africa, a number of ongoing ILC programs are working to build national collaboration to advance a pro-poor land agenda. The ILC secretariat also launched a series of global consultations to develop strategies to strengthen the tenure rights of poor people who are particularly at risk of becoming landless.

The ILC gave high priority in 2006 to the International Conference on Agrarian Reform and Rural Development, held in Porto Alegre, Brazil. During the inaugural session, IFAD's president renewed IFAD's commitment to ensuring equitable, efficient and sustainable access to and use of land and other natural resources. ILC members have formulated a new *Strategic Framework 2007–2010* for putting its pro-poor land agenda into practice. ILC supports civil society organizations (CSOs) toward the promulgation of policies and laws that protect poor people's land tenure rights through its Knowledge Network on Agrarian Reform, which focuses on sharing knowledge and building networks for collective empowerment. ILC also seeks to identify successful and innovative civil society experience to scale-up through its Community Empowerment Facility (CEF), a catalytic co-financing grant fund that supports the capacity-building and institutional strengthening of CSOs. In 2006, eight new projects were approved under the CEF, which brought the number of partners working with the facility to a total of 49 in 25 countries.

The Global Mechanism (GM)

At the UN Conference on Environment and Development held in Rio de Janeiro, Brazil in 1992, governments requested the UN to hold negotiations for an international legal agreement to prevent the degradation of dry lands. The resulting International Convention to Combat Desertification in those Countries Experiencing Serious Drought and/or Desertification, Particularly in Africa, entered into force in December 1995. Under article 21 of the convention, the Global Mechanism was established as a subsidiary body in 1997 to provide financial advisory services to the country parties to the convention. Its purpose is to promote actions in the mobilization of financial resources to address land and natural resource degradation, and promote rural development and poverty reduction, in keeping with the spirit of the convention.

IFAD has hosted the director of the GM since its inception in 1997. By the end of 2007, IFAD had contributed $7.5 million for GM's operations, making it the largest financial contributor. IFAD's grants have enabled the GM to support activities related to sustainable land management (SLM) in 29 counties and 12 sub-regions. To name an outstanding example, the GM was a partner in the development of the Central Asian Countries Initiative for Land Management, a 10-year program with planned financing of $1.4 billion. In 2006, the GM began implementing its Consolidated Strategy and Enhanced Approach to mobilize increased funding and effectiveness through strategic programs and special initiatives. Through integrated financing strategies, the GM is focusing strongly on knowledge management and capacity-building at the country level to enable governments and stakeholders to arrive at a substantive increase in investments in SLM. GM's strategy and approach were established in response to the Paris Declaration on Aid Effectiveness and Harmonization. Since IFAD has fully subscribed to integrating its aid portfolio into country development programming, the hosting of the GM in IFAD becomes increasingly an effective partnership in which the Global Environment Facility plays a major role. Evidence of the effectiveness of this partnership is provided by the results of a portfolio review of IFAD on SLM investments, which show substantively increased resource allocations over the past years.

152 *Policies, programs, and projects*

The Global Environment Facility (GEF)

The idea of the GEF was launched in Paris, France in March 1990 as an independent financial arrangement to help developing countries fund programs and projects to protect the global environment. The GEF provides grants for projects related to biodiversity, climate change, international waters, land degradation, the ozone layer, and persistent organic pollutants. The GEF also helps developing countries promote sustainable livelihoods in local communities. Since it was established in 1991, the GEF has provided $6.2 billion in grants and has generated over $20 billion in co-financing to support over 1,800 projects in 140 developing countries or countries in transition that have produced global environmental benefits.

IFAD is an executing agency for the GEF. An IFAD-GEF unit was established at IFAD headquarters in 2004 to play a catalytic role in addressing the links between poverty and global environmental degradation. IFAD helps governments in developing countries develop and implement projects that address global environmental concerns. With the onset of climate change, GEF-financed projects aim to help the transition from a climate-vulnerable to a climate-resilient developmental environment. A workshop was held at IFAD in May 2007 to better explain and to offer guidance on how to access funding under the GEF management program. Activities to mark World Environment Day, 5 June 2007, were jointly funded by IFAD and the GEF.

CGIAR

The 1974 World Food Conference passed a resolution on "Food and agricultural research, extension and training," which, among other things, recommended that the CGIAR:

> be substantially enlarged to enable it to augment the number and scope of international and regional research programmes in and for the developing countries, with the objective of complementing and helping to strengthen research in the developing countries through promoting co-operative research networks, assisting the adaptive research at the national level and in training programmes, and the dissemination of research information at all levels.[44]

The resolution was approved by the UN General Assembly. The number of CGIAR centers was increased to 18 and then consolidated to 15.

Policies, programs, and projects 153

By 2006, with an expenditure of $458 million and over 8,000 research scientists and support staff, the CGIAR had become a strong "strategic alliance" for agricultural development and poverty reduction in the developing world. At its heart is a group of 15 autonomous international agricultural research centers (Figure 4.2), 13 of which are located in developing countries, backed by a Science Council of internationally renowned scientists, and supported by 64 member countries and organizations.

The CGIAR provides the world's largest investment in generating public goods for the benefit of poor agricultural communities in developing countries. Its developmental benefits can be traced through five pathways that form the main focus of its activities:

- Sustainable production of crops, livestock, fisheries, forests, and natural resources.
- Enhancing national agricultural research systems through joint research, policy support, training, and knowledge sharing.
- Germplasm improvement for priority crops, livestock, trees, and fish.
- Germplasm collection, characterization, and conservation, as the genetic resources that the CGIAR holds in trust and makes available to all, including some of the world's largest gene banks.
- Policy research on matters that have a major impact on agriculture, food, health, disseminating new technologies, and managing and conserving natural resources.

In assessing the CGIAR's work in these five fields, reference has been made to the various external reviews and evaluations made of the CGIAR, the latest by the World Bank Operations Evaluation Department in 2004.[45]

Sustainable production

The CGIAR was originally established to maintain and widen the momentum that had led to the Green Revolution through the application of agricultural science to produce high-yielding varieties of staple cereals. The number of international agricultural research centers was increased from 4 to 15, to encompass a wide range of staple foods in addition to cereals, on an eco-regional basis, but also to bring in other parts of the agricultural sector—livestock, fisheries and forests—and concern for the management of natural resources, including water, essential for sustainable agricultural production. The added focus on

154 Policies, programs, and projects

Center	Date established (Joined CGIAR)	Location	Funding (Trend*) 2006 ($ millions)	Staffing 2006 Int./Other	Main area of focus
Original members, founded before the CGIAR:					
IRRI International Rice Research Institute	1960 (1971)	Los Banõs, Philippines	27.2 (0)	73/832	Rice (global); rice-based ecosystems (Asia)
CIMMYT International Maize and Wheat Improvement Center	1966 (1971)	Mexico City, Mexico	36.0 (0)	83/437	Wheat, maize, triticale (global)
IITA International Institute of Tropical Agriculture	1967 (1971)	Ibadan, Nigeria	45.1 (+)	107/1,128	Sustainable production systems for the humid lowland tropics; soybean, maize, cassava, cowpea, banana, plantain, yams (sub-Saharan Africa)
CIAT International Center for Tropical Agriculture	1967 (1971)	Cali, Columbia	36.5 (+)	96/640	Sustainable land use in tropical America; beans, cassava, forages and pastures (global), rice (Latin America and the Carribbean)
Founded or adopted by the CGIAR after 1971:					
ICRISAT International Crops Research Institute for the Semi-arid Tropics	1972 (1972)	Patancherm, India	32.3 (+)	59/873	Sustainable production systems for the semi-arid tropics; sorghum, pearl millet, finger millet, chickpea, pigeonpea, and groundnut (Asia)
CIP International Potato Center	1971 (1973)	Lima, Peru	22.3 (+)	60/493	Potato (global), sweet potato, other root and tuber crops (Latin America, Asia)
IPGRI International Plant Genetic Resources Institute	1974 (1974)	Rome, Italy	31.2 (+)	69/179	Plant genetic resources of current and potential crops and forages, collection and gene pool conservation (global)
WARDA West Africa Rice Development Association	1970 (1975)	Bouaké, Côte d'Ivoire	11.1 (0)	49/151	Rice (West Africa)
ICARDA International Center for Agricultural Research in the Dry Areas	1977 (1977)	Aleppo, Syria	24.4 (+)	104/397	Wheat, barley, chickpea, lentil, pasture and forage, legumes, small ruminants (West Asia–North Africa)

Center	Date established (Joined CGIAR)	Location	Funding (Trend*) 2006 ($ millions)	Staffing 2006 Int./Other	Main area of focus
Founded or adopted by the CGIAR after 1971 (contd):					
IFPRI International Food Policy Research Institute	1975 (1980)	Washington, DC, USA	37.2 (+)	89/121	Food policy, socio-economic research related to agricultural development, strengthening national agricultural research systems (global)
Founded or adopted by the CGIAR after 1990:					
World Agroforestry Center	1977 (1991)	Nairobi, Kenya	29.9 (0)	45/421	Agroforestry; multi-purpose trees (global)
IWMI International Water Management Institute	1984 (1991)	Battarmulla, Sri Lanka	20.0 (−)	115/259	Irrigation management (global)
CIFOR Center for Forestry Research	1993 (1993)	Bogor, Indonesia	15.7 (−)	41/137	Sustainable forestry management (global)
World Fish Center	1977 (1992)	Penang, Malaysia	14.8 (0)	44/278	Sustainable aquatic resource management (global)
ILRI International Livestock Research Institute	1995 (1995)	Nairobi, Kenya	26.7 (−)	81/693	Livestock disease (global), tickborne diseases, trypanosomiasis (sub-Saharan Africa)

* Funding trend: (+) increasing; (0) no change; (−) decreasing

Source: *CGIAR Secretariat*

Figure 4.2 The CGIAR centers

poverty reduction also meant that the improvements that the CGIAR sought to achieve were accessible to the abjectly poor rural people. Some of the lessons of the Green Revolution were that while spectacular results had been obtained in terms of dramatically increased cereal production, its impact on the poor was less than expected.[46] In addition, it had not reduced, and in some cases had encouraged, natural-resource degradation and environmental problems, its geographical impact was localized, and there were worrying signs of diminishing returns as it lost its momentum.

The work of IFAD and IFPRI, among others, has shown that agricultural research can benefit the poor in many ways. It can increase farm production and marketed output and provide more food and nutrients for consumption. Employment for landless laborers and small farmers can be increased. Opportunities for economically beneficial migration can be improved. Rural non-farm and urban income can be induced. Food prices can be reduced, helping the poor in their access to food. Economic and physical access of poor women to better food could be enhanced. And in the process, the poor could be empowered. But research also showed that there were vital steps in the pathway from research to impact, especially for the poor. The outputs or outcomes of research had to be adopted efficiently and effectively at the producer level. Even then, policies, markets, and institutions needed to be in place to ensure that the benefits of increased agricultural production accrued equitably to the poor, and in sustainable ways. This involved going beyond the CGIAR's comparative advantage in agricultural research, hence the emphasis on establishing partnerships with multilateral and bilateral bodies, the private sector, and civil society organizations, which was the theme of CGIAR's last annual general meeting in Beijing, China in 2007.

Linked to CGIAR's original priority and continuing focus on increasing agricultural production has been its concern with the management of natural resources to ensure that production increases are sustainable. This concern was heightened after the UN Conference on Environment and Development in 1992, and has been increased further by the threat of climate change and global warming. This is a matter of considerable and continuing debate in the CGIAR, raising issues of strategic focus. A particular problem is that unlike its work on plant breeding or germplasm research (see below), which can be carefully controlled in field trials and laboratories, natural resource management involves many diverse issues, its benefits are spread over a long period of time, and there can be broad spillover effects. Nevertheless, the CGIAR considers that research in this area is central to sustainable increases in agricultural productivity and to improvement in rural livelihoods worldwide. It therefore advocates that integrated natural resource management, together with integrated genetic resource management (see below), are its twin pillars supporting the enhancement of agricultural productivity.

The CGIAR's priorities in natural resource management research have been: (1) the management of the earth's resources (soils, flora, fauna) to enhance sustainable agricultural productivity; (2) integrated water management as a major input to agricultural and aquatic productivity; (3) management of forests for enhancing rural livelihoods and providing sustainable sources of fuelwood and non-timber forest products; and (4) incentives and policies for improved natural resource management. The CGIAR successes in research on earth resources cover several areas and underscore its complementarity with

Policies, programs, and projects 157

germplasm improvement research. Among the best known are the achievements in integrated pest management, especially by IRRI and FAO in rice production in Southeast Asia. The CGIAR's pioneering role has now been spread globally for the effective control of pests, while minimizing the necessary use of potentially dangerous agro-chemicals. Similar yield-enhancing achievements have been made through research on land management practices. The CGIAR has stressed the central importance of water to agriculture and as the biggest single environmental challenge facing the rural poor. The setting up of the International Water Management Institute in Sri Lanka in 1984, which joined the CGIAR in 1991, was in recognition of the strategic and pivotal roles that water plays throughout its work. But like its work in increasing agricultural productivity sustainably, its work on natural resource management calls for close collaboration with many other organizations with specific competences in this field.

Enhancing national agricultural research systems

The 15 CGIAR international agricultural research centers (Table 4.9) are each legally constituted as an independent, self-governing institution with its own charter, research responsibilities or mandate, and with its own board of trustees, director-general, staff, and budget. Each center functions under legal agreements with its current host country. Together, they function interdependently as members of the CGIAR system.[47] The centers are the full-time research units of the CGIAR. They are the functional and operational scientific core of the CGIAR system. And they are supported by CGIAR's Science Council and the CGIAR secretariat.

Collectively, the centers are responsible for planning, developing, and implementing a research agenda that is approved and funded by the CGIAR, as well as for producing the research results sought by the CGIAR system and partners. The centers have formed an "Alliance of the CGIAR Centers" to enable them to contribute more effectively and efficiently to the CGIAR's mission by cooperating and pooling their resources whenever and wherever needed. Over 75,000 developing country scientists have received training at the CGIAR centers. The centers are financed primarily through annual grants from CGIAR members who contribute to the centers or research programs of their choice. Increasingly, members have restricted their funding to particular centers or programs. In 2006, 58 percent of total funding was restricted, affecting the work of some centers more than others. All centers operate primarily in a centralized mode, with regional outposts,

158 *Policies, programs, and projects*

bearing key responsibilities, and closely involved with research networks and consortia. The CGIAR encourages inter-center collaboration and partnerships with other agencies, including the national agricultural research system of the countries in which they are located. The CGIAR is committed to enhancing national agricultural research systems through joint research, policy support, training, and knowledge sharing. The CGIAR center, the International Service for National Agricultural Research (ISNAR), set up in 1980 for this purpose, was absorbed into IFPRI in 2004. To understand more the needs of the national agricultural research systems and their capacities to conduct research, the CGIAR Science Council commissioned a series of four evaluations by developing country authors in Brazil, Colombia, India, and Kenya. Several issues were highlighted. First, despite the major contributions of national research institutions to CGIAR's successes, the limited credit awarded to them weakened the mutual trust needed to sustain that outcome and detracted from the identification and prioritizing of their needs. Second, the CGIAR was not keeping pace with the global challenges facing the national research systems in such matters as modern biotechnology, intellectual property rights, private sector growth, trade liberalization and the impact of non-tariff barriers, and agricultural subsidies in industrialized countries, to which should now be added climate change. Third, the donor community had funded more activities at the regional, national, and local levels that appeased their constituencies, causing the CGIAR and its centers to pursue research and activities more appropriately carried out by national research systems through increasingly restricted and tied contributions. And, fourth, the CGIAR centers reported that they were becoming a conduit for donor funding to national research systems to avoid the many difficulties of funding them directly.

There is a fundamental difference in the CGIAR's roles in small and large developing countries. In small countries, the CGIAR plays a crucial role in the development and strengthening of their national agricultural research systems. The CGIAR centers facilitate links with the international scientific community and access to the results of the latest agricultural research. They provide access to germplasm for crop improvement programs, offer invaluable research inputs and expertise, and generally stimulate an active national research program through training and encouragement. The downside is that the CGIAR centers may offer an excuse to national government to invest less in their own national research programs, forcing the CGIAR centers to bring their resources to bear on national agricultural development issues, and diverting their efforts at institution building. Another problem relates

Policies, programs, and projects 159

to a teacher–student relationship that has built up between some CGIAR centers and national research institutions, which could stifle development and initiative, and the creation of a genuine partnership. Concern has also been expressed over the quality of research carried out by national institutions, leading donors to turn to the CGIAR centers even when the research concerned is mostly of a national nature.

The CGIAR, and its co-sponsors FAO, IFAD, UNDP, and the World Bank in particular, are consciously aware of the importance of capacity-building in the national agricultural research institutions for agricultural development in the long term. The co-sponsors have their own largely uncoordinated programs of capacity-building. For the short term, the national institutions are also important in helping to see to it that the work of the CGIAR centers finds expression on the ground in national implementation programs. It is essential that the national institutions have a forum to express their views and concerns, and bring their problems to the CGIAR for solution.

The relationship between the CGIAR and the larger and more advanced developing countries, with considerable and well-established national agricultural systems, is very different but has not been fundamentally addressed. Clearly, the CGIAR cannot undertake the task of developing capacity in national research systems in all developing countries, nor should it be expected to do so. What it can do, however, is to use its unique status to address the special needs of the small developing county national research systems and encourage collaboration from the larger developing countries in a global network that could better address regional and global concerns. This may be addressed in the CGIAR evaluation of training and capacity-building that is now being undertaken.

Germplasm improvement

The importance of germplasm improvement was exemplified in the CGIAR's lauded and well-known achievement, the introduction of improved cereal varieties and complementary resource management techniques during the Green Revolution. The increase in cereal production through a doubling of rice and wheat yields in Asia and Latin America, a doubling of rice and wheat production in Asia, and similar gains in Latin America, demonstrated the contribution of enhanced germplasm to agricultural productivity, land savings, and poverty reduction.

The decline in funding for this research is counterintuitive, given its well-documented impacts. Impact studies provide convincing evidence

160 *Policies, programs, and projects*

that breeding research, mostly on conventional crops, of the CGIAR centers, together with follow-up work with national agricultural research systems, generates returns ranging from 40 to 78 percent, well above the return attainable for many alternative uses of public funds. Important progress has also been made in improving the yields of the staple and emergency crops sorghum, millet, and cassava, not readily amenable to productivity enhancement because of the marginal agroclimatic environments in which they are grown. New technologies have been generated and their adoption by poor people is said to be considerable, even in sub-Saharan Africa where successes have been more limited. There have also been cases of high estimated rates of return to research on maize (corn), wheat, and other crops in Africa.

The strategic allocation of scientific efforts in germplasm research is especially important for the CGIAR and public research programs throughout the developing world, given the huge incidence of rural poverty and the contribution of agricultural productivity to poverty reduction. The rural poor occupy both resource-rich and poor land. As the experience of the Green Revolution showed, farmers on better endowed land have benefited more from research than those on poor land. These benefits accrue primarily from increased productivity and lower food prices, but flow unevenly when poorer households are unable to adopt new technologies. Research also takes longer to produce benefits in resource-poor areas.

Reduced food prices resulting from increased productivity provide an opportunity to shift resources from food to non-food production, leading to wider economic development and benefits. Studies suggest that productivity gains resulting from germplasm improvement has also had a beneficial environmental impact through land savings. The area needed to cultivate food in developing countries for a rapidly growing population has been reduced, with estimates ranging between 2.6 and 3.6 billion hectares of crop and pasture land since the 1960s. A CGIAR study estimated land savings in Asia, Africa and Latin America attributable to all Green Revolution research at 426 million hectares. But studies also suggest that not all germplasm improvement research results in land savings. In land-surplus, labor-short economies, the introduction of new agricultural technology will likely lead to increased land clearing. In addition, liberalization of trade and investment is likely to provide additional incentives to clear land for agriculture and for timber, as in the Amazon region of Brazil and the outer islands of Indonesia.

Another concern of growing significance is evidence of a slowdown in yield growth from germplasm improvement. This has been

Policies, programs, and projects 161

attributed to several factors, including: environmental degradation caused by decaying irrigation infrastructure; falling groundwater tables and increasing salinity; micronutrient depletion; and low-level pest build-up. Resource degradation, often associated with productivity growth, can be alleviated through research pointing to the need to establish links between germplasm improvement and the improved management of natural resources to achieve sustainable, high-productivity production systems. In addition, breeding to improve the nutrient content of staple crops is an area with both past successes and future potential for the CGIAR.

Germplasm collection and conservation

Genetic resources lie at the heart of the CGIAR system. The CGIAR established a Genetic Resources Policy Committee in 1994 to advise it on genetic resources policy and assist the CGIAR chair in dealing with genetic resources issues. Until 2008, the CGIAR held the largest single collection of plant genetic material, comprising 650,000 accessions (about 10 percent of the world's collection) at 11 CGIAR centers. In October 2006, these centers signed agreements under the International Treaty on Plant Genetic Resources for Food and Agriculture for policy guidance relating to their collections, guaranteeing their protection and use under United Nations/FAO auspices. These genetic resources are an essential input to complementary research carried out by national agricultural research systems throughout the developing world. They have played an important, but largely unrecognized and unknown, role in agricultural reconstruction in countries afflicted by natural and man-made disasters.[48]

These collections make a significant contribution to preserving the world's biodiversity for use by present and future generations. They have the attributes of a pure public good with almost unlimited potential for producing large global economic benefits. The outstanding contribution of the CGIAR pioneers was to crossbreed indigenous genetic material resistant to pests and diseases with higher-yielding varieties to develop more productive plants and, more recently, animals. Successes led to a collection of valuable material from a wide range of developing countries to support further breeding efforts.

Yet the CGIAR faces many challenges in the continued maintenance and use of these genetic resources. The CGIAR's priorities, governance system and financial prospects limit its ability to effectively manage and use its vast collection. At the end of 2006, the CGIAR's work in

162 Policies, programs, and projects

biodiversity was carried out by 69 internationally recruited and 179 other staff. CGIAR funding since the system became operational in 1972 had reach $391 million but showed a reduction from $35.6 million in 2005 to $31.2 million in 2006. Over half (51 percent) of the funding provided was restricted by donors for use in areas of their choosing. At the same time, rapidly changing market, institutional, and technological conditions in which the CGIAR operates require dynamic responses and interactions

The CGIAR's genetic resources still represent a strategically important input for increasing agricultural productivity and reducing poverty, two elements that are central to its mission, but serious internal and external problems impede their effective management and use. The question of the funding of the gene banks has been raised, and whether it is adequate to avoid deterioration and loss of precious material. There are competing demands from CGIAR centers for financing genetic resource management relating to the full range of genetic material relating to crops, livestock, aquaculture, and forestry. Donor interest in genetic resource management is limited and may even be falling, despite its vital importance. While they have been willing to fund physical structures for gene banks, donors have expected the CGIAR centers concerned to fund the recurrent costs through unrestricted contributions that have been declining in recent years. And as restricted contributions have increased, donors have given higher priority to other elements in the increasing spectrum of the CGIAR mandate, such as policy and natural resource management, at the cost of gene bank operations.

As in other fields, and as external assistance has fallen, donors seem to favor increasingly the funding of final-product technologies that produce immediate and tangible results that can be communicated to their constituencies, rather than longer-term activities that take more time to deliver a product, no matter how vitally important it might be. Allocation of responsibility for genetic resource management is an additional issue. The management of genetic resources collections is governed by a standard agreement between FAO and each of the 11 CGIAR centers that hold genetic material. The CGIAR system-wide Genetic Resources Programme (SGRP) is charged with assisting the CGIAR centers in fulfilling their obligations under the agreement with FAO, but has no independent authority.

The CGIAR also faces external constraints that affect the management and use of its genetic resources. Among them are the number of, and increasingly complex international agreements on, genetic resources; the difficulty of mobilizing and maintaining international support

Policies, programs, and projects 163

and funding for long-term genetic resource conservation; and the need to ensure access to its collection by the national agricultural research systems. A Global Conservation Trust was initiated with the endorsement of the CGIAR, FAO, and the World Bank in 2000, with an initial target of $260 million to sustain a global system of gene banks, including those of the CGIAR centers, but the long-term prospects for such a system are unclear. Informed sources suggest that $400 million to $500 million may be required to maintain the proposed global system of gene banks. An IFPRI study of the cost of conserving and distributing the current holdings of the 11 CGIAR center gene banks in perpetuity estimated a required endowment of $149 million, although variations in interest rates and regeneration cycles of genetic material could cause this estimate to range from $100 to $175 million.

An additional concern relates to the CGIAR's policies and strategies for meeting the needs of developing country national agricultural research systems for genetic resources. A related issue is whether these national systems should have their own germplasm collections and how they might be funded and related to the CGIAR collection. The World Bank and some bilateral donors have supported the operations of some national-level gene banks, but others have argued that the maintenance of international collections inadvertently reduces the incentive for developing countries to save their own biodiversity and undertake their own breeding programs, leaving such work to the CGIAR.

The rapidly changing market, institutional, and technological context in which the CGIAR operates presents other challenges. Breakthroughs in genetics and genetic engineering that have led to a new round of biological innovation in agriculture, the increasing importance of proprietary knowledge, intellectual property rights in agricultural research, and the rapid growth of the private sector, especially the large multinational agricultural corporations, in agricultural inputs, markets, and agricultural research and development, represent critical opportunities and challenges for the CGIAR. The CGIAR has agreed to give increasing importance to engaging with the private sector at its annual general meeting in 2007. This can have especial importance for future germplasm research and the future management and maintenance of genetic resources, and adequate and sustainable funding arrangements based on the principles of universal access and multilateral ownership.

In a dramatic new development in 2008, over 200,000 crop varieties from Asia, Africa, Latin America, and the Middle East were shipped to a remote island near the Arctic Circle, where they will be stored in the Svalbard Global Seed vault, a facility capable of preserving their vitality for thousands of years. The vault, which opened in February 2008, was build by the Norwegian government as a service to the global community. Its operation is funded by the Rome-based international NGO, the Global Crop Diversity Trust.

Policy research

While IFPRI is the CGIAR's premier policy research body, other CGIAR centers also carry out substantial policy research. Commodity centers conduct policy research related to the crops on which they concentrate. The CGIAR Science Council brief of 2006 noted that policy-oriented research occupied a large and growing portion of the CGIAR's portfolio, from less than $30 million (9 percent) in 1995 to $70 million (18 percent) in 2006. Using a more liberal definition based on listings of potential users of policy-related research outputs, the portion could be substantially more. The work of four CGIAR centers, the Center for International Forestry Research, the International Plant Genetic Resources Institute, the International Water Management Research Institute, and the International Food Policy Research Institute, was almost entirely policy-related.

Policy research has grown more rapidly than any other research area in the CGIAR since IFPRI's entry into the system in 1980. In 2007, IFPRI's work was carried out by 89 senior researchers and 182 other staff. CGIAR cumulative funding for IFPRI's policy work reached $384.9 million by the end of 2006. Funding has grown from $26.5 million in 2003 to $44.1 million in 2007, when 72 percent of its funding was restricted by donors to uses of their choice. IFPRI was established in 1975 in recognition of the need for an independent research institute that would deal with the socio-economic aspects of agricultural development. It was also perceived that the policy framework within which individual projects were implemented had an important determining role in their impact.

IFPRI's mission is to provide policy solutions that reduce poverty and end hunger and malnutrition. It focuses on three main activities. First, to identify and analyze alternative international, national, and local policies in support of improved food security and nutrition, especially for low-income countries and poor people, and the sound management of the natural resource base that supports agriculture. Second, to contribute to strengthening the capacity of people and institutions in developing countries. Third, to actively engage in communicating successful policies by making the results of research available to all in a position to apply or use them, and by carrying out

Policies, programs, and projects 165

dialogues with those users to link research to policy action. These three overarching focus areas and nine research themes support the crosscutting themes of "policy, communications and capacity strengthening." Priority is given to benefiting the greatest number of poor people in greatest need in the developing world, with a special focus on vulnerable groups. IFPRI is committed to providing access to global food policy knowledge as an international public good, for which it has established links with academia, and excellence in other institutions.

In the fourth external program and management review of IFPRI of 2006, IFPRI was congratulated by CGIAR's Science Council for its "stellar performance" and for being considered by many to be the "premier institution for food and agriculture policy research."[49] The review found that IFPRI's mission continued to fit centrally into the CGIAR goal of achieving sustainable food security and poverty reduction in developing countries. A number of notable accomplishments had been achieved, including: generating outputs and services of high relevance to developing countries; substantially increasing its publications; successfully integrating its research, capacity strengthening, and outreach; showing exemplary leadership in work with CGIAR centers; providing global leadership in impact assessment methodology for policy research; maintaining a high reputation among its peers and partners; and smoothly managing the absorption of the International Service for National Agricultural Research (ISNAR). The CGIAR had decided to merge ISNAR into IFPRI in 2003. In 2004, IFPRI opened the ISNAR division and located it at the second principal campus of the International Livestock Research Institute (ILRI) in Addis Ababa, Ethiopia.

A major contribution of IFPRI has been to bring a social science dimension and perspective to what formerly was a largely agricultural, science-driven CGIAR. Since its establishment, the institute has produced a large number of seminal studies and reports, which have become essential reference points in the international community. These publications have covered a wide range of concerns and have been grouped into eight broad categories.[50] Projections of the world food situation (covering cereals, livestock, and fish) have been made by moving from trends and variability analysis toward models and scenarios. Development strategies and the role of food and agriculture have been analyzed, ranging from growth linkages to institutions and economy-wide policy analysis. Markets and trade have been a special focus, involving international commodities and trade policy and the analysis of domestic and regional markets. As a CGIAR center, special consideration has been given to increasing agricultural production and productivity, involving an assessment of the Green Revolution and broader technology policy research. Given the increasing concern with managing natural resources sustainably, land and water issues have been examined as well as institutional innovations. Ensuring poor households' access to food has been analyzed, from subsidies to safety nets and insurance. And nutrition and health concerns have been examined, from intra-household processes to HIV/AIDS and nutrition deficiencies.

In its endeavor to show the impact of policy on achieving sustainable solutions for ending hunger and poverty, IFPRI has made available 27 of its impact assessment discussion papers along with other related publications.[51] They range from individual developing country studies to broad perspectives, including: an interdisciplinary assessment of new agricultural technologies and their dissemination; the impact of agricultural research on poverty; the impact of policy-oriented social science research; strengthening policy research capacity around the world; food policy and gender issues; food subsidies in developing countries; and school feeding programs.

Among IFPRI's many activities, its 2020 Vision for Food, Agriculture and the Environment, launched in 1995, deserves special mention.[52] This high-profile research and advocacy initiative has played a major role in keeping food and agriculture on the international policy agenda, raised the profile of agriculture among policy-makers, stimulated the development and refinement of global food projections, including IFPRI's IMPACT model, and called attention to the need for increased investment in agricultural development as an essential step toward the reduction of poverty. IFPRI's publications in its 2020 Vision series continue to make contributions toward its realization of the conquest of hunger and malnutrition. A major undertaking in 2004 was an all-Africa conference organized by IFPRI as part of its 2020 Vision program on Assuring Food and Nutrition Security in Africa by 2020: Prioritizing Actions, Strengthening Actors, and Financing Partnerships.[53] To assure its relevance, impact, and follow-up, the conference, which was held in Kampala, Uganda, was designed in close consultation with key partners in Africa. Another major undertaking in 2007 was a conference organized by IFPRI, again as part of its 2020 Vision program, on Taking Action for the World's Poor and Hungry People, which was held in Beijing, China.[54]

In 2003, IFPRI embarked on a program of greater decentralization of its operations through the establishment of offices in Addis Ababa, Ethiopia, New Delhi, India, and San Jose, Costa Rica. The objective is to bring its work closer to the people whom IFPRI researchers study and serve and with whom they collaborate. The fourth review noted that there could be tradeoffs between strong sets of research teams at IFPRI headquarters in Washington, D.C., and greater staff distribution by region. It also suggested that there was need to examine what the optimal discipline mix should be for research on approved themes. In addition, priorities and operational strategies should be established for carrying out IFPRI's far-reaching research agenda, given that there are also heavy and increasing demands for its services by other organizations, resulting in its research staff spending increasing time on indirect activities related to their work.

IFPRI's director-general, Joachim von Braun, is committed to adhering to the institute's comparative advantage, which lies in its ability to respond to demands for high-quality research, to apply lessons leaned in one part of the world to others, to provide international public goods, to offer a wide set of skills, and to remain an independent voice as part of a larger policy research community. As he puts it: "Our goals are to remain a trusted global research center that provides the knowledge needed for food and nutrition policy serving poor people and to be a source of in-depth analysis."

An external review of the ISNAR division in 2007 found that funding had declined from $3.4 million in 2004 to $2.1 million in 2007, with restricted funding at about 30 percent of the total budget.[55] Its work was conducted with continuity by six internationally recruited researchers and consisted of four programs: agricultural science and technology policy; institutional change in agricultural innovation systems; the organization and management of agricultural research; and learning and capacity strengthening to alleviate poverty. The review recommended the recruitment of additional high-caliber senior researchers and the secondment of more IFPRI senior staff to the division. Greater incentive should be given to encourage staff to undertake capacity-strengthening research and outreach. There had been some successes in capacity-strengthening, especially in sub-Saharan Africa, which had been greatly appreciated by its clients. There would be increasing demand, but a better balance was required in the region, with greater emphasis on francophone Africa. The focus should be shifted from the provision of services to undertaking research for which a larger network of collaborating institutions, researchers, and users had been established.

The merger of ISNAR into IFPRI posed many strategic, tactical, and operational questions. Among them were the tradeoffs between service provision and research, the relevance of ISNAR's research to the generation of international public goods, the definition of its niche and its comparative and competitive advantages within the CGIAR system, and the impact of its research and services on capacity-strengthening. The division's primary focus has shifted from national agricultural research systems to a broader focus on agricultural innovative systems, from services to research in the service–research continuum, and to sub-regional and regional organizations.

A major CGIAR system-wide initiative, which is still evolving, is the Global Open Food and Agricultural University (GO-FAU).[56] The objective is to support and facilitate university teaching in agriculture and related disciplines in the developing world. The initiative, which was launched in 2004, plans to provide training and course modules for African and Asian universities, which will take the lead in selecting and designing courses, supporting students, providing accreditation, and awarding degrees. Concern has been expressed whether IFPRI and its ISNAR division have the comparative advantage to manage the GO-FAU initiative. IFPRI's response is that in the long run, some of the high-quality postgraduates will become research collaborators with IFPRI and other CGIAR centers, resulting in more relevant, sustainable agricultural and policy research in the future. ISNAR's role has been redefined as one of coordinator and manager of a developing country universities-driven program.

GO-FAU is a program with considerable potential that presents major challenges. Distance learning is a complex process and is still in its infancy, especially in Africa. Financial sustainability would need to be assured for the universities involved and the GO-FAU secretariat. An International Program Advisory Committee for GO-FAU has been established to monitor and review its progress. The returns from relatively modest funding are considered to be "immense." The targets are that by the end of 2010, five master's programs will be in place, over 30 universities in Africa, Asia, and Latin America will be involved, over 5,000 students, at least half of whom will be women, will have passed through the system, and over 500 students would be carrying out postgraduate research studies with the assistance of CGIAR staff and facilities. The Gates Foundation has requested the CGIAR secretariat to prepare a comprehensive proposal for the next five years to implement this initiative with the participation of all CGIAR centers.

The Global Challenge Programs

The Challenge Program (CP) concept was developed as part of the CGIAR's reform program to bring about a programmatic approach to take on global challenges in cooperation with a wider range of partners. The CGIAR agreed to adopt a flexible and learning-by-doing approach to developing CPs. The formal process of selecting a CP involves three steps: a concept note, a pre-proposal, and a full proposal. The CGIAR has used its unique position to stimulate and encourage the international research community to join forces to implement programs of critical global importance. This "challenge program" concept is a time-bound, independently governed program of high-impact research. It targets the CGIAR goals in relation to complex issues of overwhelmingly global or regional significance that require partnerships among a wide range of institution. Four programs in this category are currently being implemented (Table 4.9).

The Water and Food Challenge Program

This is an international, multi-institutional research initiative focused on growing more food with less water. Water scarcity is one of the most pressing problems facing humanity. The goal is to increase the productivity of water for agriculture, leaving more water for other users and the environment. Typically, the most extreme shortages are experienced by those least able to cope, the most impoverished inhabitants of developing countries. The initiative brings together research scientists, development specialists, and river basin communities in Africa, Asia, and Latin America and disseminates international public goods that improve the productivity of water in ways that are pro-poor, gender-equitable and environmentally sustainable and contribute to achieving food security, poverty alleviation, improved health and farming systems, and environmental security.

Table 4.9 Investments in the CGIAR Challenge Programs (U.S.$ millions)

Challenge Program	2003	2004	2005	2006
Water and food	5.0	5.8	10.5	10.5
Generation Challenge	0.8	6.5	12.1	14.6
HarvestPlus	2.0	6.9	9.9	11.6
Sub-Saharan Africa	0.0	0.4	2.4	3.0
Total	7.8	19.6	34.9	39.7
% of total CGIAR funding	2	4	8	9

Source: CGIAR secretariat.

170 *Policies, programs, and projects*

The Generation Challenge Program (GCP)

The GCP uses advances in molecular biology and harnesses the global stock of crop genetic resources to create and provide a new generation of plants that farmers' need. Farmers in the developing world have limited access to improved crop varieties, irrigation, fertilizers, and pesticides. Access to improved plants is regarded as a critical "tipping point" between healthy and hungry families. The GCP aims to bridge the gap by creating and providing a new generation of plants that meet farmers' needs. Its vision is a future in which plant breeders have the tools to breed crops in marginal and resource-poor environments with greater efficiency and accuracy for the benefit of poor farmers.

HarvestPlus

This is an international, interdisciplinary research program that seeks to reduce micronutrient malnutrition by harnessing agricultural and nutritional research to breeding nutrient-rich staple foods. More than half the world's population, mostly the poor in developing countries, suffer from the consequences of micronutrient deficiencies, such as in Vitamin A, zinc, and iron that are required in very small amounts but are essential to good health. This program is a global alliance of institutions and scientists seeking to improve human nutrition by breeding new varieties of the staple food crops that are consumed by the poor that have a higher level of micronutrients through a process known as "biofortification."

Sub-Saharan Africa Challenge Program

This program addresses significant constraints to reviving agriculture in Africa, including the failure of markets, inappropriate policies, and the degradation of natural resources, through an Integrated Agricultural Research for Development initiative. The objectives are to: develop technologies for sustainably intensifying subsistence; develop smallholder production systems that are compatible with sound natural resource management; improve the accessibility and efficiency of markets for smallholders and pastoralists; and formulate and adopt policies that will encourage innovation to improve the livelihoods of smallholders and pastoralists.

Conclusions

Even in this condensed and highly summarized form, this chapter has shown the considerable scope and dimensions of the policies,

Policies, programs, and projects 171

programs, and projects undertaken by each of the global food and agricultural institutions. While most of the work carried out has reflected to the mandates and missions of each institution, there have been overlapping concerns and activities, reflecting areas in which closer cooperation between them could yield significant results. These possibilities will be considered in the next chapter.

5 Future directions

This final chapter looks to the future directions that the global food and agricultural institutions described in this book might take. They were founded between 30 and 60 years ago. In the meantime, many significant changes have taken place in the world in which they operate. It is understandable, therefore, that questions are increasing being asked about their continuing relevance, and the need for reform, to face the challenges of the twenty-first century. Independent external evaluations have been undertaken of three of the institutions (FAO, IFAD, and the CGIAR). A major joint evaluation of WFP was carried out by three of its prominent donor countries in the early 1990s. While no independent external evaluation has taken place of the World Bank, a large number of views have been expressed about the future directions it should take, increasingly in recent years. These evaluations and views provide rich material for identifying the problems now faced by these institutions, the future directions they might take, and how they might cooperate in the future.

Evaluations, views and opinions

FAO

Independent external evaluation

The first, and only, independent external evaluation of FAO in its 60-year history was completed in 2007.[1] Only some of its main highlights can be given here. Its principal conclusion was the need for "reform with growth." FAO was in a "financial and programme crisis" that "imperils its future in delivering essential service to the world." If FAO disappeared, "much of it would have to be re-invented but with much more precise priorities and a concentration of its efforts in areas of demonstrable need, which corresponded to its comparative advantage." The world needed a renewed FAO. The challenge was to move forward on reform with growth before further decline inflicted irreversible damage on FAO. The evaluation report made 109 separate recommendations in its over 400 pages, aimed at "transformational change" over three to four years through an action plan to secure FAO's future.

A major concern was that the many activities that FAO carried out lacked a broad strategy, fragmenting its efforts, reducing their impact, and undermining confidence and financial support. FAO had been challenged over the past six decades to respond to ever increasing changes in the world context in which it worked, and to an array of new demands. Its original focus on increasing food production had been expanded to include wider concerns, such as food security, poverty reduction, rural development, international codes and standards, intellectual property rights, and a range of issues relating to the environment, including conservation, climate change, and sustainable management of natural resources. The promise of the Green Revolution had faltered, leading to a call for a new and "doubly green revolution." At the same time, new organizations and institutions had been created, which impinged on FAO's mandate and constitution. Strategic choices had, therefore, to be made and efforts concentrated in areas that benefited from FAO's comparative advantage.

Changes in the governance, structure, and management of the organization were required. FAO's overall governance by member countries was "failing the organization," the main factor being the "low level of mutual trust and understanding" within the membership and between some parts of the membership and the secretariat. FAO had a "heavy and costly" bureaucracy. Its management was highly centralized and risk-averse. The election of the present and previous directors-general for periods of 18 years each was "clearly not in the best long-term interest of FAO." Staff initiatives were not encouraged. Relations between FAO headquarters and its field operations were severely fragmented, and the current aim of decentralization "was not working well."

The evaluation noted that despite the steady decline in its resources, FAO continued to provide many valuable technical inputs. It recommended that the three goals of FAO's *Strategic Framework 2000–2015*: (1) reduction of the number of hungry people by half by 2015; (2) the continued contribution of sustainable agricultural and rural development to economic and social progress and the well-being of all; and (3) the conservation, improvement, and sustainable utilization of natural resources for food and agriculture; should provide the ultimate goals for the organization. One of FAO's greatest potential strengths was its capacity for cross-cutting integrated approaches, as shown in its integrated pest management program. But FAO was insufficiently focused and its impact was often not visible because it worked on relatively small projects. Partnerships should be formed with selected developing countries and donors for concentrated attention to programs of major priority to the developing countries concerned.

One of FAO's principle tasks was to ensure that the world's knowledge of food and agriculture was available to everyone. This required balancing interests between knowledge generated, often in the private domain, and knowledge availability in the public domain, especially for the least developed countries. FAO's work in emergencies deserved priority, for which an overall strategy should be formulated for those emergency functions in which FAO was strong. Increasing proportions of FAO resources should go to forestry, fisheries, and livestock. Crop production expertise in plant nutrition, especially important for sub-Saharan Africa, and small-scale urban and peri-urban horticulture for supplementing income and nutrition, should be retained. FAO should continue its lead role in water databases and agricultural water management, focusing on multidisciplinary approaches. Policy support should be strengthened and a capacity-building strategy developed following an assessment of needs. Collaboration and partnerships with other UN bodies, especially the three UN organizations based in Rome, and with NGOs and civil society organizations, should be pursued.

The evaluation represents a major milestone in FAO's history. In their "in principle" response, FAO's management agreed with most of the evaluation's recommendations as well as its major findings and the broad thrust of the report. FAO's director-general is committed to leading a process of transformation. Arrangements have been put in place in FAO's governing bodies to discuss and reach agreement on the steps to be taken to implement the evaluation's recommendations.

World Bank

Although an independent external evaluation of the World Bank has not been undertaken, there is no shortage of views and opinions on its future.[2] Increasingly, calls have been made by many, including former senior bank staff, for major reforms in the ways in which the bank is managed and operated.[3] Others have been more hostile, suggesting that the bank has outlived its usefulness.[4]

Proposals for change

The appointment and abrupt departure of the bank's last president, Paul Wolfowitz (2005–7), exacerbated the call for change. On his appointment, a working group of the Washington, D.C.-based think-tank, Center for Global Development (CGD), under its president, Nancy Birdsall, a previous director of the bank's Research Department, presented him with a report entitled *The Hardest Job in the World: Five Crucial Tasks for the New President of the World Bank*.[5]

The report did not focus on internal management issues, including the way in which the president is appointed, which led to Wolfowitz's dramatic departure, but on "structural changes in its mandate, instruments, pricing and governance" that were considered to be "critical to a revitalized Bank." The five "crucial tasks" were: (1) revitalizing the bank's role in China, India, and the middle-income countries; (2) bringing new discipline and greater differentiation to low-income country operations; (3) taking the lead in ensuring truly independent evaluation of the impact of the bank and other aid-supported programs; (4) obtaining an explicit mandate, an adequate grant instrument, and a special governance arrangement for the bank's work on global public goods; and (5) pushing the member governments to make the bank's governance more representative, and thus more legitimate and democratic.

The report acknowledged that conflicting demands on the bank and its president from many quarters made it impossible to satisfy all constituencies. It identified the biggest challenge, in the words of the bank's motto, to "work for a world free of poverty," and to provide global leadership in the fight against poverty. To do this, the bank should concentrate more on supporting effective local economic and political institutions, strengthen its role as a "knowledge bank" with over 60 years of experience, and transform itself from a development agency of contributors and beneficiaries, in which the former had the upper hand, into an organization in which developing as well as developed countries would have a keen sense of ownership and financial responsibility.

The bank should continue to be active in middle-income countries and in emerging developing countries such as China and India. Its lending operations should support policy reforms and development results, reformers within government, and strengthen democratic institutions in emerging market economies. Major changes were needed in the bank's operations if it was to be effective and relevant in middle-income countries. At the same time, the bank should take more of a lead in helping donors discriminate across low-income countries and

176 *Future directions*

formalize a third, fully grant-based, window for countries with very low per capita incomes. Longer-term commitments should be made to the best performing countries. And the bank and IMF should cooperate in making IDA countries eligible for automatic additional transfers in the event of external shocks caused by sudden weather, price or market changes.

Fully independent evaluations would improve the credibility of the bank-supported programs. The bank's president should take the lead in creating an external, independent, multi-donor aid evaluation mechanism. Regarding the bank's work on global public goods, the report suggested that an explicit mandate, an adequate grant instrument, and a special governance structure, should be obtained. No issue fundamentally undermined the legitimacy and effectiveness of the bank, however, as much as its governance structure. These factors were undermined by the continuing lack of involvement and influence of its borrowers, the developing countries.

These "crucial tasks" and their implication, while wide-ranging, have by no means been the only criticisms of the bank, and many proposals have been made for its reform. The majority report of the International Financial Institutions Advisory Commission, mandated by the U.S. Congress in 2000, recommended that the bank become a "world development agency," stop lending to emerging market economies and middle-income countries with ready access to private capital markets, and move from lending to providing grants for small technical-assistance programs targeted on the poorer countries. Reducing the number of borrower countries would sharpen the bank's operations, but this should be taken further by reducing the sectors for which the bank would provide assistance, thereby supporting fewer but larger assistance programs in a smaller recipient base.[6]

Long-term strategy exercise

In 2007, the World Bank published a paper on "Laying the ground for a long-term strategy for the World Bank Group" as part of its "Long-term strategic exercise."[7] The exercise was conducted by a team of bank staff drawn from across the institution. It was guided by the bank's chief economist and senor vice-president, Francois Bourguignon, who held a series of informal consultations around the world on the future strategy of the World Bank. The purpose of the exercise was to lay the groundwork for selecting a strategy that would enhance the developmental value of the World Bank Group over the next decade and beyond. Four focus areas were proposed for the bank in the future: sub-Saharan Africa, fragile states, social inclusiveness in middle-income countries, and global public goods. This meant, in practical terms, going beyond the status quo by: strengthening IDA and leveraging IDA's funds and capacities; making IBRD services more flexible and attractive; moving towards a "global public good bank"; capitalizing on the bank's coordination and knowledge management skills; enhancing research, data analysis, and knowledge management; and strengthening evaluation.

The paper noted that despite progress, "the end of poverty is not imminent." The number of people in extreme poverty was projected to decline by a quarter by 2015, concentrated in sub-Saharan Africa and South Asia. By 2015, some 720 million people would continue to subsist in extreme poverty on less than $1 a day. Deep poverty, at $2 a day, would remain widespread, with numbers staying close to 2 billion people. The paper stressed that the international development community must ensure that global development proceeded equitably. Development assistance was being shaped by an increasingly complex aid architecture (it was estimated that 280 international organizations and institutions competed directly or indirectly with each other for donor resources) in which donations from the private sector, including considerable funding from private foundations, were now greater than ODA. Historically, low borrowing costs were likely to continue, although many countries could not access global financial markets. While much had been learned about how development works, there remained a big gap on governance and institutions that stood out as priority areas for research. In sum, the services provided by the four constituent parts of the World Bank Group fell into three categories: finance, knowledge, and coordination. On finance, trust funds now amounted to about half the value of IDA disbursements, bank disbursements had fallen, and capital was under-utilized. Knowledge remained to be better disseminated and used, and coordination strengthened.

The results of discussions on the fifteenth replenishment of IDA (2008-11) in December 2007 were encouraging. They resulted in a historical record of $41.6 billion, an increase of $9.5 billion over the previous replenishment, at a time when many aid organizations faced financial difficulties, and signaling support for the new bank president. What seems to be emerging from the plethora of advice and opinion about the future direction of the bank was a very different development institution, more decentralized, better prepared to cooperate with other organizations and institutions, strong on social justice and social inclusion, better governed and more accountable, more efficient in

178 *Future directions*

using its unique knowledge and better disseminating it, prepared to integrate public and private funding through a closer working of the bank's constituent parts, and fully committed to working with others in programs of global and regional public goods that would be more effective in meeting the challenges of an increasingly globalizing world.

Part of the problem is that discussion has been focused on the bank rather than on how best to solve the world's problems, particularly those of the poorest countries and people, and then refashioning the bank accordingly. The international economic and social architecture established after the Second World War is now buckling under the weight of globalization, trade disputes, international terrorism, and violations of human rights. And institutional incoherence remains, arising from the multitude of aid organizations continuing to work in isolation, even competition, when solutions call for common and cohesive policies and programs (see below). This has led to radical calls for the existing aid architecture to be wrapped up, closed down, and re-emerged in a different form.

The bank is the self-appointed standard bearer in the fight against poverty yet, by its own calculations, the number of people in abject poverty is just under 1 billion, with another 2.5 billion subsisting on $2 a day. Bank statistics show that the overwhelming number of poor people live in rural areas, and depend on agriculture for their survival. Yet, its assistance for agricultural development has declined to less that 8 percent of total IBRD/IDA lending. Its assistance to the poorest countries in 2006 amounted to only about 7 percent of total aid from all sources as larger amounts are made available through the private sector. The bank's cumulative lending to China is about $40 billion for some 270 projects, while China has become an exporting superpower, sitting on reserves worth more than $1 trillion, and has its own aid program to African countries of $210 billion. Major reforms are necessary both within the bank and in its relationships with other UN bodies and aid agencies. Will the appointment of a new president lead to the reforms that are long overdue, or will the World Bank sink back into its old, outmoded, and, given the major changes that have taken place in the world since its creation, now inappropriate ways?

New bank president's initial impressions and ideas

At the end of his first 100 days in office, the new bank president, Robert B. Zoellick, who had previously served as the United States trade representative, gave his initial impressions and ideas for the bank's strategic future directions in an address at the National Press

Club in Washington, D.C. in October 2007.[8] He acknowledged that after 60 years of operation, the bank "must adapt to vastly different circumstances in a new era of globalization." He identified six strategic themes for the bank in support of the goal of an inclusive and sustainable globalization:

- First, the challenge of helping to overcome poverty and spur sustainable growth in the world's poorest countries, especially in Africa, focused "intensively with our partners" on achieving the MDGs.
- Second, the special problems of states coming out of conflict or seeking to avoid breakdown.
- Third, a more differentiated business model for middle-income countries.
- Fourth, a more active role in fostering regional and global public goods that transcend national boundaries and benefit multiple countries and people.
- Fifth, to support those seeking to advance development and opportunities in the Arab world.
- And finally, to better use its knowledge and learning of applied experience to address the five strategic themes above. This last challenge required humility and intellectual honesty, recognizing that "many development schemes and dreams have failed." This was not a reason to quit trying but to focus on results and on the assessment of effectiveness. "This was the best way to earn the confidence and support of our shareholder, stakeholders, and development clients and partners."

In pursuing these themes, the new bank president said that the World Bank Group "must also squarely face its own internal challenges," use its capital more effectively, focus more on client services, and strengthen ties with civil society organizations and NGOs, and learn from them. Reflecting on the new aid architecture, the bank needed to work more effectively with national aid programs, funds focused on particular projects, such as diseases, foundations, NGOs in the field, and private businesses. Bank staff should be assisted with better professional development and improved mobility within the institution, and stronger human resource policies to support its field staff as greater decentralization was encouraged. The bank could offer leadership by integrating good governance and rule of law policies into the development agenda and move toward operational improvements, recognizing the importance of its governance and anti-corruption agenda.

180 *Future directions*

The new bank president followed up his October 2007 address with a speech at the Center for Global Development in Washington, D.C. on 2 April 2008. He highlighted four immediate needs that also offered longer-term opportunities.[9] In the face of soaring food prices, he called for a "new deal for global food policy" that would incorporate a number of initiatives, including: meeting the WFP's call for at least $500 million of additional food supplies to meet current emergencies, and to support WFP's proposal to shift from traditional food aid to a broader concept of food and nutritional assistance (see below); investing more to meet the first MDG, which he called the "forgotten MDG," of reducing the proportion of poor and hungry people by half by 2015, which he thought had the greatest multiplier effect; creating a stronger delivery system to overcome fragmentation, which would intertwine agriculture, water, sanitation, rural infrastructure, and gender policies; increasing food production through a "green revolution" in sub-Saharan Africa that would help smallholders out of poverty, for which the bank would almost double it lending from the current $450 million; and scaling-up the advisory services of the IFC to support agribusinesses. To be successful, he recognized that there would be need to integrate and mobilize a diverse range of partners, including WFP and IFAD, other multilateral development bodies, private donors such as the Gates Foundation, agricultural institutes, developing countries with great agricultural experience, and the private sector. Zoellick linked three other immediate measures to the new deal for global food policy: a "global trade deal" that would break the impasse in the Doha development agenda; devising a "one percent solution" for equity investment in Africa, which would draw on the sovereign wealth funds of emerging developing countries that currently hold about $3 trillion in assets; and reversing the resource curse of developing countries by launching an Extraction Industries Transparency Initiative.

After the turbulent days of his predecessor, although it is still early days, the new president seems to be just what the doctor ordered, very good for staff morale, giving a sense of a return to stability and a strong sense of direction. Among other things, he regularly requests news from his senior management regarding progress in putting the *World Development Report 2008* into operation. His six themes and his four immediate initiatives should gain wide consensus in the development aid community. He has also gained the initial support of the major donor countries, as shown by the record pledges for IDA replenishment. Clearly, the new president is searching for a new constructive role for his institution. He is asking the right questions and identifying the right priorities, but indicates that the bank alone does not have all the answers, resources, or experience.

Global Partnership Programs

A development that could, among other things, give a major boost to the World Bank's work in agricultural and rural development has been the rapid growth in the number and size of global and regional partnership programs. The bank is involved in 125 Global Partnership Programs and 50 Regional Partnership Programs. The bank's Independent Evaluation Group is deeply involved in the evaluation and review of this important and growing line of business. In FY 2007, some $4 billion were spent on these programs, some 5 percent from the bank.

Why are these programs increasing?[10] There is a growing awareness of the need for collaborative action to provide global or international public goods in such areas as: research and development on food crops and diseases of the poor; mitigating the spread of communicable diseases; and mitigating the effects and adapting to global climate change. These programs are developing policy and knowledge networks to facilitate communications, generate and disseminate knowledge, improve donor coordination, and support advocacy. They are providing financial and technical assistance to support national policy and institutional reforms, capacity-strengthening, training, and catalyzing public and private investment. And they are encouraging investments at the country level for national and global public goods and at the global level for global public goods.

These programs contribute to the global governance of, and response to, major development problems. They are characterized by three features. Partners contribute and pool their resources, financial, technical, staff and skills, and reputations, toward achieving agreed objectives over time. The activities of the programs are global, regional or multi-country. And the partners have established new organizations with a governance structure and management unit to implement their activities. Bilateral donors are the principal partners at the governance level. The major donors, participating in the largest number of partnership programs, are Canada, the United Kingdom and the United States. The major foundations contributing to these programs include: Conservation International, Ford, Gates, McArthur, and Rockefeller. The principal international organizations involved in these programs are FAO, IFAD, ILO, OECD, UNDP, UNEP, UNESCO, UNICEF, and WHO.

The three largest programs, accounting for half the total expenditure, are: the Global Fund to Fight AIDS, Tuberculosis and Malaria (GFATM) with $1 billion; the Global Environment Facility (GEF) with $500 million; and the Consultative Group on International Agricultural Research (CGIAR) with $500 million. Some of the other large programs include: the Global Alliance for Vaccination and Immunization (the GAVI Alliance) with $400 million; the Multilateral Fund for the Implementation of the Montreal Protocol (MLF) with $100 million; and the Joint United Nations Program on HIV/AIDS (UNAID) with $100 million.

An evaluation report on the Global Partnership Programs of 2004 showed that selection and oversight was weak, most were donor-driven, and most are advocacy/technical assistance programs supporting national/urban public goods.[11] Global–country linkages and incentives to foster such linkages were weak, leading to the conclusion that "under-managed partnerships pose significant reputational risks for program partners." The key issues to arise from the evaluation were financing, governance and management, ensuring a voice for developing countries, establishing global–country linkages, and establishing appropriate evaluation and feedback mechanisms.

WFP

Donors' comprehensive evaluation (1991–93)

An independent external evaluation of WFP has not been carried out. However, between 1991 and 1993, a comprehensive evaluation was carried out by three of its prominent and consistent donor countries, Canada, the Netherlands, and Norway. WFP staff at headquarters and at selected country offices provided insights, views, and documentation throughout the evaluation process. Opinions and information were also sought from senior officers in other UN organizations and from NGOs. The result was perhaps one of the most detailed assessments of any UN body up until that time.[12]

The evaluation did not produce recommendations but "shared judgements" that might be taken into consideration in discussions and decisions concerning WFP's future. Its findings were not discussed in WFP's governing body. The evaluation found that WFP's performance in providing relief food during emergencies was "impressive." The judgments put forward aimed at incremental improvements rather than radical change. The conclusion was that: "it would be in the interest of all countries, both donor and recipient, to maintain and strengthen

WFP as the principal international organization for handling food relief."

The analysis of WFP's development activities noted some successes but also identified a number of weaknesses. While WFP performed well in the physical movement of food, it was considered to be less successful in the developmental aspects of the projects it supported. Three alternatives were suggested for improving WFP's development performance: reducing the number of countries in which it operated, by concentrating on those with the lowest incomes, and especially those which were disaster-prone; keeping the wide spreads of countries, but limiting activities to a much narrower band of project types in which food aid functioned well; or phasing out all types of development project except for those that were relief-related, such as disaster-preparedness, rehabilitation, and settlement of repatriated refugees. The evaluation concluded:

> A development programme targeted at the poorest people in the poorest countries organized by the UN system, based on bringing food to the hungry, and aimed at long-term impact as well as short-term benefits should surely be maintained by the donors as long as it can be run effectively and efficiently. The WFP membership should be thinking about improving their effectiveness and efficiency, not about winding up the Programme.

Taking relief and development together, the evaluation concluded:

> there is clear value in retaining WFP as a hybrid organization. If relief is accepted as the main focus there is still a strong case for combining—as a minimum development profile—an active programme oriented towards disaster preparedness, mitigation and rehabilitation.

The role of WFP's governing body as a forum for inter-governmental discussion on food aid from all sources, multilateral, bilateral, and NGOs, was considered to be "not impressive." This was partly attributed to the fact that food aid policies were not high on the international agenda. This could change if developed countries implemented agricultural policies that lowered their agricultural production, which led to a decline in food surpluses and a rise in international food prices, and if concern over food security in the poorest countries was more actively pursued.

New mission statement (1994)

The findings of the evaluation were taken in to account when WFP's new mission statement was drawn up and adopted in 1994. The "hybrid" nature of WFP was retained, enabling WFP to be "well-placed" to play a major role in the continuum from emergency relief to development assistance. WFP's core policies and strategies were defined as: saving lives in emergency situations; improving the nutrition and quality of life of the most vulnerable people at critical times in their lives; and building assets and promoting the self-reliance of poor people, particularly through labor-intensive works programs.

At the end of a long-standing debate, which extended over most of the decade of the 1990s, WFP's executive board agreed that WFP would focus its development activities on five objectives. They would be selected and combined in country programs in accordance with the specific circumstances and national strategies of each recipient country.[13] The five objectives were to:

- enable young children and expectant and nursing mothers to meet their special nutritional and nutrition-related health needs;
- enable poor households to invest in human capital through education and training;
- make it possible for poor families to gain and preserve assets;
- mitigate the effects of natural disasters in areas vulnerable to recurring crises; and
- enable households which depend on degraded natural resources for their food security to make a shift to more sustainable livelihoods.

This was based on the perception that food aid had a critical role to play in enabling marginalized, food-insecure people to participate in the board process of development. Food was a form of assistance which met one of the most basic needs of poor families. Food was essential for health, growth, and productivity. Nothing could replace it. The prospect of food security in a few years could not compensate for inadequate nutrition today. Targeted food aid was a fast track to reach the poor. It reached them directly and immediately in a way much other assistance did not, providing help until the benefits of economic growth and increased productivity relieved food insecurity.

WFP undertook to provide its assistance only when and where food consumption was inadequate for good health and productivity. Every WFP development intervention would be targeted on poor, food-insecure households. They would be designed to encourage investment and leave behind physical assets or improved human capital to help households and communities after food aid came to an end. Urban and peri-urban areas with high concentrations of malnutrition as well as food-insure rural areas would be targeted. WFP would endeavor to intervene early, and would explicitly take seasonality into account in areas with wide fluctuations in food security. A greater understanding of beneficiaries' problems would be sought through participatory approaches. And WFP would be proactive in seeking partnerships with other aid organizations, in increasing cost-effectiveness, and in developing new approaches in project design.

Despite these assurances and the approval of WFP's executive board, WFP's involvement in development projects remains an area of controversy, exacerbated by the increase in the size and frequency of natural and man-made emergencies, and growing problems in its resources (see below).

IFAD

Independent external evaluation (2005)

While a rapid external assessment of IFAD was undertaken in 1994, a full independent external evaluation of IFAD was carried out in 2005, two decades after the decision was made to create the new institution (see Chapter 4).[14] The evaluation noted that during that period, major changes had taken place in the global context for agricultural and rural development. Poverty reduction had been reaffirmed by the international community as a central development objective, as expressed in the MDGs, but external assistance for the agricultural sector had plummeted. A much wider set of enabling actions for rural growth and development was favored, accompanied by a sharper focus on partnership and policy performance in support of national poverty reduction strategies. The working environment for development organizations at country level had dramatically changed with the appearance of many donors, aid agencies, and NGOs focusing on poverty reduction as a central theme, often competing rather than cooperating with each other, through a program rather than project approach to development planning.

At the same time, IFAD had expanded it mandate and mission. From a funding institution with a special focus on improving food production, IFAD had broadened its vision as a full-fledged development organization. By combining the roles of an international financing institution and that of a specialized agency of the UN system,

186 Future directions

IFAD looked to "lead global efforts in helping the world's poorest" though innovation, greater policy engagement, partnerships, and scaling-up. Its latest strategic framework charted an increasingly ambitious agenda, emphasizing the fund's catalytic role in "enabling the rural poor to overcome their poverty" through harnessing knowledge gained through innovation, building regional and international coalitions, and helping to establish policies and institutions that focused on the poor helping themselves out of poverty.

A central message to emerge from the evaluation was that while these were noble and essential objectives, the institutional arrangements set up when IFAD was first founded had not been changed concomitantly. Changes were required in the ways in which the fund was governed, organized, and managed, and in how it conducted its business. What was described as the "low-cost, arms-length, individual project format and approach" was ill suited to the new challenges encompassed in IFAD's new and broadened mandate that called for learning and replicating empowerment programs for the rural poor. In its first 20 years, a series of reforms and initiatives had been undertaken, some called for by the fund's executive board, others proposed by senior management, which recognized the need to improve performance. But these had been largely carried out in an ad hoc way without a fundamental recognition of what broadening the fund's mandate and direction implied, and with insufficient regard for its limited capacity in terms of staff and resources.

Against the background of declining resources, and a major restructuring of members' voting rights, the consultative process of replenishing contributions to IFAD had become the major driver of internal policy change. Whereas initially replenishment consultations focused almost exclusively on financial pledges to IFAD, a framework was put in place for monitoring actions to enhance its operations. But the process, together with the increasing emphasis on creating and maintaining partnerships, absorbed considerable staff and management time. It also suggested that a period of consolidation was required to ensure the full impact of the latest initiatives before moving on in a new policy direction.

IFAD's executive board is responsible for executive management of the fund. Meeting three times a year for two days each session, with a crowded agenda and large volumes of written material, often provided at short notice, especially in translated versions, the board's meetings resembled more those of other UN bodies than other international financial institutions. Board members differed in their experience, skills, and training, and there were no terms of reference for the post. These factors reduced the executive board's effectiveness.

Human resources are central to the success of a knowledge-based organization such as IFAD. Management of these resources impacts directly on the organization in achieving its objective. The evaluation found that the number of staff in IFAD's Programme Management Division, the hub of the organization, were too few to develop the processes and skills to conduct its widening mandate, which required it to be an innovator, a knowledge institution, a catalyst, and a leader. Poor human resource management was seen to be a major contributor to the variable performance of IFAD-supported projects. The introduction of a new human resource policy addressed many of these problems, but radical changes were needed in the culture of the organization that required priority attention from senior management.

Innovation and partnership are now the two signature features of IFAD. Partnerships are intended to make IFAD more effective and to support the fund's objectives of being a catalyst and innovator, and to scale-up the benefits of the programs and projects it supports. But uncritical use of the term "partnership," and failure to foster clear objectives and to improve ways of working from the inception of a partnership, led to the evaluation's finding that, with a few notable exceptions, there was no evidence of enhanced impact through partnerships that would bring strategic benefits to the fund, its partners and, especially, to poor rural people. IFAD has been a knowledge organization since it recognized the need to design and implement its own project. As the evaluation recognized, realization that IFAD needed to apply its own experience and skills if projects were to be effective at rural poverty alleviation was an early driver in the shift away from co-financing projects identified, designed, and implemented by other aid organizations, to a predominantly self-identified approach. But this required effective ways of collecting and storing the knowledge acquired, ensuring its use in the formulation and implementation of new projects, and its dissemination to partners and others involved in the reduction of rural poverty. IFAD's broadening and specific mandate provided a "powerful imperative" for the fund to play a central role in demonstrating how different approaches to rural development sustainably reduce poverty and contribute to the achievement of the MDGs.

The evaluation made a number of recommendations arising from its findings. These related to: managing the changes that were considered to be necessary; addressing the causes of the low impact of IFAD-supported projects; developing a new business model for carrying out its functions and responsibilities; adopting "smarter ways" to encourage skills and learning; clarifying IFAD's strategic niche among the galaxy of development organizations; and providing direction for development effectiveness. IFAD's president is committed to implementing the evaluation's recommendations. As was shown in Chapter 4, IFAD has already carried out a series of reform measures under its Action Plan.

CGIAR

The CGIAR has an impressive tradition of self-assessments through external program evaluations, often involving outside consultants, managed by its former Technical Advisory Committee, now its Science Council, and the CGIAR secretariat. Three reviews of the CGIAR system as a whole were undertaken in 1976, 1981, and 1998. A fourth one is underway (see below).

Vision statement for international agricultural research: a doubly green revolution (1994)

In 1994, the CGIAR Oversight Committee commissioned an external panel to develop a "vision statement" for international agricultural research that would lead to sustainable agriculture for a food-secure world.[15] Its report was presented to, and adopted at, a meeting of ministers of overseas development from developed countries and ministers of agricultural resources from developing countries held in Lucerne, Switzerland in February 1995. At the heart of the panel's report was the call for a "doubly green revolution" that would be even more productive than the first Green Revolution and even "greener" in terms of conserving natural resources and the environment. Over the next three decades, it would aim to repeat the successes of the Green Revolution, on a global scale, and in many diverse localities. At the same time, learning from the experiences of implementing the first Green Revolution, it would aim to be equitable, sustainable, and environmentally friendly. The first Green Revolution took as its starting point the biological challenge of producing new high-yielding food crops and then looked to see how the benefits could reach the poor. The new revolution would start with the socio-economic demands of poor households and then identify the appropriate research priorities. The goals would be the creation of food security and sustainable livelihoods for the rural poor.

Success would be achieved through a combination of applying modern science and technology with implementing economic and social reform in innovative and imaginative ways. It would require concerted effort by the world community, in both developed and developing countries, the application of new scientific and technological discoveries in a manner that was environmentally sensitive, and the creation of new partnerships between natural and social scientists that would respond to the needs of the poor. In essence, the new priorities would be: food security, income and employment generation, and the conservation of natural resources and the environment, whose outcome would be the creation of sustainable livelihoods for the poor. Multidisciplinary research teams would need even greater integration, and a wider span of disciplines, than in the past, encompassing both the natural and social sciences.

Two developments were driving changes in biological and agricultural research institutions. First was the emergence of molecular biology and its associated technologies. Second was an ecological approach that in tandem with economics, sociology, and anthropology, rapidly increased an understanding of the structure and dynamics of agro-ecosystems comprising domesticated plants, animals, and the people who husbanded them. What were the implications for the future of the CGIAR? The CGIAR and its centers would need to focus increasingly on new and different partnerships that worked toward well defined outcomes. These would include research institutions, universities, private companies and consortia in the developed countries, and regional and national research institutions, universities, private companies, NGOs, and farmers in developing countries.

A portfolio of programs rather than reliance only on a set of centers should constitute the business prospectus of the CGIAR system and should ultimately be the basis for fund allocation. Three principles—subsidiarity, partnership, and transfer—should apply in defining the CGIAR's specific responsibilities and roles within the international research effort. The CGIAR would contribute to international research activities through regional action programs and global programs that were long-term and center-based, and also include multi-center and collaborative strategic research. The collective responsibility would be to eradicate hunger in ways that protected the environment. The new mandate would assure food security for all through agricultural research that not only added to food production but generated employment and income that, in turn, increased the market demand for food.

In *The Lucerne Declaration and Action Program* that was adopted at the end of the ministerial-level meeting in Lucerne, Switzerland in February 1995,[16] ministers, heads of agencies, and delegates representing the CGIAR membership, among other things:

endorsed the vision of the renewed CGIAR of helping to combat poverty and hunger in the world by mobilizing both indigenous knowledge and modern science, and through sharply focused research priorities, tighter governance, greater efforts at South–North partnership, and flexible arrangements, as an appropriate response to the challenges of the coming century [and gave their] strong support for the revitalized CGIAR.

"Collegiality and informality" were regarded as "important and durable assets of the CGIAR." Therefore, "the CGIAR should not be established as a formal international organization, but could benefit from strengthening its decision-making processes and consultative mechanisms."

Third system review of the CGIAR system (1998)

A third review of the CGIAR system as a whole was carried out in 1997–98 by an independent external panel. The panel was led by Maurice Strong of Canada, who was secretary-general of the UN Conference on Human Environment in Stockholm, Sweden in 1972, secretary-general of the UN Conference on Environment and Development in Rio de Janeiro, Brazil in 1992, a former executive director of UNEP, and special adviser to the UN secretary-general and the World Bank president.[17] It is understandable, therefore, that the review had a visible environmental and sustainability focus.

The review came 17 years after the second system-wide review in 1981. Significant advances had taken place since that time in modern science and information and communications technologies, providing the setting, as the panel put it, "for a frontal assault on poverty, food security and environmental degradation." The panel added that there was a "compelling moral and ethical imperative" that underpinned the need for a "global research effort to harness the best of science to meet the needs of the poor in an environmentally sustainable manner ... reinforced by economic, social and security imperatives." The persistence of extreme hunger was "indefensible." FAO had estimated the over 800 million people lacked adequate food. By 2005, food for an additional 3 billion people would be needed. Agricultural production would have to be "greatly increased." Nobel laureate Norman Borlaug believed that average yields of all major crops would have to be increased by 50 percent by 2025 if food and agricultural needs were to be met. FAO estimated that two-thirds of the growth in agricultural production would have to come from the intensified use of land already under cultivation, while protecting natural resources.

The review found that the CGIAR was well placed to address these issues. In its view, the CGIAR had already established a "universally acknowledged record of success in international agricultural research." Investment in the CGIAR had been the single most effective use of ODA. The panel predicted that: "There can be no long-term agenda for eradicating poverty, ending hunger and ensuring sustainable food security without the CGIAR." The future effectiveness of the CGIAR system lay in "continuing to nurture scientific credibility, build on scientific strengths and mobilize scientific partnerships to meet the goals of eliminating poverty and hunger and protect the environment."

On the cusp of a new millennium, the review made 29 recommendations, focused on issues the panel considered to be of the highest priority for setting the future direction of the CGIAR. It began by recommending a new mission statement, significantly broadening its original focus, which read: "to contribute to food security and poverty eradication through research promoting sustainable agricultural development based on the environmentally sound management of natural resources." The panel added that: "This mission will be achieved through research leadership, partnerships, capacity building and policy dialogue."

The panel recommended five priorities for the CGIAR's future work:

- launching a global initiative for integrated gene management with the CGIAR collections of major crop species (about 10 percent of global collections) as the centerpiece;
- establishing a coordinating and servicing unit for biosafety, bioethics and biosurveillance so that the latest developments in biotechnology were applied in ways that were pro-poor and pro-environment;
- creating a legal entity for the CGIAR, in place of the informal association, which could hold patents, and develop "rules of engagement" (involving both the public and private sectors) based on the premise that access to the means of production was as much a human right as access to food;
- creating a global network of integrated natural resource management, which would link productivity research with the environmentally sound management of natural resources; and
- developing an effective global information and communications system for food security to make science and technology accessible as a free good to scientists, NGOs and farmers.

The panel emphasized that to succeed, initiatives in agricultural research required an appropriate policy environment. CGIAR experience had shown that agricultural progress took place only if mutually reinforcing packages of technology, services and public policies, and producer-oriented marketing opportunities, were introduced. The panel recommended that the CGIAR launch a special collaborative program to strengthen the capacities of the national agricultural research systems (NARSs) for policy research and formulation covering economic and well as environmental, science, and technology research policy.

Implementation of the above priorities would only be possible through CGIAR leadership in creating and expanding partnerships not only with NARSs but beyond, including with the private sector, NGOs, regional and sub-regional organizations and advanced research institutions. The panel recommended, where appropriate, broadening the range of CGIAR's partnerships and that the CGIAR increase its emphasis on capacity-building, particularly the policy-making capacity of NARSs.

Special priority for sub-Saharan Africa was recommended, not just as "more of the same" but to include the establishment of an "Inter-Center African Capacity Building Initiative for Sustainable Food Security." Greater inter-CGAIR center cooperation should be promoted to achieve the CGIAR's goals.

A new model of CGIAR governance was called for, formalizing and streamlining the existing structure. The panel found that the current system involved high transaction costs, lack of timeliness and effectiveness in decision-making, and lack of a clear system of accountability. It recommended that the informal governance structure be formalized through the creation of a legal entity that would serve as a new "central body" of the CGIAR. This would include members, a board of directors, an executive committee, the CGIAR chair, a finance committee, and a chief executive officer. The CGIAR chair should also serve as the chief executive officer, should be a vice-president or equivalent of the World Bank, and should devote attention full-time to the CGIAR's work. CGIAR membership should be broadened to include more governments and other representative stakeholders. The CGIAR co-sponsors should no longer have a separate category but should have a permanent seat in the proposed central body and the executive committee.

The international development community was requested to reverse the declining trend for funding for agriculture and for agricultural research, and wider sources of finance were sought. In 1996, the CGIAR received 0.7 percent of ODA. To fulfill its mission, the panel estimated that it would require about $400 million annually by 2000. It recommended that the World Bank continue to provide it financial and policy support and intellectual leadership, which the panel considered

Future directions 193

was "indispensable" for CGIAR's future. The panel noted that the World Bank had contributed $600 million over the period 1972–97 that had mobilized over $4 billion from other sources.

The panel was asked to consider whether the CGIAR system would still be required through the early years of the next century. The answer was a resounding "yes," but the CGIAR system needed to change substantially to meet the challenges of a changing world. The commercialization of science had created a disincentive to produce public goods through agricultural research and development that would hit the poor and hungry hardest. Through its scientific research, capacity-building, and knowledge dissemination, the CGIAR had a critical leadership role to play in the twenty-first century.

The CGIAR at 31: an independent meta-evaluation (2004)

In 2004, another CGIAR system-wide evaluation was carried out, this time by the World Bank Operations Evaluation Department, an independent unit within the bank that reports directly to the bank's board of executive directors.[18] The evaluation also reviewed the bank's contribution to the CGIAR as part of its involvement in Global Partnership Programs.

The evaluation concluded that the CGIAR's productivity-enhancing research had had "sizable impacts on reducing poverty," and was "critical to meet the MDG of halving poverty by 2015." But the CGIAR had considerably broadened its agenda (see Figure 3.2) and was less focused on enhancing agricultural productivity than it was originally. The mix of activities in CGIAR's broadened mandate reflected "neither its comparative advantage nor its core competence." The CGIAR's expenditure on productivity-enhancing agricultural research, which was regarded as "a global or regional public good ideally suited to a publicly funded global network," had declined by 6.5 percent annually in real terms between 1992 and 2001, while expenditures on improving policies and protecting the environment had increased by 3.1 percent annually over the same period. Overall, CGIAR funding had declined by 1.8 percent, while the share of restricted funding (funding tied by donors) had increased from 36 to 57 percent, over this period of time.

Several factors explained the CGIAR's changing research mix and the increasing donor restrictions and influence. These included: the waning in popularity of germplasm improvement and biotechnology research in the constituencies of some key donor countries due to negative perceptions of the Green Revolution; the rise of

194 *Future directions*

environmentalism and the importance of protecting the environment for sustainable agricultural development; the weakening of many national agricultural research systems in developing countries, which led donors to turn to the CGIAR centers to carry out tasks ideally performed by national center; and to lack of support for the CGIAR gene banks of 600,000 accessions, a unique public good.

Changes in the funding mechanisms of the CGIAR since the mid-1990s also increased donor influence on the CGIAR's reseach agenda. The World Bank shifted the allocation of its own, important, financial contribution from being a "donor of last resort" to a matching-grant arrangement in response to a funding crisis in 1993–94. This change, and a redefinition of the CGIAR's research agenda, resulted in a fundamental transformation from a science-driven program, based on the independent advice formerly of the CGIAR's Technical Advisory Committee and later by its Science Council, to a donor-driven program, and a shift from the CGIAR producing global and regional public goods toward providing national and local services.

At the same time, other factors, such as the growing importance of genetic resource management, the biotechnology revolution, intellectual property rights, and private sector research called for CGIAR system responses, strategies, and policies to deal with these CGIAR system-wide challenges. But the CGIAR had no formal definition of responsibilities, charter or even a memorandum of understanding, preferring, in the words of the Lucerne Declaration, "collegiality and informality." The evaluation recommended that the time had come for the CGIAR to draw up a charter delineating the roles and responsibilities of the parties involved. (The "Charter of the CGIAR system" was adopted by the CGIAR at its annual general meeting in 2004 and revisions approved in 2006 and 2007.)

The evaluation examined the multiple roles of the World Bank/ IBRD in the CGIAR including: as co-sponsor; a key leadership role in CGIAR governance; providing a vice president, nominated by the bank's president, to serve as the CGIAR chair; appointing a bank director to serve as head of the CGIAR secretariat to exercise day-to-day leadership and shape overall policies and procedures; the housing and functioning of the CGIAR secretariat as a department of the bank; and lender to developing countries for complementary activities. The evaluation found that the bank "has been the guardian of the CGIAR and the catalyst that makes the System coherent." Other donors viewed the bank's roles as a seal of approval, giving them confidence to invest in the CGIAR system, attracting an amount of funding that exceeds bank support by a factor of 10. But a conflict of interests had compromised the bank's capacity to exercise strategic leadership and press for reforms at the scale and speed that might be warranted. The evaluation recommended that the bank should address its corporate governance responsibilities in the management of the CGIAR, separate oversight for management, and exercise a degree of oversight

Other systemic reforms were also needed. The CGIAR's priorities should respond more actively to changes in the global agricultural research context. More prominence should be given to basic plant breeding and germplasm improvement. Natural resource management research should be focused sharply on increasing productivity and the sustainable use of natural resources in developing countries. The World Bank should lead a concerted effort "at the highest level" to achieve fundamental reforms in CGIAR's governance, finance, and management, particularly to encourage donors to reverse the trend toward restricted funding. The bank itself should abandon its matching grant model and ensure that its resources were allocated strategically in support of global and regional public goods that contributed to agricultural productivity and poverty reduction. The bank should also make sure that a strong, qualified, and independent Science Council (in place of the CGIAR's Technical Advisory Committee) was established and invested with appropriate responsibilities for providing the CGIAR system with transparent advice on priorities, strategies, and resource allocation.

The evaluation ended by making the case for increased funding for the CGIAR system. This included exploring the use of grant funds for the provision of regional public goods that reduced poverty, if reforms were made to address the radically changed external and internal environment facing the CGIAR. As a lender to developing countries, the bank should increase lending to agricultural research, education, extension, and training, especially in sub-Saharan Africa, in order to enhance the performance of the national agricultural research systems there.

Science Council priorities for CGIAR research (2005–2015)

The CGIAR established a Science Council (SC), consisting of six members and a chair, in 2004, all identified through an international search by an independent selection committee of experts, supported by a secretariat located at FAO headquarters in Rome. Its recommendations are reviewed by the CGIAR's executive council, which nominates the SC chair and SC members for consideration and confirmation by the CGIAR. The SC chair and members are eminent scientists in the biological, physical, and social sciences, with science policy and development experience.

The SC recommended priorities for CGIAR research for the period 2005–15 to contribute to the MDGs in 2005.[19] Three key criteria were employed to help identify the priorities: (1) the expected impact on poverty alleviation, food security and nutrition, and sustainable management of natural resources, taking into account the expected probability of success and expected impact of successful projects; (2) whether the research is of an international public good nature; and (3) whether there are alternative sources of funds for the research, and whether the CGIAR has the comparative advantage in undertaking the research. Based on these criteria, five unranked priority areas were recommended for research in the CGIAR system over the ten year period:

- sustaining biodiversity for current and future generations;
- producing more and better food at lower cost through genetic improvement;
- reducing rural poverty through agricultural diversification and emerging opportunities for high-value commodities and products;
- poverty alleviation and sustainable management of water, land, and forest resources; and
- improving policies and facilitating institutional innovation to support sustainable reductions in poverty and hunger.

Each priority area had four contributing priority programs, giving a total of 20 priority programs for the 10-year period to 2015. It was expected that cross-cutting programs would be developed from elements of the 20 research priorities, with any additional research needed being provided by partners. The SC identified four principal ways in which this prioritized CGIAR research contributed the the MDGs (Box 1.1). First, by maintaining the past emphasis on research to help smallholders produce more staple food and fodder per unit of land, labor, and water in an environmentally sustainable way. Second, by placing greater emphasis on research to enhance incomes of smallholders through the production of high-value commodities and products. Third, research on sustainable management of natural resources would be designed to ensure environmental sustainability. And finally, research on institutions, markets, and policy would help to develop a global partnership for development.

The SC proposed that the Alliance of CGIAR Centers and CGIAR members agree to allocate 80 percent of the total CGIAR budget to the five priority areas. Of the remaining 20 percent, at least half should be spent by the CGIAR centers on exploratory, innovative research work to develop new science and potential new future priorities. Center programs were expected to be time-bound and increasingly to include exit strategies so that the programs would be taken over by national agricultural research systems. The gendered nature of agricultural production would influence research in areas with large numbers of women farmers, as in sub-Saharan Africa. The proposed priority research programs would be carried out in strong partnerships, including between the public and private sectors. Implementing the programs would also require that the CGIAR augment its agricultural research system. The SC's recommendations were endorsed by the CGIAR executive council and subsequently approved by CGIAR members.

Science Council review of CGIAR Challenge Programs

In 2007, the SC also conducted a review of the lessons learnt from the selection and implementation of the CGIAR Challenge Programs.[20] Concerning the selection process, the SC found that the open competitive calling for CP concepts was not successful in generating a sufficient number of exciting and innovative research ideas, especial from advanced research institutions. A prerequisite for approving a CP was that the research challenge a CP can feasibly solve needed to be carefully identified at the start of the program. Those CPs that had a clear and tractable challenge defined from the outset were able to attract and engage research institutions that saw their role in taking up the challenge. Waiting for a competitive grants process to attract partners could lead to a dilution of efforts and loss of focus. There was also a need to carefully consider what level of engagement with national research systems was optimal for increasing a CP's likely success in delivering relevant outputs and outcomes, for implementation, and for out-scaling and impact after a CP was terminated. The SC reinforced the original principles of the CPs, "to engage new partners and new science in impact oriented and time-bound programs for addressing high priority research challenges."

Regarding the governance of CPs, the SC found that a governance body that was composed of independent individuals with no institutional connection to consortium members or CP partners appeared to have more advantages and higher potential for effective and efficient performance. The organizational structure of a CP should allow for independent governance but should also take into account the need for support provided by as host institution as a legally constituted entity. Programmatic decisions should be left entirely to the CP's steering

198 *Future directions*

committee. The management of CPs (director/coordinator) needed to play a stronger leadership role, and be given primary responsibility for performance evaluation of the CP staff and management team.

On funding issues, the SC found that the CPs had neither caused a decrease in CGIAR center funding nor did they divert resources from unrestricted contributions to the CGIAR. They had generated new funds and earned a strong level of support from traditional and non-traditional donors. In general, CPs had been regarded in a positive light by partners. There was consensus that the partnership model for their implementation had been effective. The national research systems partners were appreciative of the skills gained through training and other capacity-building activities of the CPs. But challenges remained.

CGIAR's future directions

There is no shortage of views about CGIAR's future directions. All agree that today's world is significantly different from when the CGIAR was established in 1971. Since that time, new actors have joined the global agricultural research and knowledge system, including the private sector and the powerful multinational agricultural and food corporations, making the creation of partnerships an indispensable way of forwarding the enlarged CGIAR agenda. The outgoing CGIAR chair, director, and senior consultant of the CGIAR secretariat have given their views on, as they put it, "revolutionizing the evolution of the CGIAR" between 2001 and 2007.[21] They identified four initial pillars of CGIAR reform: the CGIAR Challenge Programs focused on key global issues; the creation of the CGIAR executive council to streamline governance and facilitate decision-making; the creation of a science-focused CGIAR Science Council replacing the CGIAR Technical Advisory Committee; and the establishment of the CGIAR System Office to develop a single, integrated strategy for coherent communication and fund-raising. But questions had been raised concerning the heavy and complex bureaucracy that has been developed to run and manage the CGIAR system, and the high overhead costs involved.

These senior CGIAR officials identified a fundamental change as the acceptance of the Consultative Group as a decision-making body and not merely as a platform for discussion. They listed the key internal issues that needed to be tackled as: simplification of governance at each of the CGIAR centers; increasing alignment among CGIAR centers and members in terms of programs, provision of services, and governance; reviewing and adjusting CGIAR priorities to meet new future challenges; and mobilizing science and technology through the work of the CGIAR Science Council. In their opinion, the CGIAR system should be prepared to plan and develop new modes of operation, governance, and management to meet the new challenges that will undoubtedly come.

In many ways, the unique origin and structure of the CGIAR make it well placed to play some increasingly important roles in the future.[22] Among these roles are: the custodian of genetic resources; assessing the consequences of technological change; providing strategic leadership and integration within the global agricultural research community; and acting as an honest broker in access to knowledge and technology. These and other roles will become increasingly important as future events, including climate change and globalization, take hold. The extent to which the CGIAR will be able to play these roles will depend on how it manages some major internal problems (see below) and the respect it retains in the international community. A major lacuna has been the pace and scale at which the research work of the CGIAR centers has been taken up by farmers, especially in sub-Saharan Africa. Discussions are now taking places with the Rockefeller and Gates Foundations, who have funded the Alliance for a Green Revolution in Africa (AGRA), to see how this problem can be overcome.

Resources and resource-related problems

With the exception of the World Bank, the other global food and agricultural institutions discussed in this book are facing increasing resource and resource-related problems. The paradox of the bank is that while its resources have increased, its support for agricultural and rural development has decreased.

In the case of FAO, over the past 10 years its total financial resources (net of special funds for emergencies) have declined in real terms by almost one-third and its total staff complement by a quarter. At the same time, extra-budgetary funding has grown to account for almost half of FAO total resources, reflecting a growing tendency for donors to tie and direct their contributions to activities that are in their domestic interest. To the extent that those interests coincide with those of the institution, this funding can be especially helpful at a time when regular contributions are declining. Where they are not, as the independent external evaluation of FAO pointed out, the challenge is to ensure the integrity and relevance of extra-budgetary funds as a whole, while maintaining overall strategic and programmatic coherence, and

200 Future directions

the multilateral character of the institution, a problem common to many UN agencies.[23]

The independent external evaluation of FAO identified a number of factors that have contributed to the fall in FAO's resources and influence. These have included: tensions in its governance as "mistrust and opposition" have developed between various groups of member countries, particularly the OECD donors, who provide a major part of FAO's regular resources, and the G77, increasing the political rather than the technical context within which the organization works; the failure of the organization to change in conformity with the changing world in which it has operated in the past 60 years, during which many new organizations and agencies have made inroads into its original mandate; and the longevity of its past and present directors-general, which, as the independent, external evaluation put out, is "clearly not in the best long-term interest of FAO." The challenge is to move forward on "reform with growth" before further declines in resources and staff cause irreversible damage to FAO in delivering essential services to the world.

In the case of IFAD, tensions have occurred that are similar to those in other institutions, as the early promise of large additional resources was not sustained. Declining resources were shared among an increasing number of different types of projects and programs, diluting their developmental impact. A similar experience was encountered in the CGIAR as its mandate was broadened, but with an additional difficulty. The emergence of a regime strongly influenced by the authority of the individual CGIAR centers on the one hand, and the sovereignty of donors on the other, has made it increasingly difficult to retain the integrity of a single system of international agricultural research that has gained worldwide recognition. As donors have increased restricted (tied) funding to activities and centers of their choice, this has distorted the overall synergies and impact of the system as a whole. One suggestion is that if the CGIAR is to continue to operate as one system, the members should decide to make it a legal international organization with one central board with affiliated centers and/or Challenge Programs.[24] While this suggestion is likely to meet with opposition, there is a strong case to modify and streamline the organizational structure of the CGIAR.

Faced with major changes in the world in which it operates, the CGIAR has launched a "change management initiative," under the leadership of the CGIAR chair, designed to introduce reforms to enhance its effectiveness and efficiency.[25] A Change Steering Team and four working groups were established in early 2008 and are expected to present their recommendations to the CGIAR executive council at its meeting in mid-October. They have been requested to address four major themes: a future vision and development challenges; strategic partnerships; governance at the center and overall CGIAR levels; and funding mechanisms. At the same time, another independent review of the CGIAR is being undertaken by an external panel, which will present its report by the end of July 2008. Its findings and recommendations will be taken into consideration in writing the report on the change management initiative.

In many ways, the resource problem of WFP is more serious, many-sided, and complex. Food aid flows have been influenced by the interplay of three factors: food production, stocks, and prices. Flows have been highest when production and stocks have been high and prices low, and lowest when production and stocks have been down and prices high, just when poor food-importing countries have needed them most. In recent years, global food aid deliveries have fallen from over 15 million tons in 1999 to 8.2 million tons in 2005. As food aid has fallen, the share delivered through WFP has increased, reaching 54 percent in 2005.

In the past, donors have pledged their contributions to WFP's resources in monetary terms, used mainly to draw from their own food stocks. While the WFP secretariat gave donors an indication of the kinds and amounts of food commodities required for WFP operations, a high degree of mutual self-interest was shown in the commodities that each donor actually provided, including high value-added products such as canned meat and fish. This tying of food aid to donor's interests was taken further by the United States, which required that the food commodities provided came from stocks declared to be in surplus from U.S. agricultural production. In addition, three-quarters should be in the form of bagged, fortified, or processed products. Under U.S. cargo preference legislation, three-quarters of its food aid commodities had to be shipped in U.S. vessels at shipping rates significantly above the international level.

A U.S. Government Accountability Office (GAO) study of the U.S. food aid program in 2006 showed that despite growing demand for food aid, rising business and transportation costs contributed to a 43 percent decline in the average volume delivered over the past five years.[26] These costs represented about 65 percent of total food aid expenditure, highlighting the need to maximize the efficiency and effectiveness of food aid deliveries, and impeding the goal of "getting the right food to the right people at the right time." The GAO recommended that the USAID and the departments of agriculture and

202 Future directions

transportation work together to institute measures to improve logistical planning, transportation contracting, and monitoring of the U.S. food aid programs.

A study commissioned by the OECD in 2005 on the tying of food aid by donors to direct transfers from their domestic food production found that the costs involved were on average about 50 percent more than local food purchases and 33 percent more than procurement of food in another developing country through triangular transactions. The overall results of the study showed that there were substantial cost inefficiencies associated with tying food aid. The most resource transfer-efficient forms of food aid were likely to be flexibly sourced, either within the recipient country or from third countries, but not necessarily always a developing country. Greater donor flexibility in sourcing food aid would benefit agricultural development in many low-income developing countries.[27]

In 2006, CARE, one of the largest international NGOs, decided to stop receiving U.S. food aid commodities, which it had used for many years for sale in developing countries to generate cash for humanitarian programs, in view of the potential harm to markets and local food production as well as the high management costs involved.[28] The only exceptions would be where it could be clearly demonstrated that food aid sales would be used to address the underlying causes of chronic food insecurity with reasonable management costs and without causing harm to markets or local production.

In recent years, WFP has appealed to donors to provide more of their contributions in cash to purchase food in developing countries, especially for emergency operations. A number of donors have responded, including the European Union, which now provides almost all its contributions to WFP in cash. While helpful, the sudden and substantial increases in the prices of basic food commodities and of oil in recent years have created further problems. Several factors have contributed to the rise in food prices. Bad harvests in the U.S.A. and European Union, and serious and prolonged drought in Australia, have reduced grain stocks. The long-promised cuts in food subsidies, most noticeably in the EU, could also have a permanent effect on food supplies and prices. International trade in edible oils and grains has been restricted as producers, such as Russia, have introduced export quotas to control domestic prices. Record oil prices have had their effects on food production through increasing the costs of running agricultural machinery, transportation, and especially the manufacture of fertilizers, and have resulted in record shipping rates to get food to poor, food-importing countries.

But the biggest structural change is using food crops to produce biofuels. This has been characterized as an attempt to provide fuel security for the rich at the expense of food security for the poor. In the space of a few years, one-fifth of the U.S. grain harvest and about 40 million tons of maize (corn) have been diverted to produce ethanol, about 4 percent of global coarse grains used to feed humans and livestock. This rapid growth is largely the result of subsidies. The environmental benefit of biofuel and its contribution to solving the energy problem are ambiguous and controversial. It remains to be seen whether this becomes a permanent problem through the enactment of the U.S. farm bill in 2008. In addition, a decision is awaited in the WTO concerning the amounts and types of food aid that will be permissible in the context of international trade.

All these factors are having a compounded effect on WFP resources, forcing attention on how it operates in order to respond to the needs of the hungry poor and the victims of man-made and natural disasters, and calling for transforming the organization from being a "food aid agency" into a "food assistance agency."[29] Of the food bought by WFP on the open market in 2007, totaling about $760 million, 80 percent came from developing countries. WFP has begun programs in developing countries to contract local farmers to produce food commodities to order. In partnership with some donor governments and NGOs, WFP has also piloted giving cash or vouchers to people in poor countries to stimulate local demand. In the meantime, as food and oil prices rise and its resources have not increased proportionately, WFP has had to contemplate cutting basic food rations to poor people in dire situations or prioritizing the emergencies to which it can respond. At the same time, WFP is making progress in broadening its donor base. In 2006, there were 96 donors, almost double the number of a few years ago, and the private sector is becoming an increasingly important partner, not only in monetary terms but in advocacy and political support.

As if this were not enough, WFP also faces a peculiar financial problem concerning the staffing and the administration of the world's largest humanitarian agency. WFP's management plan rests on the basic and crucial assumption that the United Nations and its member states require, and are ready to fund on a voluntary basis, its global humanitarian operations and program activities.[30] The funding model for WFP differs significantly from most UN bodies in that it has no predictable income for its program support and administrative (PSA) expenditures. The PSA budget covers all staff and non-staff costs at

204 *Future directions*

WFP headquarters and liaison offices, the majority of costs at its regional bureaux, and some management costs of its country offices. These costs are solely funded by income derived from a certain percentage, currently set at 7 percent, of the voluntary contributions received from donors.

Given the uncertainties inherent in this funding model, a main challenge facing WFP member states and leadership is to maintain a managerial and operational support capacity that has certain basic features. It has to be both robust and flexible, be able meet the commitments made to its beneficiaries in operations and programs approved by its executive board, and maintain a rapid response and preparedness capacity in terms of people, equipment, and systems, ready to be mobilized immediately at the onset of unforeseen emergencies. This funding model served well in recent years when the volume of WFP work and resources increased considerable with the onset and frequency of major natural and man-made disasters. When fewer or no major emergencies occurred, the 7 percent formula was unable to meet the management costs that had built up in crisis years. The most immediate problem with this funding model has been the lack of a mechanism to compensate for exchange rate variations. The U.S. dollar exchange rate against the European euro has fallen sharply in recent years. Most of WFP's PSA expenditures are incurred at its headquarters in Rome and thus based on euro costs. A fixed 7 percent overall income has been unable to cope with PSA cost increases related to exchange rate variations, unrelated to volume of work or increased real costs.

As a result, the PSA budget for the 2008–9 biennium was reduced by 21 percent in real terms and WFP staff cut by around 290 posts, mostly at its headquarters. With retirements and voluntary early separations, around 50 staff will not have their contracts extended. While every effort is being made to ensure that this reduction will not impair the efficiency of WFP's operations, they may not be sufficient to ensure adequate resourcing of all critical areas. WFP will have to explore new ways to maintain a sustainable core budget, which includes specific funding for initiatives that it is asked to undertake on behalf of the humanitarian community or costs arising from global United Nations decisions, such as cluster leaderships and in the "Delivering as One" UN initiative. All this adds up to the need for donors to help WFP face what its executive director has called the "perfect storm" of higher food and fuel prices, climate change, and population growth, and rising absolute numbers of the hungry poor. At the time of writing (March 2008), WFP launched an "extraordinary emergency appeal" to governments to donate at least $500 million, later raised to $750 million, for ongoing emergency operations to avoid rationing food aid in response to the spiralling cost of food, shipping, and fuel. The donor community more than met this appeal: Saudi Arabia alone made a contribution of $500 million.

Institutional incoherence, cooperation, and coordination

In preparations for the 1974 World Food Conference, it was proposed to create a new body, perhaps called a "World Food Authority," to implement or coordinate the implementation of the recommendations and decisions of the conference.[31] Such an authority would have three functions. It would mobilize international financial assistance for agricultural development. It would provide support to a wider system of world food information and food security and facilitate observance of the International Undertaking on World Food Security that had been approved by the FAO council in 1973 and by the conference. And it would facilitate implementation of the longer-term food aid policy proposed for adoption by the conference. The proposed authority would consist of: a permanent inter-governmental council with half its members elected by the UN General Assembly and half by the FAO Conference; an agricultural development fund to provide assistance for increasing food production in developing countries, with weighted voting rights in proportion to contributions; a committee on food information and food stocks; and a committee on food aid. The main purpose of the proposed authority would be to strengthen effective action by existing agencies and provide a mechanism whereby governments could better coordinate international action.

At the final session of the Preparatory Committee that met shortly before the conference began in November 1974, the secretary-general of the conference, Sayed Ahmed Marei, who at the time was special adviser to the Egyptian president, Anwar Sadat, said that a "high-level political body" was essential to get the decisions needed, and that an institutional framework was necessary that "would have to reflect the world community's political will to eliminate the scourge of hunger. It would have to be a credible organ for mobilizing the new resources needed and speak with greater authority to both developed and developing countries than any existing mechanism."[32] During the conference, contrasting views were expressed concerning the proposed new authority. One suggestion was that a "world food security council" should be established with powers to act on matters of food security similar to those of the UN Security Council on matters relating to world peace.

The World Food Council: its work and demise

In the event, the conference recommended, and the UN General Assembly approved, the setting up of a World Food Council (WFC) at the ministerial or plenipotentiary level. The council would function as an organ of the United Nations and report to the UN General Assembly through the Economic and Social Council (ECSOC). It would serve as a coordinating mechanism "to provide overall, integrated and continuing attention for the coordination and follow-up of policies concerning food production, nutrition, food security, food trade and food aid and other related matters by all the agencies of the UN system."[33] In taking this step, the conference appreciated the complex nature of the world food problem, which could only be solved through an integrated multidisciplinary approach within the framework of economic and social development as a whole. Crucially, the United States supported adoption of the conference recommendation, but noted significantly that the council "would have no authority beyond moral suasion to force action on the part of governments or UN bodies."[34] It was agreed that the council would consist of 36 members, nominated by ECOSOC and elected by the UN General Assembly, each member serving for three years on a rotating basis. An executive director was appointed by the UN secretary-general in consultation with WFC members and the FAO director-general for a period of four years.[35] Its headquarters was located at FAO in Rome, with a small secretariat and operating budget.

The establishment of the WFC promised a new beginning in the quest for world food security. From the outset, however, the council represented a compromise between those who did not want any new UN machinery to address the problems of world food security and the more rigorous proposals for a "world food authority" and a "world food security council." Nevertheless, it was the only UN body to be specifically set up at the ministerial or plenipotentiary level, reporting directly to the UN General Assembly through ECOSOC on matters relating to world food security. In essence, WFC was to be a political overview body, serving as the eyes, ears, and conscience of the UN system regarding world food security issues. In the selection of WFC members, its executive director and executive bureau, and secretariat staff, careful consideration was to be given to geographical and political balance between developing and developed countries, reflecting the concern of the G77 that the council should not become a tool of the powerful developed nations.

WFC ministerial sessions were held once a year, and lasted four or five days, preceded by a preparatory meeting of a similar duration. The first session was held in Rome in June 1975. Thereafter, they were held at locations in the developing and developed countries at the invitation of governments that agreed to defray the costs involved, after consultation with the UN secretary-general.[36] In preparing documentation and providing administrative, operational and other services for the council, the WFC secretariat was to cooperate "to the maximum extent," and rely on, existing international bodies in the field of food and agriculture, especially FAO. Funding of WFC activities was met out of the UN administrative budget and was closely controlled. In conducting its work, WFC would maintain contact with, and give advice and make recommendations to, UN bodies regarding the formulation and follow-up on world food policies. It was also to receive periodic reports from the UN agencies and other bodies concerned with food security issues including: FAO's Committee on World Food Security; the FAO Commission on Fertilizers; FAO on progress in implementing its Global Information and Early Warning System on Food and Agriculture; WFP, IFAD, the CGIAR, and the United Nations Conference on Trade and Development (UNCTAD) on the world food trade situation, and on progress to increase trade liberalization and access to international markets for food products from developing countries.

The main tasks of the WFC were perceived as:

- reviewing major food and hunger issues with a view to advancing international understanding of them, and the resolutions adopted by the World Food Conference of 1974, and to monitor steps taken by governments and the UN system;
- recommending remedial action through WFC initiatives, thereby providing global policy direction; and
- monitoring and coordinating the relevant UN bodies and agencies.

The council undertook a considerable amount of work and made a number of initiatives in its 18 years of existence as the political overview body in the UN system in the fight against hunger and malnutrition.[37] As a ministerial body, it lent its weight to: the establishment of IFAD; an increase in food aid through an enlarged Food Aid Convention; the establishment of an International Emergency Food

Reserve with agreed modalities; and the creation of a cereal financing facility in the IMF. Among its major initiatives, the council: established criteria for the classification of "food priority countries" as a primary focus of attention; urged that particular concern be given to the special food problems of Africa; developed the concept of "national food strategies"; attempted to keep international attention focused on the various dimensions of the goal of eradicating hunger and malnutrition; advocated food crisis contingency planning; recommended establishing developing country-owned food reserves; drew attention to the importance of environmental management in the quest for food security; warned of the possible diversion of assistance from developing countries to countries of Eastern Europe with the beak-up of the former Soviet Union; and addressed the problem of international migration and its threat to food security. It also developed strategic perspectives on future prospects for eliminating hunger and malnutrition. And it issued four resounding declarations as clarion calls to ECOSOC, the UN General Assembly, and the international community on the elimination of hunger and malnutrition. The council's contributions toward helping to shape and promote an effective world food policy focused on the elimination of hunger were therefore significant.

An important function of the WFC was to act as a coordinating mechanism for all the relevant UN bodies concerning policies on food production, nutrition, food security, and food aid. The scale and complexity of this function was revealed when in 1990 the council requested the WFC secretariat to review coordination among the UN agencies toward meeting the common objective of eliminating hunger and malnutrition. The review found that well over 30 multilateral institutions were "in a significant way" interested in food and nutrition security issues (Table 5.1).

Given the multi-institutional structure and "sectorization" of the UN system, efforts were made to ensure coordination among the system's constituent parts. Despite these various coordination arrangements, extensive reviews had found coordination within the UN system to be deficient. The UN agencies were perceived to "compete excessively," and joint programming of their operations remained "mostly inadequate." From its review, the WFC secretariat drew two general conclusions. First, the need for a central focus on hunger elimination in the UN system remained as important as when the WFC was established in 1975. To meet the challenges ahead, the council would need to strengthen further its monitoring, assessment, and promotional roles. Second, improved coordination was most critically needed at the country level. Multilateral and bilateral aid agencies could support

Table 5.1 United Nations bodies with an interest in food and nutrition security

UN body	Special interest*
FAO	Agricultural protection, rural development, employment, income generation, marketing, trade, food security, nutrition, food emergencies/early warning, agrarian reform, structural adjustment, environment
IAEA	Irradiation of food
IBRD/IDA	Macro policy, structural adjustment, program and project lending for food security and nutrition improvement; management of consultative groups
IFAD	Agricultural production, rural development, agrarian reform, structural adjustment, employment, income generation, environment
ILO	Employment, income generation, training, social protection, entitlement programs, structural adjustment, rural development
IMF	Macro policy, structural adjustment, financing of food imports
INSTRAW	Women and food security
UNFPA	Food security and population questions
UNHCR	Refugees and food security and nutrition issues
UNICEF	Food security and nutrition programs, mothers and children, structural adjustment
UNIDO	Agro-industry, food processing
UNITAR	Training programs in food security, nutrition and related issues
UN regional commissions (5)	Food security and nutrition in regional policy and context
UNRISD	Research on food security and related issues
UN Centre for Human Rights	Food security as a human right
UN Centre for Human Settlements (Habitat)	Food security and viable and sustainable settlements
UN Centre for Social Development and Humanitarian Affairs	Food policy in context of social development
UNCTAD	Food trade and agricultural subsidies
UNCTC	Food production and trade of transnationals
UNDHA	Humanitarian operations
UNDP	Technical cooperation and grant aid for programs and projects for food security and nutrition, management of round-table process
UNEP	Food production, food security, environment and sustainability
UNESCO	Formal and informal education on food and nutrition and related issues

(continued)

Table 5.1 (continued)

UN body	Special interest*
UNRWA	Food security and nutrition for Palestinian refugees
UN secretariat and departments (New York)	UN General Assembly and Security Council, general oversight, political questions, macro policy, structural adjustment, population, environment, sustainability
UNU (includingWIDER)	Research and teaching on food security issues
WFP	Development and emergency food aid for food security and nutrition
WHO	Health and nutrition programs, food standards (with FAO)

* The special interest indicated for each UN body is illustrative and not definitive. There are also 15 international centers of the Consultative Group on International Agricultural Research (CGIAR) including the International Food Policy Research (IFPRI). In addition, there are three regional banks and the World Trade Organization (WTO), whose special interests relate to food security that have cooperative arrangements with the United Nations system.

Source: D. John Shaw, *World Food Security, A History since 1945* (Basingstoke, UK and New York: Palgrave Macmillan, 2007), 207.

developing countries' efforts by adjusting their own aid management and coordination procedures to meet developing countries' needs. This could include improvements in the internal coordination of hunger-focused action within the agencies themselves, and providing management support to improve developing countries' capacity to plan and manage their national polices and programs, and external aid. The council agreed that in the light of the growing complexity of hunger and poverty problems, its role in providing "a central, undivided focus on hunger within the UN system" was even more important than at the time when it was established. It agreed to encourage an enhanced hunger focus and improved coordination among all relevant international agencies and governing bodies. In this spirit, council members welcomed the proposal, endorsed by the UN secretary-general, for the creation of an inter-secretariat consultative mechanism among the four Rome-based food organizations, FAO, IFAD, WFC, and WFP.

Although much was achieved, there was disquiet both within and outside the council about the way in which it functioned from as early as 1979, five years after its establishment. The UN secretary-general, Perez de Cuellar, appointed a small advisory group in 1986 to evaluate the effectiveness of the WCF and recommend ways in which the council might more effectively accomplish its objectives, but with the financial situation of the UN worsening, no follow-up action was taken. Meeting at its 18th ministerial session in 1992, which turned out to be the last time the council met, ministers agreed that "the Council has fallen short of achieving the political leadership and coordination role expected from its founders at the 1974 World Food Conference."

There was consensus that the objectives of that conference were as important in 1992 as they were in 1974 and that "food and hunger issues must remain at the centre of national and international development efforts." There was also "broadly based agreement" that in a rapidly changing world "there can be no continuation of the *status quo* for the World Food Council or for the United Nations as a whole." Therefore, there was "general agreement" on the need for review of the role and functioning of the council in the wider context of global food security management and the overall restructuring of the social and economic activities of the UN system, which the UN secretary-general, Boutros Boutros-Ghali, had initiated.

For this purpose, the council agreed to establish an ad hoc committee, which would be open to all WFC members at the level of minister or his/her delegate. The council proposed that the UN General Assembly review the mandate, operations, and future role of the WFC, taking into account the report of the ad hoc committee, in the debate of the restructuring of the UN economic and social system at its session in September 1992. Council members met in New York shortly before the start of the UN General Assembly session to discuss a report prepared not by the WFC secretariat but by the secretariat of the UN, that fell short of what WFC members had requested the ad hoc committee to do. Eighteen council members made interventions at the New York meeting. Fourteen were in favor of retaining the WFC but with various proposals for its reform. Four members (Canada, Denmark, Japan, and the United States) supported the distribution of its functions and responsibilities along the lines outlined in the UN secretary-general's statement to the meeting, which involved strengthening the role of ECOSOC as a "central forum" for major economic, social, and related issues, and making the "most cost-effective use" of the resources available to the UN in a "revitalization process."

In the ensuing debate in ECOSOC and the UN General Assembly, with no fanfare or ceremony, after almost two decades, the council was disbanded, one of the few UN bodies to be closed after its creation. A number of reasons have been put forward for its demise. In many ways, the council and its work served as a microcosm of the complexities and difficulties of achieving world food security. For some, the council was seen as the victim of a restructuring process in the UN system that had to demonstrate to the major developing countries, particularly the United States, who made the largest contributions to the world organization, that the UN secretary-general meant business in cost-cutting and streamlining the UN decision-making apparatus. For others, the council had served its time, had demonstrated its ineffectiveness, and interest had moved on to other priorities.

It was the ministerial character, and the political weight it carried, that made the council a unique policy forum. The WFC president, and especially its executive director, backed by a small, dedicated staff, played important roles in formulating and advocating WFC policy proposals and consensus building. Despite their Herculean efforts, they were given neither the authority nor the means to carry out the coordinating role expected of the WFC for all relevant bodies of the UN system. Some pointed to the compromise that led to the establishment of the council at the 1974 World Food Conference. In setting up the compromise council, delegates were as much influenced by what they did not want to create as by what they intended to do. As a result, the council was given the far reaching roles and responsibilities of the originally conceived "World Food Authority" without the authority and resources to carry them out. The council was therefore never able to command the leadership and coordinating roles expected of it, and the respect and attention that was necessary for it to fulfill its functions.

Born out of a world food crisis, which quickly passed, its utility for both developing and developed countries also waned. Crucially, the council was never really able to distinguish between the world food problem and the world food security problem. Members consisted mostly of ministers of agriculture who had neither the mandate nor the experience to cover the range of food security issues outside the agricultural sector, nor legally binding control over the activities of the large number of UN agencies whose work related to food security. WFC's role became a confused mixture of general advocacy and action plans. Its four-or-five day sessions, once a year, preceded by a brief preparatory meeting, covered too many agenda items, were often broad in scope, and insufficiently focused on monitoring key action programs. Insufficient attention was given to inter-sessional activities to keep the focus and maintain the momentum.

Cooperation from key UN agencies was essential for the secretariat to carry out its work. Yet there was resentment of the council's establishment, which was seen by some as unnecessary, adding to the institutional incoherence that already existed among the numerous bodies concerned with world food security. Its location, as a UN agency, at

FAO headquarters in Rome, away from UN headquarters in New York, was a major impediment, particularly as FAO saw itself as playing a major and coordinating role in the UN system for policies and activities related to food security and nutrition. The experience of the WFC has shown that the solution does not lie in the establishment of a separate body without executive authority and with a mandate that cuts across that of other agencies. Nor does it lie in giving coordinating responsibilities to a single agency with restricted sectoral membership and a limited sectoral mandate. A number of proposals have been made for UN reform, including the establishment of a "UN Economic Security Council," to overview future world food security. Whatever decisions are taken on UN reform, it will be necessary to have a focal point at the highest political level to ensure that food security and nutrition are advocated and managed as central issues embedded in world and national action for achieving economic and social development and peace, with cohesive and coordinated programs of international development assistance.

Conclusions

As this book was being written, a world food crisis was unfolding, caused by unprecedented increases in the price of basic foods and of oil. The cost of wheat, rice, maize (corn) and vegetable oil all hit record highs in the first quarter of 2008. The food import bill of developing countries rose by 25 percent in 2007 as food prices rose to levels not seen in a generation. Many countries have imposed controls on food exports to ensure domestic food supplies. The use of bilateral agreements and barter contracts to secure food supplies is rising, undermining world agricultural trade. Over 30 countries are said to be at risk of social unrest because of the rising price of food. The hungry poor who spend a large part of their meager income on food have been particularly affected, wiping out any recent gains in poverty reduction, and worsening the trend toward meeting the MDG of reducing the proportion of the world's hungry people by half by 2015.

The 1.5 billion small farmers in the developing world will not gain from these unprecedented food price rises. The majority of them buy more food than they produce and so will suffer along with the urban poor and rural landless people. The challenge is to assist them raise their low productivity and at the same time protect their food security until they can fend for themselves. Adequate arrangements should also be established to ensure that the urban poor have access to the food they need and that victims of natural and man-made disasters receive their basic needs, including appropriate food rations. In a post food surplus era, old tools that have been forgotten and new tools will be required to assist the hungry and food-insecure.

As described in this book, the world food crisis has been caused by a mixture of factors. Ultimately, it is the outcome of prolonged neglect by governments in developing countries and donors to invest in agricultural development. They will no longer be able to ignore the effects of this inaction. Hopefully, this wake-up call will lead to positive action in which the global food and agricultural institutions will have a vital part to play. The president of the World Bank has proposed a "new deal for global food policy" in which they should be intimately involved.

As the first publication to review these global food and agricultural institutions together, this gives an opportunity to see how they cooperate and how that cooperation might be strengthened in the future. It also enables a perspective to be taken on how these institutions fit into the galaxy of aid organizations both with and outside the UN system.

The five institutions share a number of common features. They all work for or with food. They all seek to end hunger and alleviate poverty. They all subscribe to contributing to the achievement of the MDGs. And, to a large extent, they share common members. Their web sites list a number of ways in which they cooperate with other aid organizations but largely as add-ons to their core programs. They all retain their own separate identities, with their own governing bodies, financing arrangements, and programs of assistance. They have broadened their mandates and have added specialists to their staff in seeking to improve their effectiveness rather than through pursuing closer working arrangements among each other and with other aid bodies.

Calls have been made for them to work closer together, especially in common programs and projects in the developing countries. This particularly applies to the three UN organizations in Rome. The high-level panel on UN system-wide coherence has recommended that "to build long-term food security and break the cycle of recurring famines, especially in sub-Saharan Africa, WFP, FAO and IFAD should review their respective approaches and enhance interagency coordination."[38] It has been suggested that they should share common services to reduce costs. The three organizations are cooperating more, although the memory of the head of one of the organizations (FAO) endeavoring to dominate another (WFP) has left an unfortunate legacy that could militate against closer working relations[39] That experience showed the importance of leadership, and the qualities required for effective leadership, of the UN bodies. It also showed the important roles that governments must play in the governing bodies of the UN agencies.

Ultimately, it showed that effective reform is possible through working together.

UN organizations also take part in the UN Development Group established after the reform of the UN system in 1997 to coordinate UN development assistance. They also are represented on the UN Standing Committee for Emergencies and cooperate with the UN Department for Humanitarian Affairs set up in 1991 to strengthen coordination of UN system-wide emergency aid. Representatives of all the UN agencies also take part in the meetings of special working groups, such as the UN Standing Committee on Nutrition. The CGIAR has established coordination with the UN bodies, which have been its co-sponsors from its inception, with its secretariat part of the administration of the World Bank and the secretariat of its Science Council located at FAO headquarters in Rome. All are committed to working closely with NGOs and CSOs and are endeavoring to strengthening ties with the private sector.

An effective way of demonstrating solidarity and establishing coordination among the five institutions would be for them to declare a common initiative on world hunger as part of the "new deal on global food policy" called for by the president of the World Bank, in which they would share their respective comparative advantages. This could take the form of a Global Partnership Program, similar to the ones that already exist in the fight against the communicable diseases of HIV/AIDS, tuberculosis, and malaria; the protection of children and of the environment; and international agricultural research. As in the other Global Partnership Programs, the institutions, to which others may be invited to join, especially IMF, WTO, and WHO, would pool their resources (financial, technical, staff, skills, and reputations) toward achieving agreed objectives over time, with a common governance and management structure.

As this book was being put to press, the report of the International Assessment of Agricultural Science and Technology for Development (IAASTD) was launched at UNESCO headquarters in Paris on 15 April 2008 (www.unesco.org). This assessment is the result of a three-year collaborative effort (2005–7), cosponsored by FAO, GEF, UNDP, UNEP, UNESCO, the World Bank, and WHO. It concludes that while agricultural science and technology have made it possible to greatly increase productivity in the last 50 years, sharing of the benefits has been far from equitable, and progress has been achieved at high social and environmental cost. Greater emphasis must be placed on safeguarding natural resources and on "agroecological" practices. The way the world grows its food will have to be changed radically also to better serve the poor and hungry, enhance rural livelihoods, and ensure food and nutrition security. At the same time, combined efforts must cope with a growing population, evolving consumption patterns, and climate change, and avoid social breakdown and environmental collapse. No single institution, nation or region can tackle these issues alone. This will place even greater pressure on the future work of the institutions covered in this book, in greater concert with others.

Postscript

Since this book was written, food and oil prices have continued to escalate, eroding the gains made in reducing the number of hungry poor and adding significantly to the import bills of food-deficit, low-income countries. A number of initiatives have been proposed or initiated to address the world food security problem. In April 2008, the UN secretary-general established a High Level Task Force on the Global Food Security Crisis primarily to promote a unified response to the global food price challenge, including by facilitating the creation of a prioritized plan of action and coordinating its implementation. The task force participants including FAO, IFAD, IMF, UNCTAD, UNDP, UNEP, UNHCR, UNICEF, World Bank, WFP, WHO, WTO and the UN Office of the High Representative for the Least Developed Countries, Landlocked Countries and Small Island Developing States. The UN Under-Secretary-General for Humanitarian Affairs has been appointed as the Task Force Coordinator.

A High-Level Conference on World Food Security was held in Rome, Italy in June 2008, convened by FAO, IFAD, WFP and the CGIAR, to address the challenges of higher food prices, climate change and bioenergy. The conference adopted a declaration committing participants to immediate and short-term measures to respond urgently to requests for assistance from affected countries and to provide immediate support for agricultural production and trade, and a number of medium and long-term measures. Arrangements were also made to monitor and analyse world food security in all its dimensions and to develop strategies to improve it. The declaration resolved "to use all means to alleviate the suffering caused by the current crisis, to stimulate food production and to increase investment in agriculture, to address obstacles to food access, and the use the planet's resources sustainably, for present and future generations". The declaration ended: "We commit to eliminating hunger and to securing food for all today and tomorrow".

Notes

Foreword

1 Thomas R. Malthus, *An Essay on the Principle of Population* (London: Printed for J. Johnson in St. Paul's Churchyard, 1798).
2 *International Assessment of Agricultural Science and Technology for Development* (IAASTD), launched at UNESCO headquarters in Paris, France on 15 April 2008. Available at www.unesco.org
3 The IAASTD was launched under the co-sponsorship of the FAO, GEF, UNDP, UNEP, UNESCO, the World Bank, and WHO.
4 Quoted in "The World Food Crisis," *New York Times* editorial, 10 April 2008.
5 See Julie A. Mertus, *The United Nations and Human Rights: A Guide for a New Era* (London: Routledge, 2005); and Bertrand G. Ramcharan, *Contemporary Human Rights Ideas* (London: Routledge, 2008).
6 See Elizabeth R. DeSombre, *Global Environmental Institutions* (London: Routledge, 2006).
7 See Thomas G. Weiss and David A. Korn, *Internal Displacement: Conceptualization and its Consequences* (London: Routledge, 2006); and Gil Loescher, Alexander Betts, and James Milner, *UNHCR: The Politics and Practice of Refugee Protection Into the Twenty-First Century* (London: Routledge, 2008).
8 D. John Shaw, *World Food Security: A History Since 1945* (Basingstoke and New York: Palgrave Macmillan, 2007) and D. John Shaw, *Sir Hans Singer: The Life and Work of a Development Economist* (Basinstoke and New York: Palgrave Macmillan, 2002); and D. John Shaw, *The UN World Food Progamme and the Development of Food Aid* (Basingstoke and New York: Palgrave Macmillan, 2001).

1 Background

1 UNICEF, *The State of the World's Children 2005: Childhood Under Threat* (New York: United Nations Children's Fund, 2005).
2 Stuart Gillespie, Milla McLachlan, and Roger Shrimpton, eds, *Combating Malnutrition: Time to Act* (Washington, D.C.: World Bank, 2003).
3 IFPRI, *Reaching Sustainable Food Security for All by 2020: Getting the Priorities and Responsibilities Right* (Washington, D.C.: International Food Policy Research Institute, 2002).

4 C. Ford Runge, Benjamin Senauer, Philip G. Pardey, and Mark W. Rosegrant, *Ending Hunger in Our Lifetime: Food Security and Globalization* (Baltimore, Md.: Johns Hopkins University Press, 2003).
5 Amartya Sen, *Development as Freedom* (New York: Alfred Knopf, 1999).
6 Lester R. Brown, *Outgrowing the Earth: The Food Security Challenge in an Age of Falling Water Tables and Rising Temperatures* (New York and London: W. W. Norton, 2004).
7 Peter Uvin, *The International Organization of Hunger* (London and New York: Kegan Paul International, 1994).
8 Klaus M. Leisinger, Karin Schmitt, and Rajul Pandya-Lorch, *Six Billion and Counting: Population Growth and Food Security in the 21st Century* (Washington, D.C.: International Food Policy Research Institute, 2002).
9 United Nations, *World Population Prospects: The 2002 Revision, Volume 1* (New York: United Nations, 2001).
10 United Nations, *World Population Prospects* (New York: United Nations, 2005).
11 UNFPA, *State of the World Population 2004: The Cairo Consensus at Ten—Population, Reproductive Health and the Global Effort to End Poverty* (New York: United Nations Population Fund, 2004).
12 World Bank, *World Development Report 2000/2001: Attacking Poverty* (New York: Oxford University Press for the World Bank, 2001).
13 World Bank, *World Development Report 2002* (New York: Oxford University Press for the World Bank, 2002).
14 Shaohua Chen and Martin Ravallion, *Absolute Poverty Measures for the Developing World, 1981–2004* (Washington, D.C.: Development Research Group, World Bank, 2007).
15 Akhter U. Ahmed, Ruth Vargas Hill, Lisa C. Smith, Doris M. Wiesmann, and Tim Frankenberger, *The World's Most Deprived. Characteristics and Causes of Extreme Poverty and Hunger* (Washington, D.C.: International Food Policy Research Institute, 2007).
16 Joachim von Braun and Rajul Pandya-Lorch, *Taking Action for the World's Poorest and Hungry People. Synopsis of an International Consultation* (www.ifpri.org/Pubs/books/oc57.asp#d1).
17 Paul Collier, *The Bottom Billion. Why the Poorest Countries Are Failing and What Can Be Done About It* (Oxford and New York: Oxford University Press, 2007).
18 UNESCO, EFA Global Monitoring Report 2002. *Education for All—Is the World on Track?* EFA Global Monitoring Report 2003/04. *Gender and Education for All—The Leap to Equality* EFA Global Monitoring Report 2005. *Education for All—The Quality Imperative.* EFA Global Monitoring Report 2006. *Education for All. Literacy for Life.* EFA Global Monitoring Report 2008. *Education for All by 2015. Will We Make It?* (Paris, France: United Nations Educational, Scientific and Cultural Organization, 2002, 2004, 2005, 2006, 2007).
19 UNICEF, *The State of the World's Children 2004. Girls, Education and Development* (New York: United Nations Children's Fund, 2004).
20 Barbara Bruns, Alain Mingat, and Ramahatra Rakotomalala, *Achieving Universal Primary Education by 2015: A Chance for Every Child* (Washington, D.C.: World Bank, 2003).

220 *Notes*

21 ILO, *Tripartite World Conference on Employment, Income Distribution and Social Progress and the International Division of Labour* (Geneva, Switzerland: International Labor Organization, 1976).
22 Amartya Sen, *Poverty and Famines: An Essay on Entitlements and Deprivation* (Oxford: Clarendon Press, 1981).
23 Joachim von Braun, ed., *Employment for Poverty Reduction and Food Security* (Washington, D.C.: International Food Policy Research Institute, 1995).
24 WTO, *Ministerial Declaration of the Doha Multilateral Negotiations* (Geneva, Switzerland: World Trade Organization, 2001).
25 Bernard M. Hoekman and Petros C. Mavroidis, *The World Trade Organization: Law, Economics, and Politics* (London and New York: Routledge, 2007).
26 UNCTAD, *Trade and Development Report 2006* (Geneva, Switzerland: United Nations Conference on Trade and Development, 2006).
27 Edward Clay and Olav Stokke, eds, *Food Aid and Human Security* (London: Frank Cass, 2000).
28 S. Neil MacFarlane and Yuen Foong Khong, *Human Security and the UN. A Critical History* (Bloomington and Indianapolis, Ind.: Indiana University Press, 2006).
29 UNDP, *Human Development Report 1994* (New York: United Nations Development Programme, 1994).
30 CHS, *Human Security Now* (New York: United Nations Commission on Human Security, 2003).
31 United Nations, *A More Secure World: Our Shared Responsibility: Report of the High-Level Panel on Threats, Challenges and Change* (New York: United Nations, 2004).
32 Worldwatch Institute, *State of the World 2005: Redefining Global Security* (New York and London: W. W. Norton, 2005).
33 D. John Shaw, *The UN World Food Programme and the Development of Food Aid* (Basingstoke and New York: Palgrave Macmillan, 2001).
34 George S. McGovern, *The Third Freedom. Ending Hunger in Our Time* (New York: Simon & Schuster, 2001). Also published in paperback (Lanham, Md.: Rowman & Littlefield, 2002).
35 UNDP, *UN Millennium Project 2005. Investing in Development: A Practical Plan to Achieve the Millennium Development Goals* (New York: United Nations Development Programme, 2005). The bulk of the analytical work for the UN Millennium Project was carried out by a number of thematic task forces comprising over 250 experts. In addition to the report of the project, 13 task-force reports were produced on hunger, universal primary education, gender equality in education and empowering women, child and maternity health, HIV/AIDS, malaria, TB, access to essential medicines, water and sanitation, improving the lives of slum dwellers, trade, environmental sustainability, and science, technology, and innovation. The 14 volumes were published in a UN Millennium Development Library set (London: Earthscan/James and James, 2006).
36 James A. Baker and Lee H. Hamilton, *The Iraq Study Group Report. The Way Forward—A New Approach* (New York: Vintage Books, 2006). Joseph E. Stiglitz and Linda J. Bilmes, *The True Cost of the Iraq Conflict* (New York: Norton, 2008).

Notes 221

37 William Easterly, *The White Man's Burden. Why the West's Efforts to Aid the Rest Have Done so Much Ill and so Little Good* (Oxford and New York: Oxford University Press, 2006).
38 FAO, *Plant Genetic Resources* (Rome, Italy: Development Education Exchange Papers, Food and Agriculture Organization of the United Nations, 1993).
39 FAO, *Statement on Biodiversity* (Rome, Italy: Food and Agriculture Organization of the United Nations, 2000).
40 FAO, *UN Statement on the Use of GM Food for Food aid in Southern Africa* (Rome, Italy: Food and Agriculture Organization of the United Nations, 2002).
41 FAO, *The State of Food and Agriculture 2003–04. Agricultural Biotechnology: Meeting the Needs of the Poor?* (Rome, Italy: Food and Agriculture Organization of the United Nations, 2004.)
42 David L. Pelletier, "FDA's regulation of genetically engineered foods. Scientific, legal and political dimensions," *Food Policy* 31, no. 6 (December 2006): 570–91.
43 Carl K. Eicher, Karim Maredia, and Idah Sithole-Niang, "Crop biotechnology and the African farmer," *Food Policy* 31, no. 6 (December 2006): 504–27.
44 FAO, *Food Outlook. Global Market Analysis* (November 2007).
45 Nicholas Stern, *The Economics of Climate Change* (Cambridge: Cambridge University Press, 2006). Also available at www.sternreview.org.uk
46 Joseph Stiglitz, *Globalization and Its Discontents* (London: Penguin Books, 2002). Also by the same author, *Making Globalization Work. The Next Steps to Global Justice* (London: Allen Lane, 2006).
47 Raphael Kaplinsky, *Globalization, Poverty and Inequality. Between a Rock and a Hard Place* (Malden, Mass. and Cambridge: Polity Press, 2005).
48 ILO, *A Fairer Globalization: Creating Opportunities for All. Report of the World Commission on the Social Dimensions of Globalization* (Geneva, Switzerland: International Labor Organization, 2005).
49 Uwe Kracht and Manfred Schulz, eds, *Food and Nutrition Security in the Process of Globalization and Urbanization* (Munster, Germany: Lit Verlag, 2005). See also the volume they edited, *Food Security and Nutrition. The Global Challenge* (Munster, Germany and New York: Lit Verlag and St. Martin's Press, 1999).
50 Wenche Barth Eide and Uwe Kracht, eds, *Food and Human Rights in Development Vol. 1. Legal and Institutional Dimensions and Selected Topics* (Antwerp, Belgium and Oxford: Intersentia, 2005). See also their *Food and Human Rights. Vol. II. Evolving Issues and Emerging Applications* (Mortsel, Belgium: Intersentia, 2007).
51 FAO, *Voluntary Guidelines to Support the Progressive Realization of the Right to Adequate Food in the Context of National Food Security.* Adopted at the 127th session of the FAO Council, November 2004. (Rome, Italy: Food and Agriculture Organization of the United Nations, 2004).
52 Edward Newman, *A Crisis of Global Institutions? Multilateralism and International Security* (London and New York: Routledge Global Institutions series, 2007).
53 For the year 2006, the combined value added of the largest 19 transnational corporations was over four times that of the combined GDP of all 50 least developed countries.

54 Gordon Conway, *The Doubly Green Revolution. Food for All in the 21st Century* (London and New York: Penguin Books, 1997).
55 World Bank, *World Development Report 2008. Agriculture for Development* (Washington, D.C.: World Bank, 2007).
56 Lester R. Brown, *Plan B 3.0. Mobilizing to Save Civilization* (New York: W. W. Norton, 2008).

2 Origins

1 Samuel I. Rosenman, ed., *The Public Papers and Addresses of Franklin D. Roosevelt*. 4 vols. (New York: Harper, 1950).
2 Townsend Hoopes and Douglas Brinkley, *FDR and the Creation of the U. N.* (New Haven, Conn. and London: Yale University Press, 1997).
3 Of all the personalities involved, Frank McDougall is especially linked with the creation of FAO. He was impressed by the "new knowledge" of nutrition that developed between the two world wars and by the paradox of large food surpluses emerging alongside hunger and malnutrition. His conviction that these two "evils" should cancel out each other was crystallized in his phrase "the marriage of food and agriculture." His memorandum on "The Agricultural and Health Problem," written in 1935, served as a first step toward bringing the findings of nutritionists before the League of Nations, which indicated that a large proportion of the world's population did not get enough of the right kinds of food, and that food production should be expanded to meet nutritional requirements. He is considered to have sold the idea of an international organization to combat hunger to President Roosevelt, which led to the Hot Springs conference and the founding of FAO. At the conference, he showed a film, *The World of Plenty*, to the delegates and asked "What are we fighting for? When he answered his own question by urging a war against want, starting with the want of foods, delegates rose to their feet and cheered. To this day, a memorial lecture is delivered in his honour by a distinguished person at each session of the FAO Conference. Addeke H. Boerma, *FAO and the World Food Problem: Past, Present and Future* (Rome, Italy: FAO, 1968). Ralph W. Phillips, *FAO: Its Origins, Foundation and Evolution, 1945–1981* (Rome, Italy: FAO, 1981). Amy L. S. Staples, *The Birth of Development* (Kent, Ohio: Kent State University Press, 2006), 76.
4 FAO, *United Nations Conference on Food and Agriculture, Hot Springs, Virginia, May 18–June 5, 1943. Final Act and Section Reports* (Washington, D.C.: United States Government Printing Office, 1943).
5 FAO, *Report of the First Conference of FAO Held at Quebec City, October 16–November 1, 1945* (Ottawa, Canada: Dominion Department of Agriculture, 1945).
6 This description of the origins of the World Bank is drawn from two extensive histories: Edward S. Mason and Robert E Asher, *The World Bank since Bretton Woods* (Washington, D.C.: Brookings Institution Press, 1973); and Devish Kapur, John P. Lewis, and Richard Webb, *The World Bank. Its First Half Century*. Vol. 1, *History* (Washington, D.C.: Brookings Institution Press, 1997).
7 United Nations, *The Charter of the United Nations*, signed at the United Nations Conference in San Francisco, California on 24 June 1945. (New York: United Nations, 1945.)

8 Brian Urquhart and Erskine Childers, *Renewing the United Nations System* (New York: The Ford Foundation, 1994).
9 A full description of how SUNFED became IDA is given in D. John Shaw, "Turning point in the evolution of soft financing: The United Nations and the World Bank," *Canadian Journal of Development Studies* XXVI, no. 1 (2005): 43–61.
10 For further details see D. John Shaw, *The UN World Food Programme and the Development of Food Aid* (Basingstoke and New York: Palgrave Macmillan, 2001).
11 The group consisted of: Dr. M. R. Benedict, professor of agricultural economics, University of California, Berkeley, U.S.A.; Dr. J. Figeres, former president of the Republic of Costa Rica; Dr. V. K. R. V. Rao, former vice-chancellor, University of Delhi, India; Dr. P. N. Rosenstein-Roden, professor of economics, Massachusetts Institute of Technology, U.S.A.; and Dr. H. W. Singer, principal officer, Office of the Under-Secretary for Economic and Social Affairs, United Nations, New York, who acted as chairman of the group.
12 FAO, "Expanded program of surplus food utilization." Report by the expert group to the FAO director-general in FAO, *Development Through Food: A Strategy for Surplus Utilization* (Rome, Italy: FFHC Basic Study no. 2, FAO, 1961), 69–117.
13 Memorandum to President Kennedy from George S. McGovern of 28 March 1961 and attached report on "Recommendations for Improvement in the Food for Peace Program," (McGovern papers, Box TK-5, Seeley G. Mudd Manuscript Library, Princeton University), 35–36.
14 "Statement of the delegate of the United States of America at the Intergovernmental Advisory Committee, 10 April 1961, FAO, Rome, Italy, reproduced in FAO, *Development Through Food: A Strategy for Surplus Utilization* (1961), 121.
15 In his first address to the UN General Assembly on 25 September 1961, President Kennedy proposed that the decade of the 1960s should be designated the "United Nations Decade for Development" through which, "the United Nations' existing efforts to promote economic growth can be expanded and coordinated." His proposal was accept. President Kennedy Speeches. Papers of the President's Office Files. Box 34. John Fitzgerald Kennedy Library, Boston, Mass.,U.S.A.
16 UN, *Report of the World Food Conference, Rome, 5–16 November 1974* (New York: United Nations), 12. Sartaj Aziz played a major role in the creation of IFAD. He made the original proposal for its establishment and was appointed executive secretary of the preparatory commission that prepared its legal instruments and lending policies, and was assistant president of IFAD (1978–84).
17 John Andrew King, "The International Fund for Agricultural Development: The first six years," *Development Policy Review* 3, no. 1 (1985): 44–65.
18 Gordon Conway, *The Doubly Green Revolution. Food for All in the 21st Century* (London and New York: Penguin Books, 1997), 44–65.

3 Mandates, governance, and finance

1 The words "and ensure humanity's freedom from hunger" were added to FAO's mandate in 1965 at the 20th FAO conference, midway through the

Freedom from Hunger Campaign that the FAO director-general, B. R. Sen, launched in 1960.
2 *FAO: The Challenge of Renewal. Report of the Independent External Evaluation of the Food and Agriculture Organization of the United Nations* (Rome, Italy: FAO, 2007).
3 World Bank, *A Guide to the World Bank*. 2nd edition (Washington, D.C.: World Bank, 2007), xvii. The inscription at the entrance to the World Bank's offices at 1850, I Street, Washington, D.C., reads, "Our dream is a world free of poverty."
4 World Bank, *Reaching the Rural Poor. A Renewed Strategy for Rural Development* (Washington, D.C.: World Bank, 2003), 8–9.
5 WFP, *WFP Mission Statement*. Document CFA; 38/P/5. (Rome, Italy: World Food Programme, 1994).
6 UN, *Report of the World Food Conference, Rome 5–16 November 1974* (New York: United Nations, 1975), 16.
7 UN, "Further Measures for the Restructuring and Revitalization of the United Nations in the Economic, Social and Related Fields." UN General Assembly Resolution 48/162, adopted on 20 December 1993.
8 IFAD's mandate is set forth in the *Agreement Establishing IFAD* and in the fund's *Lending Policies and Criteria* (Rome, Italy: International Fund for Agricultural Development, 1977).
9 Idriss Jazairy, Mohiuddin Alamgir, and Theresa Panuccio, *The State of World Rural Poverty* (New York and London: New York University Press and Intermediate Technology Publications, 1992).
10 IFAD, *Rural Poverty Report 2001. The Challenge of Ending Rural Poverty* (Rome, Italy: published for IFAD by Oxford University Press, 2001).
11 Prabhu Pingali and Tim Kelly, "The role of international agricultural research in contributing to global food security and poverty alleviation: The case of the CGIAR," in Robert Evenson and Prabhu Pingali, eds, *The Handbook of Agricultural Economics: Volume III* (Amsterdam, the Netherlands: Elsevier Press, 2007).
12 CGIAR, *Charting the CGIAR's Future: A New Vision for 2010* (Washington, D.C.: CGIAR secretariat, July 2000).
13 Prabhu Pigali and Tim Kelly, "The role of international agricultural research in contributing to global food security and poverty alleviation." Nearly half of the recipients of the annual World Food Prize have been CGIAR researchers.
14 IFAD later became a co-sponsor of the CGIAR.
15 CGIAR, *The Charter of the CGIAR System*. Adopted b y the CGIAR at its Annual General Meeting in 2004, with revisions approved in 2006 and 2007 (Washington, D.C.: CGIAR Secretariat, March 2007).

4 Policies, programs, and projects

1 For an account of the early pioneering work of FAO, see D. John Shaw, *World Food Security: A History since 1945* (Basingstoke and New York: Palgrave Macmillan, 2007), 15–111.
2 Craig Murphy, *The United Nations Development Programme* (Cambridge: Cambridge University Press, 2006).
3 UN, *Report of the World Food Conference, 1974* (New York: United Nations, 1975), 18.

4 Edouard Saouma, *FAO in the Front Line of Development* (Rome, Italy: FAO, 1993).
5 FAO, *World Food Summit. Rome Declaration on World Food Security* and *World Food Summit Plan of Action* (Rome, Italy: FAO, 1996); and FAO, *World Food Summit: Five Years On* (Rome, Italy: FAO, 2002).
6 FAO, *Livestock's Long Shadow* (Rome, Italy: FAO, 2006).
7 FAO, *The State of World Fisheries and Aquaculture 2006* (Rome, Italy: FAO, 2007).
8 FAO, *The State of the World's Forests 2007* (Rome, Italy: FAO, 2007).
9 FAO, *Status and Lessons Learned from Special National and Regional Programmes for Food Security and other Related FAO Food Security Programmes.* Document CFS: 2007/3. Committee on World Food Security, Twenty-third Session, Rome 7–10 May, 2007 (Rome, Italy: FAO, 2007).
10 FAO, *Emergency Action: Technical Handbook Series. The Emergency Sequence. What FAO Does—How FAO Does It* (Rome, Italy: FAO, 1998).
11 "Voluntary guidelines to support the progressive realization of the right to adequate food in the context of national food security." Adopted by the 127th session of the FAO council, November 2004.
12 FAO, *FAO Investment Centre. A Better Future for the Rural Poor* (Rome, Italy: FAO, 2003).
13 Edward S. Mason and Robert E. Asher, *The World Bank since Bretton Woods* (Washington, D.C.: Brookings Institution Press, 1973), 739–48; and Devish Kapur, John P. Lewis, and Richard Webb, *The World Bank. Its First Half Century. Vol. 1: History* (Washington, D.C.: Brookings Institution Press, 1997), 379–447. Katherine Marshall, *The World Bank. From Reconstruction to Equity* (London and New York: Routledge, 2008).
14 ILO, *Employment, Incomes and Equality. A Strategy for Increasing Productive Employment in Kenya* (Geneva, Switzerland: International Labour Office, 1972).
15 World Bank, *World Development Report 2008. Agriculture for Development* (Washington, D.C.: World Bank, 2007), 42. Kevin Cleaver, "Contemporary issues of agriculture and rural development in developing countries," presentation at the Berlin European Forum on Agriculture and Rural Development, July 2007, and to the United States Treasury, August 2007.
16 Giovanni A. Cornia, Richard Jolly, and Francis Stewart, *Adjustment with a Human Face. Protecting the Vulnerable and Promoting Growth. A Study by UNICEF.* 2 vols. (Oxford: Clarendon Press, 1987.)
17 FAO, "The effects of stabilization and structural adjustment programmes on food security," Economic and Social Development Paper no. 89 (Rome, Italy: FAO, 1988).
18 World Bank, "Adjustment lending. An evaluation of ten years of experience," Policy and Research Series no. 1 (Washington, D.C.: World Bank Country Economics Department, 1988).
19 Michael Lipton and Robert Paarlberg, *The Role of the World Bank in Agricultural Development in the 1990s* (Washington, D.C.: International Food Policy Research Institute, October 1990), 43–44.
20 World Bank, *World Bank Assistance to Agriculture in Sub-Saharan Africa.* An Independent Evaluation Group review (Washington, D.C.: World Bank, 2008).
21 World Bank, *From Vision to Action in the Rural Sector* (Washington, D.C.: World Bank Group, March 1996).

22 World Bank, *Reaching the Rural Poor. A Renewed Strategy for Rural Development* (Washington, D.C.: World Bank Group, December 2003).
23 World Bank, *Agricultural Growth for the Poor. An Agenda for Development* (Washington, D.C.: World Bank, 2005).
24 World Bank, *World Development Report. Agriculture for Development* (Washington, D.C.: World Bank, 2007).
25 WFP, *Strategic Plan 2004–2007*. Document WFP/EB.3/2003/4-A/1. (Rome, Italy: World Food Programme, 2003.)
26 Jon Margous, *Building the World's Largest Humanitarian Agency* (Rome, Italy: World Food Programme, 2002).
27 UNHCR, *The State of the World's Refugees 1993: The Challenge of Protection* (London: Penguin Books, 1993); and UNHCR, *The State of the World's Refugees, 1997–98: A Humanitarian Agenda* (Oxford: Oxford University Press, 1997).
28 "Strengthening the Coordination of Humanitarian Emergency Assistance in the United Nations." United Nations General Assembly Resolution 46/182, adopted on 19 December 1991.
29 WFP, *Global School Feeding Report 2006* (Rome, Italy: World Food Programme, 2006). See also WFP, *Hunger and Learning. World Hunger Series 2006* (Rome, Italy: World Food Programme, 2006).
30 WFP, *People Living with AIDS. Food as the First Line of Defence* (Rome, Italy: World Food Programme, 2004).
31 FAO, *Disposal of Agricultural Surpluses. Principles recommended by FAO* (Rome, Italy: FAO, 1954). Subsequently revised and expanded in five versions, Last edited in 2001. The *Principles* are not legally binding but provide guideline, a code of conduct, or what are called "consultative obligations." An FAO Consultative Subcommittee on Surplus Disposal was created to monitor adherence to the *Principles*.
32 ACC/SCN, "ACC/SCN statement on nutrition, refugees and displaced persons," in ACC/SCN, *Nutritional Issues in Food Aid. Symposium Report. Nutrition Policy Discussion Paper no. 12* (Geneva, Switzerland: ACC Subcommittee on Nutrition, 1993).
33 WFP, *Food for Nutrition: Mainstreaming Nutrition in WFP*. Document WFP/EB.A/2004/5-A/1. (Rome, Italy: World Food Programme, 2004.)
34 UN, *Report on the World Food Conference 1974* (New York: United Nations, 1975), 9.
35 WFP, *Nutrition in Emergencies: WFP Experience and Challenges*. Document WFP/EB.A/2004/5-A/3. (Rome, Italy: World Food Programme, 2004.)
36 WFP, *Micronutrient Fortification: WFP Experience and the Way Forward* (Rome, Italy: World Food Programme, 2004).
37 Agnes R. Quisumbing, Lynn R. Brown, Hilary S. Felstein, Lawrence Haddad, and Christine Pina, *Women: The Key to Food Security* (Washington, D.C.: International Food Policy Research Institute, 1995).
38 WFP, *The Contribution of Food Aid to Improving Women's Status*. Document WFP/IGC: 27/15 (Rome, Italy: World Food Programme, 1975).
39 WFP, *Breadwinners at Home and at Work. World Food Programme Support during the Decade for Women*. Document WFP/CFA: 20/INF/5. (Rome, Italy: World Food Programme, 1985. Also published as WFP Occasional Paper no. 4, 1985.

40 WFP, *Gender Policy 2003–2007. Enhancing Commitment to Women to Ensure Food Security* (Rome, Italy: World Food Programme, 1992).
41 WFP, *Ending Child Hunger and Undernutrition Initiative.* Document WFP/EB.1/2007/5-A; and *Global Framework for Action: Ending Child Hunger and Undernutrition Initiative.* Document WFP/EB.1/2007/5-A/Add.1. (Rome, Italy: World Food Programme, 2007).
42 IFAD, *An Independent External Evaluation of the International Fund for Agricultural Development* (Rome, Italy: Office of Evaluation, International Fund For Agricultural Development, 2005). The evaluation was prepared by a consulting firm based in the United Kingdom and consisted of a team of 26 consultants from 14 countries, plus 10 national evaluation teams, conducted under the overall supervision of the director of IFAD's Office of Evaluation.
43 IFAD, *Annual Report 2006* (Rome, Italy: International Fund for Agricultural Development, 2007), 68.
44 UN, *Report of the World Food Conference 1974*, 8.
45 World Bank, *The CGIAR at 31. An Independent Meta-Evaluation of the Consultative Group on International Agricultural Research* (Washington, D.C.: World Bank Operations Evaluation Department, 2004).
46 Gordon Conway, *The Doubly Green Revolution. Food for All in the 21st Century* (London and New York: Penguin Books, 1997), 62–63.
47 CGIAR, *The Charter*, 16.
48 Surendra Varma and Mark Winslow, *Healing Wounds. How the International Centers of the CGIAR Help Rebuild Agricultural in Countries Affected by Conflicts and Natural Disasters* (Washington, D.C.: Consultative Group on International Agricultural Research, 2005).
49 CGIAR, *Report of the Fourth External Program and Management Review of the International Food Policy Research Institute* (Rome, Italy: CGAIR Science Council, February 2006).
50 Joachim von Braun and Rajul Pandya-Lorch, eds, *Food Policy for the Poor. Expanding the Research Frontier. Highlights from 30 Years of IFPRI Research* (Washington, D.C.: International Food Policy Research Institute, 2005).
51 IFPRI, *Impact Assessment Publications* (Washington, D.C.: International Food Policy Research Institute, 2007). www.ifpri.org/impact/impactpubs.asp. Most of the publications are available for download in PDF format.
52 IFPRI, *A 2020 Vision for Food, Agriculture and the Environment. The Vision, Challenge and Recommended Action* (Washington, D.C.: International Food Policy Research Institute, 1995).
53 IFPRI, *Assuring Food and Nutrition Security in Africa by 2020: Prioritizing Action, Strengthening Actors, and Facilitating Partnerships—Proceedings of an All-Africa Conference, Kampala, Uganda, 1–3 April, 2004* (Washington, D.C.: International Food Policy Research Institute, 2004).
54 IFPRI, *Taking Action for the World's Poor and Hungry People, 17–19 October 2007, Beijing, China* (Washington, D.C.: International Food Policy Research Institute, 2007). www.ifpri.org/2020chinaconference
55 IFPRI, *Report of the Center-Commissioned External Review of the International Service for National Agricultural Research (ISNAR)* (Washington, D.C.: International Food Policy Research Institute, September 2007).

56 Karen Rosskopf, *Implementation Plan for Distance Learning Material Development and Delivery in the Global Open Agriculture and Food University* (Washington, D.C.: CGIAR Secretariat, 2004).

5 Future directions

1 *FAO: The Challenge of Renewal. Report of the Independent External Evaluation of the Food and Agriculture Organization of the United Nations.* Submitted to the Council Committee for the Independent External Evaluation of FAO, September 2007 (Rome, Italy: FAO, 2007). The evaluation core team consisted of: Leif E. Christoffensen (Norway), team leader, Keith Bezanson (Canada), former team leader and principal author of the report, Ume Lela (India), Michael Davis (United Kingdom), Carlos Perez del Castillo (Uruguay), and Thelma Awori (Uganda).
2 The amazon web site, www.amazon.com, lists over 1,300 entries of publications relating to the World Bank.
3 See, for example, William Easterly, *The White Man's Burden. Why the West's Efforts to Aid the Rest Have Done So Much Ill and So Little Good* (Oxford and New York: Oxford University Press, 2006); and Joseph Stiglitz, *Globalization and Its Discontents* (London and New York: Penguin Books, 2002).
4 Kevin Danaher, ed., *50 Years Is Enough: The Case Against the World Bank and the International Monetary Fund* (Cambridge, Mass.: South End Press, 1994).
5 Nancy Birdsall, ed., *Rescuing the World Bank. A CGD Working Group Report and Selected Essays* (Washington, D.C.: Center for Global Development, 2006).
6 World Bank, *Meeting the Challenges of Global Development. A Long-Term Strategic Exercise for the World Bank Group* (Washington, D.C.: World Bank, 2007).
7 Jeffrey C. Hooke, *The Dinosaur Among Us. The World Bank and Its Path to Extinction* (North Charleston, S.C.: BookSurge, 2007).
8 Robert B. Zoellick, "An inclusive and sustainable globalization," The National Press Club, Washington, D.C., 10 October 2007.
9 Robert B. Zoellick, "A challenge of economic statecraft," Center for Global Development, 2 April 2008.
10 Chris Gerrard, "Global governance without a global government: The growth and implications of Global Partnership Programs." 11 January 2008. (www.worldbank.org/ieg/grpp).
11 World Bank, *Addressing the Challenges of Globalization. An Independent Evaluation of the World Bank's Approach to Global Programs* (Washington, D.C.: World Bank Operations Evaluation Department, 2004). This report was written by Uma Lele and Chris Gerrard and built on case-study analyses by the World Bank.
12 Chr. Michelsen Institute, *Evaluation of the World Food Programme* (Bergen, Norway: Chr. Michelsen Institute, 1994). The evaluation, which took three years to complete at a cost reported to be over U.S.$3 million (excluding the cost of extensive support and documentation provided by the WFP secretariat), was conducted by 16 international consultants, assisted by national consultants in nine country case studies. The first phase of the evaluation, completed in late 1992, was conducted by the North–South

Institute of Canada. The second phase, completed in December 1993, was coordinated by the Chr. Michelsen Institute of Bergen, Norway. The evaluation report consisted of an abridged version, a main report, and nine country case studies.
13 WFP, *Enabling Development* (Rome, Italy: World Food Programme, 1999).
14 IFAD, *An Independent External Evaluation of the International Fund for Agricultural Development* (Rome, Italy: Office of Evaluation, IFAD, 2005). The evaluation report was prepared by ITAD Ltd., a consulting firm based in the United Kingdom. The firm assembled a team of 26 consultants from 14 countries, plus 10 national evaluation teams. The evaluation was conducted under the overall supervision of the director of IFAD's Office of Evaluation, on behalf of IFAD's executive board.
15 Gordon Conway, Uma Lele, Jim Peacock, and Martin Pineiro, *Sustainable Agriculture for a Food Secure World. A Vision for International Agricultural Research* (Washington, D.C., and Stockholm, Sweden: Consultative Group on International Agricultural Research and Swedish Agency for Research Co-operation with Developing Countries, 1994). The panel consisted of Gordon Conway (chair), Uma Lele, Jim Peacock, and Martin Pineiro, with Selcuk Ozgediz as panel secretary, Michael Griffin and Peter Hazell, resource persons, and Henri Carsalade and Johan Holmbery as co-convenors of the panel on behalf of the CGIAR Oversight Committee.
16 CGIAR, *Renewal of the CGIAR. Sustainable Agricultural for Food Security in Developing Countries.* Ministerial-level meeting, Lucerne, Switzerland, 9–10 February 1995 (Washington, D.C.: Consultative Group on International Agricultural Research, 1995).
17 CGIAR, *The International Research Partnership for Food Security and Sustainable Agriculture. Third System Review of the Consultative Group on International Agricultural Research* (Washington, D.C.: CGIAR System Review Secretariat, 1998). The review panel consisted of Maurice Strong (Canada) (chairman), Bruce Alberts (United States), Kenzo Hemmi (Japan), Klaus Leisinger (Switzerland), Yolana Kakabadge (Ecuador), Whitney MacMillan (United States), Bongiwe Njobe-Mbuli (South Africa), Emile Salim (Indonesia), and M. S. Swaminathan (India).
18 World Bank, *The CGIAR at 31: An Independent Meta-Evaluation of the Consultative Group on International Agricultural Research* (Washington, D.C.: World Bank Operations Evaluation Department, 2004). The work for this review was led by Uma Lele, senior adviser, Operations Evaluation Department Global Team.
19 CGIAR Science Council, *System Priorities for CGIAR Research 2005–2015* (Rome, Italy: Science Council Secretariat, 2005).
20 CGIAR Science Council, *Lessons Learnt from Selection and Implementation of the CGIAR Challenge Programs* (Rome, Italy: Science Council Secretariat, 2007).
21 Francisco J. B. Reifschneider, Ernest Corea, and Ian Johnson, *Revolutionizing The Evolution of the CGIAR 2001 to 2007. A Contribution to the Institutional Memoir and Some Thoughts for the Future* (Washington, D.C.: Consultative Group on International Agricultural Research, 2007).
22 Prabhu Pingali and Tim Kelly, "The role of international agricultural research in contributing to global food security and poverty alleviation: The case of the CGIAR," in Robert Evenson and Prabhu Pingali, eds,

Handbook of Agricultural Economics, vol. 3 (Amsterdam, the Netherlands: North Holland, 2007), 381–418.
23 Edward Newman, *Crisis of Global Institutions? Multilateralism and International Security* (London and New York: Routledge Global Institutions series, 2007).
24 Bo M. I. Bengtsson, *Agricultural Research at the Crossroads. Revisited Resource-poor Farmers and the Millennium Development Goals* (Enfield, N.H.: Science Publishers, 2007), 244.
25 A note on the CGIAR's "change management initiative" can be found at www.cgiar.org/changemenagement/index.html
26 GAO, *Foreign Assistance. U.S. Agencies Face Challenges to Improving the Efficiency of Food Aid* (Washington, D.C.: United States Government Accountability Office, 2007).
27 OECD, *The Development Effectiveness of Food Aid. Does Tying Matter?* (Paris: Organization for Economic Cooperation and Development, 2005). The study was undertaken by Edward Clay in collaboration with Barry Riley and Ian Urey.
28 CARE, *White Paper on Food Aid Policy: CARE USA* (New York: CARE, 2006).
29 Ugo Gentilini, *Cash and Food Transfers: A Primer* (Rome, Italy: World Food Programme, 2007).
30 WFP, *WFP Biennial Management Plan (2008–2009)*. Document WFP/ EB.2/2007/5-A/1. (Rome, Italy: World Food Programme, 2007.)
31 United Nations, United Nations World Food Conference. The World Food Problem. Proposals for National and International Action. Document E/ CONF. 65/4 (New York: United Nations, 1974).
32 UN, *Report of the Preparatory Committee for the World Food Conference on Its Third Session* (New York: United Nations, 1974).
33 UN, *Report of the World Food Conference, Rome, 5–16 November, 1974* (New York: United Nations, 1975), 18.
34 U.S., *Report on the World Food Conference. Hearings before the Committee on Foreign Affairs, House of Representatives, Ninety-Third Congress, Second Session, November 26, 1974* (Washington, D.C.: United States Government Printing Office, 1974).
35 Three executive directors were appointed during the WFC's 18 years of operations: John A. Hannah (United States), 1975–78; Maurice J. Williams (United States), 1978–86; and Gerald I. Trant (Canada), 1986–92.
36 Of the 18 annual WFC ministerial sessions, three were held in Rome, one at the UN headquarters in New York, nine in developing countries, and five in developed countries.
37 For a comprehensive account of the work of WFC, see D. John Shaw, *World Food Security. A History since 1945* (Basingstoke and New York: Palgrave Macmillan, 2007), 167–221.
38 UN, *High-Level Panel Report on UN System-Wide Coherence* (New York: United Nations, 2006).
39 James Ingram, *Bread and Stones. Leadership and the Struggle for Reform in the United Nations World Food Programme* (North Charleston, S.C.: BookSurge, 2006).

Web sites and select bibliography

Each institution has its own copious literature, which can be accessed via their well-designed web sites. The web sites and a select bibliography for each institution are given below.

FAO

Web site: www.fao.org

FAO, *World Food Summit. Rome Declaration on World Food Security and World Food Summit Plan of Action* (Rome, Italy: FAO, 1996).

——— *Report of the World Food Summit: Five Years On* (Rome, Italy: FAO, 2002).

——— *The State of Food Insecurity in the World* (Rome, Italy: FAO). Published annually since 1999.

——— *The State of Food and Agriculture 2003–2004. Agricultural Biotechnology. Meeting the Needs of the Poor?* (Rome, Italy: FAO, 2004).

——— *The State of World Fisheries and Aquaculture 2006* (Rome, Italy: FAO, 2007).

——— *State of the World's Forests 2007* (Rome, Italy: FAO, 2007).

——— *The Challenge of Renewal. Report of the Independent External Evaluation of the Food and Agriculture Organization of the United Nations* (Rome, Italy: FAO, September 2007).

World Bank/Agricultural and Rural Development Department

Web site: www.worldbank.org

Edward S. Mason and Robert E. Asher, *The World Bank since Bretton Woods* (Washington, D.C.: Brookings Institution Press, 1973)

Devish Kapur, John P. Lewis, and Richard Webb, *The World Bank. Its First Half Century. Vol. 1. History* (Washington, D.C.: Brookings Institution Press, 1997).

Csaba Csaki, *Reaching the Rural Poor: A Renewed Strategy for Rural Development* (Washington, D.C.: World Bank, 2003).

World Bank, *Agricultural Growth for the Poor. An Agenda for Development* (Washington, D.C.: World Bank, 2005).
———*A Guide to the World Bank. Second Edition* (Washington, D.C.: World Bank, 2007).
———*World Development Report 2008. Agriculture for Development* (Washington, D.C.: World Bank, 2008).

WFP

Web site: www.wfp.org

WFP, *WFP Mission Statement*. Document CFA: 38/P/5. (Rome, Italy: World Food Programme, 1994).
———*Enabling Development*. Document WFP/EB. A/99/4-A. (Rome, Italy: World Food Programme, 1999).
D. John Shaw, *The UN World Food Programme and the Development of Food Aid* (Basingstoke, U.K. and New York: Palgrave Macmillan, 2001).
James Ingram, *Bread and Stones. Leadership and the Struggle for Reform in the United Nations World Food Programme* (North Charleston, S.C.: BookSurge, 2006).
Ugo Gentilini, *Cash and Food Transfers: A Primer* (Rome, Italy: World Food Programme, 2007).
WFP, *World Food Programme Annual Report 2006* (Rome, Italy: World Food Programmed, 2007).

IFAD

Web site: www.ifad.org

Idriss Jazairy, Mohiuddin Alamgir, and Theresa Panuccio, *The State of World Rural Poverty. An Inqury into Its Causes and Consequences* (New York: published for the International Fund for Agricultural Development by New York University Press, 1992).
IFAD, *Rural Poverty Report 2001. The Challenge of Ending Rural Poverty* (Rome, Italy: published for the International Fund for Agricultural Development by Oxford University Press, 2001).
———*An Independent External Evaluation of the International Fund for Agricultural Development* (Rome, Italy: Office of Evaluation, International Fund for Agricultural Development, September 2005).
———*Annual Report 2006* (Rome, Italy: International Fund for Agricultural Development, 2006).

CGIAR

Web site: www.cgiar.org

Warren C. Baum, *Partners against Hunger: The Consultative Group on International Agricultural Research* (Washington, D.C.: published for the Consultative Group on International Agricultural Research by the World Bank, 1986).

Gordon Conway, *The Doubly Green Revolution. Food for All in the 21st Century* (London and New York: Penguin Books, 1997).
Uma J. Lele, *The CGIAR at 31. An Independent Meta-Evaluation of the Consultative Group on International Agricultural Research* (Washington, D.C.: World Bank Operations Evaluation Department, 2004).
Joachim von Braun and Rajul Pandya-Lorch, *Food Policy for the Poor. Expanding the Research Frontier. Highlights from 30 Years of IFPRI Research* (Washington, D.C.: International Food Policy Research Institute, 2005).
IFPRI, *Impact Assessment Publications* (Washington, D.C.: International Food Policy Research Institute, 2007) (www.ifpri.org/impactpubs.asp).
Joachim von Braun and Rajul Pandya-Lorch, *Taking Action for the World's Poorest and Hungry People. Synopsis of an International Consultation*, Beijing, China, 2007. (www.ifpri.org/Pubs/books/oc57.asp#d1).
CGIAR, *The Gateway to Evidence that International Agricultural Research Is Making a Difference.* (http://impact.cgiar.org).
—— *Focus on Partnerships for Effective Research: CGIAR Annual Report 2006* (Washington, D.C.: Consultative Group on International Agricultural Research Secretariat, 2007).

Some general references

Peter Uvin, *The International Organization of Hunger* (London and New York: Kegan Paul International, 1994).
George McGovern, *The Third Freedom. Ending Hunger in Our Time* (New York: Simon & Schuster, 2001).
IFPRI, *Reaching Sustainable Food Security for All by 2020: Getting the Priorities Right* (Washington, D.C.: International Food Policy Research Institute, 2002)
C. Ford Runge, Benjamin Senauer, Philip G. Pardey, and Mark W. Rosegrant, *Ending Hunger in Our Lifetime: Food Security and Globalization* (Baltimore, Md.: Johns Hopkins University Press, 2003).
Lester R. Brown, *Outgrowing the Earth: The Food Security Challenge in an Age of Falling Water Tables and Rising Temperatures* (New York and London: W. W.Norton, 2004).
UNDP, *UN Millennium Project 2005. Investing in Development. A Practical Plan to Achieve the Millennium Development Goals. Overview* (New York: United Nations Development Programme, 2005).
Nicholas Stern, *The Economics of Climate Change* (Cambridge: Cambridge University Press, 2006).
Akhter U. Ahmed, Ruth Vargas Hill, Lisa C. Smith, Doris M. Wiesmann, and Tim Frankenberger, *The World's Most Deprived. Characteristics and Causes of Extreme Poverty and Hunger.* 2020 Discussion Paper 43 (Washington, D.C.: International Food Policy Research Institute, October 2007).
Paul Collier, *The Bottom Billion. Why the Poorest Countries are Failing and What Can Be Done About It* (Oxford: Oxford University Press, 2007).

D. John Shaw, *World Food Security. A History since 1945* (Basingstoke and New York: Palgrave Macmillan, 2007).

Lester R. Brown, *Plan B 3.0. Mobilizing to Save Civilization* (New York and London: W. W. Norton, 2008).

Index

Africa (Sub-Saharan Africa) 6, 10, 22, 35
agricultural subsidies, United states and European Union 28–9
agricultural trade 27–30
al-Qaeda terrorist attack in United States on 11 September 2001 30
AIDS 11–12
Alliance for a Green Revolution in Africa (AGRA) 199
Annan, Kofi A. (United Nations Secretary-General, 1997–2006) 35
Atlantic Charter (signed by US President Roosevelt and British Prime Minster Churchill, August 1941) 53
Aziz, Sartaj (Director, FAO Commodities and Trade Division, Deputy Secretary-General 1974 World Food Conference, first deputy Executive Director, World Food Council, Assistant President, IFAD, Pakistan Minister of Agriculture, Finance and Foreign Affairs) xix

Beckmann, David (NGO Bread for the-World president) 14
Biofuels 42–3
Birdsall, Nancy (Center for Global Development president) 175
Black, Eugene (World Bank president, 1949–62) 112
Borlaug, Norman (Nobel Peace Prize laureate, 1970) 65
bottom billion (world's poorest people) 20–3
Braun, Joachim von (IFPRI director general) 14, 167
Brown, Lester R. (Earth Policy Institute president) 16

CARE white paper on food aid policy (2006) 202
Center for Global Change, Washington, DC: Hardest Job in the World. Five Crucial Tasks for the new President *of the World Bank* (2005) 175–6
CGIAR (Consultative Group on International Agricultural Research):
  Alliance of the CGIAR Centers 157
  Charter of the CGIAR 91:
  CGIAR centers 92, 154–5
  CGIAR chairman 91
  CGIAR consultative group 91
  co-sponsors of CGIAR 90–1
  director 92
  membership 91
  Science Council 92
  Secretariat 92
  Technical Advisory Committee 90
  core programs 65
  enhancing national agricultural research systems 157–9
  enlarging the CGIAR, 1974 World Food Conference resolution 152

236 *Index*

founding conferences, Bellagio, Italy (1970–1) 60
funding arrangements: restricted funding 93; unrestricted funding 92
Genetic Resources Policy Committee 161
genetic resources program 161
germplasm collection and conservation 161–4
germplasm improvement 159–61
global challenge programs: HarvestPlus 170
Sub-Saharan Africa Challenge Program 170
The Generation Challenge Program 170
The Water and Food Challenge Program 169
Global Conservation Trust 163
Global Open Food and Agriculture University Initiative 168
Global Seed Vault, Svalbard, Norway 163–4
guiding principles of operations 90
inaugural meeting of CGIAR (July 1971) 66
independent evaluation: CGIAT at 31 (2004) 193–5
International Center for the Improvement of Maize and Wheat (1971) 66
International Centers for Tropical Agriculture, Colombia and Nigeria (1967) 66
International Food Policy Research Institute (IFPRI) 14: Assuring Food and Nutrition Security in Africa Conference, Kampala, Uganda, 2004 166
decentralization and establishment of regional offices 166
Ending Hunger in our Lifetime (2003) 14
external review 2006, findings of 165–6
funding and staffing 164
mission 164–5
publications 166
Reaching Sustainable Food Security for All by 2020 (2002) 14
Taking Action for the World's Poor and Hungry People Conference, Beijing, China, 2007 20, 166
The World's Most Deprived study (2007) 20–3
2020 Vision for Food, Agriculture and the Environment 14, 166
international public goods, concept of 88
International Rice Research Institute (1960) 65
International Service for National Agricultural Research (ISNAR), merged with IFPRI in 2004, external review 2007, findings of 167–8
Lucerne Declaration and Action Program (1995) 189
management of natural resources, priorities for 156–7
mandate: expanded 89–90; original 89
origins: the Green Revolution 65
joint venture in Mexico (1943) 65
outreach programs 65
research priorities 2005–2015 195–7
resource problems 200–1
review of CGIAR challenge programs (2007), 197–8
revolutionizing the evolution of the CGIAR (2007) 198–9
sustainable agricultural production programs, benefits of 155–6
third review of the CGIAR system (1998) 190–3
vision statement for future international agricultural research (1994) 188–90
World Bank roles in the GIAR, assessment of 194–5

Charter of the United Nations (1945) 58
climate change and global warming 43–7:
economics of, the Stern review (2006) 45
Convention on Biological Diversity (1995) (see FAO)
cooperation among global food and agricultural institutions, proposals for 214–5

DALYS (disability-adjusted life years concept) 12
decent work, concept of 26
Declaration of the United Nations (1942) 53
Diouf, Jacques (present FAO director-general, 1994 –) 98,103
Doha Development Agenda 27–9
doubly green revolution, concept of 52

ECOSOC (Economic and Social Council of the United Nations) 206, 211
education for all (EFA): concept of 24; aid for 25–6
employment for hunger and poverty reduction 26–7
Energy Independence and Security Act (United States, 2007) 43

FAO (Food and Agriculture Organization of the United Nations):
agricultural biotechnology (*State of Food and Agriculture 2003–04*) 107
Codex Alimentarius Commission (with WHO) 106
Committee on Agriculture: agricultural and nutritional priorities 99–100
Committee on World Food Security (CFS) 97
decreasing authority of FAO 96
early technical assistance (1946–76) 95–6
emergency and rehabilitation programs:

Index 237

Emergency Prevention System for Transboundary Animal and Plant Pests and Diseases 105
Food Insecurity and Vulnerability Information and Mapping System 105, 128
Global Information and Early Warning System for Food and Agriculture 105
International Strategy for Disaster Reduction 105, 128
Special Fund for Emergency and Rehabilitation Activities 105
extra-budgetary and trust funds 69–71
financial contributions to regular program 69–70
first FAO Conference (Quebec City, Canada, October 1945) 67.
FAO Conference 68
FAO Council 68: independent chairman 68; panels of experts 69; technical and special committees 69
FAO constitution 67
FAO mandate 67–8
FAO secretariat 69:
decentralization: regional, sub-regional and country offices 97
headquarters departments 69
Fisheries Department 100: Code of Conduct for Responsible Fishermen 101
Food Security Action Programme 102
Food Security Assistance Scheme 102–3
Forestry Department 101–2: Collaborative Partnership on Forests 101
Global Forest Resources Assessment 2005 101
State of the World's Forests 2007 101
Freedom from Hunger Campaign (1960–70) 59
funding from other UN bodies for FAO field activities 96

Global Strategy for the Management of Farm Genetic Resources 99
independent external evaluation of FAO (2007) 172-4
Intergovernmental Advisory Committee (1961) 61
Interim Commission to draw up detailed plans for FAO (1944-45) 55
International Alliance Against Hunger (2005) 98
International Conference on Nutrition (with WHO) (1992) 98
International Institute of Agriculture library 55, 111
Investment Centre (IC) 97, 107-8
knowledge organization:
 FAO's statistical databases 111-2
 FAO's virtual library 111-2
origins (UN Conference on Food and Agriculture, Hot Springs, Virginia, United States, May/June 1945) 53-5:
 declaration of the conference 54-5
plant health and genetic resources programs 105-7:
 Code of Conduct on the Distribution and Use of Pesticides 106
 Commission on Phytosanitary Measures 106
 Convention on Biodiversity (1995) 107
 farmers' field schools 106
 integrated pest management programs 106
 Intergovernmental Task Force on Foods Derived from Biotechnology 106-7
 International Plant Protection Convention 106
 International Undertaking on Plant Genetic Resources for Food and Agriculture 107
Principles of Surplus Disposal (1954) 132

Special Action Programme for the Prevention of Food Losses after Harvest 102
Special Programme for Food Security 102-4
State of Food Insecurity in the World (annual publication since 1999) 98
state of the world's animal genetic resources for food and agriculture 98
statement on biotechnology (2000) 40
Strategic Framework (2000-2015) 98-9, 173
Technical Cooperation Programme (TCP) 97, 109-10
Trust Fund for Food Security and Food Safety 71, 107
World Conference on Agrarian Reform and Rural Development (1979) 98
World Food Board proposal (1946) 95
World Food Summit (1996) 98
World Food Summit + 5 (2002) 98
Fast Track Initiative (aid for education) 26
Food and nutrition security 8-18
food price rises, causes of 42-3, 213-4, 216
Ford Foundation 65-6
Fourth World Conference for Women (Beijing, China, 1995) 137

Gates Foundation 199
Global Alliance for Vaccination and Immunization 182
Global Crop Diversity Trust 182
Global Environment Facility (see IFAD)
Global Fund to Fight AIDS, Tuberculosis and Malaria 182
Globalization 47-50: differing views on 47-8; effects of 48
GM crops and food 37-41:
 Ad Hoc Intergovernmental Task Force on Foods Derived from Biotechnology (*see* FAO); access by farmers in the

Index 239

developing world 41; debate on 38–40;
United States policy on 41
Gore, Al (former US Vice President and Nobel Peace Prize holder 2007) 46
Gorbackev, Mikhail (former President of the Soviet Union, Nobel Peace Prize holder, and chairman, Green Cross International) 32
Green Revolution 65, 159
Guterres, Antonio (UN High Commissioner for Refugees and chair, Ending Child Hunger and Undernutrition Initiative) 141

Havana Charter on Trade and Development (1948) 29
High-Level Conference on World Food Security (2008) 217
human rights approach, concept of 50–1
human security, concept of 30
Human Security Network (founded 1999) 31
hunger and malnutrition: costs of 12–13; effects on children 11
hungry poor: classification 10; livelihoods 11; location 11

Ioanes, Raymond (Senior Official of the US Department of Agriculture and member of the US delegation to the Intergovernmental Advisory Committee meeting at FAO in Rome, Italy in April 1961) 61
IFAD (International Fund for Agricultural Development)
action plan management team 146
action plan to improve development effectiveness (2005) 146
agreement establishing IFAD (1976) 63
assistance: loans and grants 87–9
Belgium Survival Fund 149–50
Consultative Group to Assist the Poor (2006) 148
country strategy opportunities paper (1995) 144
Executive Board 85
Farmers' Forum 149
Global Environment Facility 152
Global Forum for Agricultural Research (1996) 148
Global Mechanism for the Convention to Combat Desertification 151
Governing Board 63
independent external evaluation of IFAD (2005) 142,185:
assessment of IFAD project performance 143–5
innovative projects, assessment of 145
partnerships, assessment of 148
recommendations on reform of governance and management 185–8
International Land Coalition 150–1
mandate: expanded 83–4; original (1974) 82
membership, categories of 85
OECD and OPEC country disagreement on 'rough parity' for IFAD funding 63
operational activities (1976–2007) 88
origins:1974 World Food Conference resolution to establish IFAD 63
outposting of staff, pilot scheme 86
president, powers and responsibilities 86
rapid external evaluation of IFAD (1994) 185
replenishment of IFAD resources 87
resource problems 200
Rural Poverty Report (2001) 83
secretariat, structure of 86
staffing numbers 86
Strategic Framework (2007–10) 84, 147
The State of World Rural Poverty (1992) 83
voting powers: original 64; revised (2007) 85–6
IFPRI (*see* CGIAR)

ILO:
  World Commission on the Social Dimensions of Globalization, report (2004) 48–50
  World Employment Conference (1976) 26
  World Employment Report (2004–05) 26–7
Improved coordination in the UN system 214–5
income factor: population living on $1 and $2 a day (*see* World Bank)
Intergovernmental Panel of Climate Change (IPPC): reports of 44
International Conference on Financing for Development (2002) 36
International Conference on Population and Development (1994) 19–20
International Monetary Fund (IMF) 56–7
international organization of hunger, accusation of 18
International Women's Year 1975 136
institutional incoherence, concept of 205
International Trade Organization (ITO), proposal for (1948)

Jacques, Sydney (US State Department official and member of the US delegation to the Intergovernmental Advisory Committee meeting at FAO in Rome, Italy in April 1961 61
Joint United Nations Program on HIV/AIDS 182

Kennedy, John F. (US President 1961–3) 59:
  Address to the UN General Assembly 25 September 1961 223n
Keynes, John Maynard (famous British economist) 29
Kyoto Protocol (1997) 45

League of Nations 53,55:
  International Standards of Food Requirements 55

Marriage of Food and Agriculture (1935) 222n
New science of nutrition 53
Nutrition and Public Health report (1935) 55
The Relation of Health, Agriculture and Economic Policy (1937) 55

Marei, Sayed Ahmed (Secretary-General, 1974 World Food Conference and Special Adviser to Egyptian President, Anwar Sadat) 205
Marshall, George C. (US Secretary of State in the Truman Administration and Originator of the Marshall Plan for European Recovery after World War II) 60
Marshall Plan (European Recovery Program, 1948–52) 60, 71
McDougall, Frank (one of the founders of FAO) 222n
McGovern, George S. (Congressman and Senator, first Director, US Food-for-Peace program, Democratic Party nominee for US president in 1972, US Ambassador to the UN Food and Agriculture Agencies in Rome, Italy, and WFP Ambassador at Large) 34, 59, 61–2:
  The Third Freedom: to end world hunger 34–5
McNamara, Robert (World Bank President 1968–81)
MDGs (Millennium Development Goals) 1, 4–6
Multilateral Fund for the Implementation of the Montreal Protocol 182

Nutrition in Times of Disaster, conference organized by SCN and Nutrition Planner Forum, Geneva, Switzerland, (1988) 132

Index 241

obesity 17–18
OECD study on donor tying of food aid (2005) 202
Orr, Sir John (later Lord) Boyd (first FAO Director-General 1946–48) 55

population growth, effects of 18–20
poverty and hunger: costs of 11–13; dimensions of 7; effects on children 11–12

Rockefeller Foundation 65–6, 199
Roosevelt, Franklin D. (US President, 1933–45) 53: State of the Union address, the four freedoms, January 1941 53
rural poverty (see IFAD)

Sachs, Jeffrey (Director, UN Millennium Project and Director, Earth Institute,
Columbia University, New York) 37
Saouma, Edouard (FAO Director-General 1976–1994) 97
Sen, Amartya (Nobel Prize in Economics, 1998) 15, 26: *Development as Freedom* (1999) 15
Sen, B. R. (FAO Director-General 1956–67) 60
Sorensen, Theodore (Special Council to US President Kennedy) 62
Stern, Sir Nicholas (Head, UK Government Economic Service and formerly Chief Economist, World Bank) 45
Strong, Maurice (secretary-general of the UN Conference on Human Environment (1972) and UN Conference on Environment and Development (1992), former UNEP executive director and special adviser to the UN secretary-general and World Bank president) 191
Symington, James (Deputy Director, US Food-for-Peace program) 61

TNT, a global mail and logistics company 131
Truman, Harry S. (US President, 1945–53) 60

UN Commission on Human Security (CHS) 31
UN Conference on Climate Change, Bali, Indonesia, December 2007 46
UN Conference on Environment and Development, Rio de Janeiro, Brazil, 1992 190
UN Conference of Food and Agriculture, Hot Springs, Virginia, United States May/June 1943 53–5
UNCTAD 29–30
UN Decade for Women (1976–85) 135
UN Development Group 215
UNDP 7, 66, 96: *Human Development Reports* (annual from 1990) 31
UNEP 44
UNESCO: *EFA Global Monitoring Reports* 23–4
UN Expanded Program of Technical Assistance (EPTA) 96
UN Framework Convention on Climate Change (1994) 45
UN Girls' Education Initiative 25
UNHCR 77
UN High-Level Panel on UN System-wide Cohence 214
UNICEF: *State of the World's Children*, annual reports 24–5
UN Millennium Project 35–7
UN Millennium Summit 2000 4
United Nations Conference, San Francisco, California, June 1945 53
UN Commissioner on Human Rights 31–2
UN organizations with an interest in food and nutrition security 209–10
UN Resolution on the Provision of Food Surpluses to Food-Deficit People through the UN System, October 1960 59

242 Index

UN Security Council 16
UN Special Fund 96
UN Special Fund for Economic Development (SUNFED) 59
UN statement on food aid and GM foods 40
US Food and Drugs Administration (FDA): US policy on GM food 41
US Government Accountability Office study on the US food aid program (2006) 201
US Intrnational Financial Institutions Advisort Commission 176

World Bank
  Agricultural and Rural Development Department (ARD) 73, 112
  Agricultural Growth for the Poor. An Agenda for Development (2005) 120–1
  aid to China 175,178
  articles of agreement 71
  Bank presidents 72
  Board of Executive Directors 72
  Board of Governors 72
  commencement of operation, June 1946 57
  comprehensive development framework 75
  country assistance strategy 76
  debt relief for heavily indebted poor countries (HIPCs) 75
  declining assistance to agriculture, reasons for 115–8
  economic adjustment programs, effect of 116–7
  fifteenth replenishment of IDA (2008–2011) 177
  George Woods' initiatives 113–4
  Global Donor Platform for Rural Development 120
  global partnership programs 181–2
  IBRD:
    financial arrangements 73–4
    largest shareholders 72
    mandate 71, 112
    operations
    origins: Bretton Woods conference 1944 56
    voting arrangement 72
  IDA:
    approval (1960) 59
    loans and grants 73–5
    mission 71
  IFC's agribusiness portfolio 180
  independent evaluation group 72
  inspection panel 76
  joint study with UNICEF on nutrition (2003) 13–14
  lending arrangement, eligibility for IBRD/IDA assistance 74–5
  location of the bank, discussions on 58
  long-term strategy exercise (2007) 176–7
  management structure of IBRD/IDA 72
  McNamara presidency (1968–81) 114–5
  national poverty reduction strategy 75
  new president's initial impressions and views (October 2007, April 2008) 178–81
  origins: Bretton Woods conference 1944 56
  population living below $1 and $2 a day estimates 20–3
  project cycle 76
  quality assistance group 76
  Reaching the Rural Poor. A Renewed Strategy for Rural Development (2003) 119–20
  Staffing: decentralization of 72; number of staff 73
  strategic framework paper 75
  treasury, borrowing and lending operations 73
  Vision to Action in the Rural Sector (1996) 118–9
  voting arrangements 74
  Wolfensohn, James D. (World Bank President 1995–2005) 118
  Wolfowitz, Paul (World Bank President, 2005–2007) 175
  Woods, George (World Bank President 1963–68) 113–4

Index   243

World Commission on Dams 116
World Development Report 2008.
  Agriculture for Development
  121
United Nations Monetary and
  Financial Conference, Bretton
  Woods, New Hampshire,
  United States, July 1944
  establishing the IBRD 56–7
WFC (World Food Council,
  1976–93):
  coordination mechanism 208–10
  demise, reasons for 211–3
  main tasks 207–8
  mandate 206
  ministerial sessions 209
  origins: 1974 World Food
    Conference resolution
    problem of 210
WFP (UN World Food
  Programme):
  constitution 77
  continuation after the
    experimental period 63
  donors: broadening the donor
    base 81
  emergencies, increasing
    involvement in, and reasons for
    76–7, 122–4
  Enabling Development: WFP
    development objectives 184
  Ending Child Hunger and
    Undernutrition Initiative
    139–41
  establishment as a joint UN/FAO
    venture (1961) 77
  evaluation of WFP (1994) 192–4
  examples of WFP large-scale and
    complex emergency operations
    126–8
  executive director, appointment
    and responsibilities 79
  *Expanded Program of Surplus
    Food Utilization*, report of
    expert group to
  FAO director-general (1961) 60–1
  FAO Conference and UN General
    Assembly resolutions
    establishing WFP,
    November/December 1961 62

FAO Conference and UN General
  Assembly resolutions on the
  continuation of WFP,
  December 1965 63
food aid management and
  modalities 128
food purchases in developing
  countries 128
gender policy and programs 135–9
governing bodies:
  Committee on Food Aid Policies
    and Programmes (CFA)
    (1975–2006) 78
  Executive Board (EB) (2006 –)
    78
  Intergovernmental Committee
    (IGC) (1963–1975) 78
HIV/AIDS: support programs
information and communications
  technology to address
  emergencies 128
mandate 76
manmade emergencies, common
  features of 125
McGovern proposal for a
  three-year experimental
  multilateral food aid program,
  April 1961 62–3
new mission statement (1994) 77,
  184–5
nutrition policies and programs
  131–5
origins: FAO Conference and UN
  General Assembly resolutions,
  1961 59–63
program support and
  administrative expenditure,
  problems of 203–4
proposals to transform WFP
  (1965) 63
protracted emergency operations
  125
protracted emergency and
  rehabilitation operations 125–6
resources 80
resource problems 81, 201–5
school feeding programs 129–31
secretariat, structure of 79
staffing, headquarters, regional
  and country offices 80

244 *Index*

Strategic Plan (2004–2007) 122
transportation and logistics arrangements 80–1
vulnerability analysis and mapping (VAM) 128
WFP/UNHCR guidelines on refugee rations 133
WMO:
 Assessment of the Role of Carbon Dioxide and other Greenhouse Gasses on Climate Variations Conference (with UNEP) (1985) 44
 first World Climate Conference (1979) 44
WHO:
 Expert Consultation on Diet, Nutrition and the Prevention of Chronic Diseases 17
Global Burden of Disease Study (with the World Bank) 12
International Task Force on Obesity 17
World Food Conference, Rome, Italy, November 1974:
 World Food Authority, proposal for 205
 World Food Security Council, proposal for 213
world food systems, changes since World War II 17
Worldwatch Institute: redefining global security, S*tate of the World* (2005) 32–3
working poverty, concept of 27
WTO: ministerial meetings 28–9

Zoelick, Robert B. (World Bank President 2007 –) 178

CPSIA information can be obtained at www.ICGtesting.com
Printed in the USA
LVOW01s1618170114

369527LV00015B/252/P

9 780415 445047